THE UNFINISHED GOSPEL

THE UNFINISHED GOSPEL

NOTES ON THE QUEST FOR THE HISTORICAL JESUS

EVAN POWELL

SYMPOSIUM BOOKS
Westlake Village, California

First Edition, 1994
Symposium Books
2899 Agoura Road, Suite 341
Westlake Village, CA 91361

© 1994 Evan Powell

Jacket design by Katina Wood

Cataloging-in-Publication Data

Powell, Evan, 1953-
     The unfinished Gospel: notes on the quest for the historical
Jesus/Evan Powell. -- 1st ed.
     p. cm.
     Includes bibliographical references and index.
     Library of Congress Catalog Card Number: 93-92849
     ISBN 0-9639650-6-9

     1. Jesus Christ--Historicity.   2. Bible. N.T. Gospels--
Commentaries.   I. Title.

     BS2553.P69 1994   226'.0663
                                          QBI94-618

Printed in the United States of America

To Richard N. Schwab
Professor of History, Emeritus
University of California, Davis

Contents

Acknowledgments

The Unfinished Gospel could not have been written without the insightful critical review of several noted scholars who took the time to analyze its ideas and arguments as they evolved from sketches on paper to a final manuscript.

For these reviews I am indebted to Birger Pearson of the University of California at Santa Barbara, Ronald Hock of the University of Southern California, Robert McKenzie of the Graduate Theological Union, Joel Green of the American Baptist Seminary of the West, Jane Schaberg of the University of Detroit, Mercy, and the Rev. Earl F. Palmer of University Presbyterian Church, Seattle. Each provided a critical commentary of the manuscript, and indicated weaknesses in its arguments. With their perceptive critiques, I was able to refine the manuscript and substantially improve the final result. They each have saved me from numerous embarrassments which would otherwise have made their way into print.

In expressing my gratitude to these individuals, I do not mean to imply that they would agree with my observations or conclusions. This book often challenges consensus opinions, and suggests new ways to interpret the gospel texts. Thus, each of those who so graciously provided critique and comment will have his or her own studied opinion of the final product.

My warmest appreciation is also extended to DeAnn Fieselman for her invaluable comments on the evolving manuscript as I struggled to give it a clear voice; and to Niki Haworth, whose exceptional editorial skills have influenced every page. A special note of thanks to my parents, Bruce and Charleen Powell, for many ideas which greatly improved the text.

Finally, I am grateful to Katina Wood for visualizing and producing the magnificent cover design which has contributed immeasurably to the quality of the finished product.

This book is dedicated to Richard N. Schwab, Professor of History, Emeritus, at the University of California, Davis. In my studies under him, I learned to analyze philosophical, religious, and historical questions in a manner that made this book possible. Our conversations on the existence of God will be remembered all my life.

I wish to acknowledge the organizations which have granted permission to reproduce excerpts from their copyrighted materials.

All scriptural references are taken from the

REVISED STANDARD VERSION OF THE BIBLE
Second Edition © 1971

Reprinted with permission of the Division of Christian Education of the National Council of the Churches of Christ in the United States of America

Excerpts from *The Gospel According to John* by **Raymond Brown,** © 1970, and from the Anchor Bible Series' *Mark,* by **C.S. Mann,** © 1986 are reprinted with permission of Doubleday, a division of Bantam, Doubleday, Dell Publishing Group, Inc. All rights reserved.

Excerpts from *The New American Commentary, Mark,* by **James A. Brooks**. Used by permission of Broadman Press (Nashville: Broadman Press © 1991). All rights reserved.

Excerpts from *Ancient Christian Gospels,* by **Helmut Koester,** © 1990 are reprinted with permission of Trinity Press International. All rights reserved.

Excerpts from *The Gospel of Thomas,* by **Marvin Meyer**. Copyright © 1992 by Marvin Meyer. Copyright © 1992 by Harold Bloom. Reprinted by permission of HarperCollins Publishers, Inc.

Excerpts from *Jesus, A Life,* by **A.N. Wilson**. Copyright © 1992. Reprinted with permission of the publisher W. W. Norton.

Excerpts from *The Gospel According to St. John, Second Edition,* by **C.K. Barrett**. Second Edition © 1978 C.K. Barrett. Used by permission of Westminster/John Knox Press.

❖ *Prologue* ❖

And they brought the boy possessed by a spirit to Jesus;
and when the spirit saw him, immediately it convulsed
the boy, and he fell on the ground and rolled about,
foaming at the mouth. And his father said to Jesus, "If
you can do anything, have pity on us and help us." And
Jesus said to him, "If you can! All things are possible to
him who believes." Immediately the father of the child
cried out and said, "I believe; help my unbelief!"

(Mark 9:20, 22-24, paraphrased)

One of the great challenges of the human mind is to reconcile belief in God, or a higher spiritual reality, with rational perceptions of a world in which divine influence is not apparent. This dilemma is reflected in the above excerpt from the Gospel of Mark. A man has brought his son, possessed by a spirit, to Jesus for healing. The man does not know whether Jesus can heal his son, but faced with the boy's potential death, the man wants to believe. Indeed he declares, *"I believe."* Yet at the same time he admits he does not know enough to overcome his doubts. He has not seen enough to satisfy his rational nature: *"Help my unbelief!"*

This man's plea is a universal cry of humankind. It reflects the profound tension that most people struggle with when they take both faith and reason seriously. It is a problem which is particularly acute in our age of science and reason. However, the problem of reconciling faith and reason is not a uniquely modern one. The gap between faith and reason exists at the historical core of Christianity.

Early church writers were well aware of the non-rationality of the Christian message. They attempted to eliminate the problem by dismissing human reason as untrustworthy and ineffectual as a means of understanding spiritual things. Paul proclaimed that faith does not "rest in the wisdom of men but in the power of God" (1Cor. 2:5). Acknowledging the non-rational character of his message, Paul writes:

> Has not God made foolish the wisdom of this world? For since, in the wisdom of God, the world did not know God through wisdom, it pleased God through the folly of what we preach to save those who believe. For Jews demand signs, and Greeks seek wisdom, but we preach Christ crucified, a stumbling block to Jews and folly to Gentiles, but to those who are called, both Jews and Greeks, Christ the power of God and the wisdom of God. For the foolishness of God is wiser than men . . ." (1 Cor. 1:20b-25a)

Paul claims that God intended to confound humankind by creating a message of salvation which could not be evaluated by normal methods of inquiry. Only those who set aside reason and embrace the "foolishness of God" would be saved. Tertullian, a prominent Christian writer at the end of the second century, also promoted faith as the antithesis of reason in the quest for true knowledge:

> The most ignorant peasant under the Christian dispensation possesses more real knowledge than the wisest of the ancient philosophers (Apologeticus, c. 197 CE)

Tertullian has also been attributed the saying, "I believe because it is impossible" although the original quotation is more accurately rendered "It is certain because it is impossible." (De Carne Christi, c. 209 CE). This suggests that human reason may be dismissed since the irrationality of the Christian message is the best argument in its favor.

To represent human reason as powerless to discern spiritual reality was effective for ancient Christian evangelists. At the time, human reason was not recognized as the reliable tool of learning and scientific discovery that it is today. Theirs was a culture in which mythologies, rituals, and traditions were more prominent as means by which people could interpret the world and their individual role in it. So it was not unusual that the ancient evangelists could characterize the unilateral self-revelation of God as something which could not be understood or evaluated effectively through reason.

However, during the last few centuries, reliance upon human reason has gained ascendancy in modern culture. In 1690, John Locke wrote in *An Essay Concerning Human Understanding*:

> Nothing that is contrary to, and inconsistent with, the clear and self-evident dictates of reason, has a right to be urged or assented to as a matter of faith, wherein reason hath nothing to do. (Book IV, Ch. XVIII)

In this same work, Locke went on to comment on Tertullian's famous rejection of reason:

> Religion, which should most distinguish us from the beasts, and ought most particularly to elevate us as rational creatures above brutes, is that wherein men often appear most irrational, and more senseless than beasts themselves. *"I believe because it is impossible"* might, in a good man pass as a sally of zeal; but would prove a very ill rule for men to choose their opinions and religions by. (Book IV, Ch. XVIII)

Ever since Copernicus proved that the Earth circumnavigates the Sun, the power of human reason to discover and define the physical universe has been demonstrated frequently and effectively. Thus Christianity can no longer survive as a religion which stands against reason, or one that must be believed because it is impossible. Though certain fundamentalist sects continue to thrive, their appeal is primarily to poor and less educated segments of society. Christianity in general has suffered a steady decline of its influence upon contemporary western culture over the last two centuries. The reason is clear: on many vital issues, the classic non-rationality of Christian faith stands at odds with the belief that logical reasoning is the most reliable and trustworthy tool for discovering the realities of the universe.

The problem has been recognized by the great minds of the church. Theologians and evangelists in this century have turned their efforts to demonstrating that faith and reason are compatible after all. Hans Kung, the distinguished Roman Catholic theologian, closes his monumental work *Does God Exist?* with this summary:

Does God exist?

After the difficult passage through the history of the modern age from the time of Descartes and Pascal, Kant and Hegel, considering in detail the objections raised in the critique of religion by Feuerbach, Marx and Freud, seriously confronting Nietzsche's nihilism, seeking the reason for our fundamental trust and the answer in trust in God, in comparing finally the alternatives of the Eastern religions, entering also into the question "Who is God?" and of the God of Israel and of Jesus Christ: after all this, it will be understood why the question "Does God exist?" can now be answered by a clear, convinced Yes, justifiable at the bar of critical reason.[1]

Perhaps the best known twentieth century Christian apologist is C. S. Lewis. Lewis also tackled the problem of faith vs. reason head on by acknowledging and affirming reason as the primary tool modern man uses to perceive truth:

> I am not asking anyone to accept Christianity if his best reasoning tells him that the weight of the evidence is against it.[2]

Lewis went on to develop a popular systematic argument that the tenets of Christian faith were entirely consistent with reason, and that Christianity should be embraced, not because it is irrational or impossible, but because it is the only truly rational solution to the great questions of life and existence.[3]

Ultimately, however, many of Lewis' arguments fail. He often relied upon startling rhetorical devices rather than solid reasoning. One of his most famous arguments is the "Lord or lunatic" dilemma:

> I am trying here to prevent anyone saying the really foolish thing that people often say about Him: "I'm ready to accept Jesus as a great moral teacher, but I don't accept his claim to be God." That is the one thing we must not say. A man who was merely a man and said the sort of things Jesus said would not be a great moral teacher. He would either be a lunatic--on a level with the man who says he is a poached egg--or

---

[1] Kung, Hans, *Does God Exist*, Vintage Books, 1981, p. 702

[2] Lewis, C. S., Mere Christianity, Collier Books, 1960, p. 108

[3] Lewis' apologetics appear in a series of works including *Mere Christianity, Miracles, The Problem of Pain, The Abolition of Man, God in the Dock, Christian Reflections, and A Grief Observed.*

else he would be the Devil of Hell. You must make your choice. Either this man was, and is, the Son of God: or else a madman or something worse. You can shut Him up for a fool, you can spit at Him and kill Him as a demon; or you can fall at his feet and call Him Lord and God. But let us not come with any patronising nonsense about His being a great human teacher. He has not left that open to us. He did not intend to.[4]

In this argument Lewis establishes a false dilemma as a rhetorical device. Note the underlying assumption: *"A man who was merely a man and said the sort of things Jesus said . . ."* If Jesus actually said everything he is documented as saying in the gospels, one might agree that Lewis has a point--either Jesus was a lunatic or the Son of God. However, the key issue is how accurately the gospels represent the actual words and deeds of Jesus. If we were to suppose that some of what the gospels record about Jesus were theological interpretations of the primitive church, we might suspect that his "claim to be God" (as Lewis puts it) could have been attributed to him after the fact. If so, we might easily conclude that the historical Jesus was neither Lord nor lunatic. Yet this option, though it is a reasonable one, is not offered by Lewis as a legitimate solution to his radical dilemma.[5]

The problem with Lewis' argument illustrates two issues of central concern in this book. First, a successful reconciliation of reason with Christian faith cannot be accomplished without identifying who the historical Jesus actually was. To say that Jesus was either Lord or lunatic based on his sayings in the gospels, without asking whether the gospels are historically accurate, is to ignore a vital part of the question.

Second, Lewis' argument fails because of an underlying assumption which cannot be defended. In general, it seems that many modern theories about the gospels and the historical Jesus suffer from the same illness. There is frequently nothing wrong with the logical arguments as far as they go, assuming the underlying presuppositions are correct. Yet there is a remarkable lack of attention to the viability of presuppositions, not only in the work of apologists such as Lewis, but also in the work of many contemporary New Testament scholars and historians.

---

[4] Lewis, C. S., Ibid., p. 41

[5] For a comprehensive critique of the work of C. S. Lewis, see John Beversluis' book *C. S. Lewis and the Search for Rational Religion*, Wm. B. Eerdmans, 1985

This oversight is startling, since it is well recognized that underlying assumptions not only influence the outcome of any inquiry, but can often predetermine its results. John Locke wrote:

> False and doubtful positions, relied upon as unquestionable maxims, keep those who build on them in the dark from truth. Such are usually the prejudices imbibed from education, party, reverence, fashion, interest, etc. (Book IV, Ch. VII)

As obvious as this is, we will find in this study that many who have attempted to reconstruct the life and teachings of the historical Jesus have done so by building upon assumptions which cannot be defended in the light of critical reason. They have fallen prey to the trap Locke cautioned against. Some have inherited their unproven assumptions through formal theological training, and others through church tradition. Many assumptions are forced upon contemporary research by the tyranny of academic convention, which frequently serves to stifle creative inquiry rather than foster it. Regardless of their source of origin, there are a host of unproven prejudices regarding the gospels and the historical Jesus which form the foundation of much modern scholarly work.

Notably, the recently published work of the Jesus Seminar, *The Five Gospels,* which has presumed to isolate the most probable sayings of the historical Jesus, is based on certain presuppositions which will be shown herein to be untrustworthy. The introduction to *The Five Gospels* highlights the fact that the Seminar's conclusions are founded on "seven pillars of scholarly wisdom." Of these seven reputed pillars, four are reliable and firmly established. However, the other three are subject to challenge. The Jesus Seminar's results are skewed radically by these three pillars. If they are proven to be in error, the Seminar's findings would be rendered invalid.

The Unfinished Gospel explores a question which ultimately must be addressed by the church: how may the doctrines and claims of Christianity be interpreted such that they (a) are compatible with modern reason, and (b) retain important meaning for contemporary society? To get at this question, we must take a fresh look at the gospels and other New Testament documents to see if the historical Jesus can actually be discovered, and to see how the doctrines which form the basis of Christianity may have evolved.

We will discover that there are remarkable patterns of literary development in the gospels which point to an entirely new vision of their origin. In drawing attention to these patterns in the texts, it will be argued that they cannot be dismissed as coincidental or irrelevant. The patterns suggest that the four gospels may fit together like pieces of a puzzle. However, New Testament scholars have generally ignored these patterns, as they are not compatible with traditional ideas about the origin of the gospels. In fact, they challenge several conventional ideas about who Jesus was, and about the origin of Christianity.

This is not the first time that an intriguing set of patterns has led to a challenge of conventional academic wisdom. There is a fascinating parallel between the present study and the experience in the world of geophysics early this century. Note that when we look at a map of the world the continents look like pieces of a puzzle which, if we could pick them up and move them, could be reassembled. In particular, the Atlantic coastlines of North and South America, Europe, and Africa are mirror images of one another. They create a pattern which requires an explanation. Why do they look so similar? For many years people wondered if this was just a coincidence or whether something had caused this pattern to exist.

In the 1960's scientists discovered that the continents used to be one gigantic land mass. Over vast geologic ages it broke apart, forming separate continents which drifted away from one another. This discovery explains the replicated coastline patterns we see today. However, though the patterns on the map had been obvious for some two hundred years, scientists did not realize that the continents had actually broken apart and moved until the late 1960's. Prior to that, the large majority of the scientific community ignored the intriguing shapes of the continents as merely coincidental. The idea that continents could move did not fit their perception of the nature of the earth.

Though it is now a hallmark of scientific wisdom, the Theory of Continental Drift was derided as ridiculous prior to the 1960's, and those who advocated it placed their academic reputations at risk. The theory was first proposed in 1858. However, the proposal was based only on the suggestive shape of the continents. Since no further supporting argument was offered, it was simply ignored. Then in 1924, Alfred Wegener published *The Origin of the Continents and Oceans*, in which he offered additional evidence in favor of the theory.

With the appearance of Wegener's book, opinion in the scientific community hardened against the idea. The Theory of Continental Drift was entirely incompatible with what scientists thought they knew about the structure of the earth. Most scientists said the evidence for the theory must be written off as coincidental, improperly researched, or mistakenly interpreted. Wegener and those few who took him seriously were ridiculed. Hostility was particularly acute in the United States, where the minority of scientists who gave credence to the theory were labeled "drifters." Those who wished to retain their academic standing as respectable scientists were well advised to keep their opinions to themselves.

As late as 1960, the large majority of scientists had consigned Wegener's theory to the dustbin of debunked crank theories of the past. However, in that decade new technologies developed which enabled scientists to study the deep sea floor in ways not previously possible. The data which flowed in from those explorations provided virtual proof that Wegener and the "drifters" had been right all along. By the end of the decade, any scientist who did *not* accept the idea that the continents had moved was considered out of touch.

As we embark upon this study of New Testament (NT) research, one may sense parallels between NT scholarship today and the world of geophysics prior to the 1960's. Many firmly established theories about the gospels enjoy a wide consensus among scholars. While these theories seem to explain much of the textual evidence, most scholars will readily concede that they do not explain it all. Yet from a practical point of view, these theories are often considered to be settled, and they form the foundation of much contemporary historical Jesus research.

At the same time, the pronounced literary patterns in the gospels which will be introduced here have largely gone unrecognized and unexplained by conventional theories. To the extent they are acknowledged, they are passed over as coincidental or irrelevant since

16

they do not fit prevailing views of the gospels. The theories presented in this work will explain some of the evidence which has thus far been overlooked. In so doing, it offers a fundamental revisualization of the gospels--and a new perspective on Jesus, the resurrection, and the origin of Christianity.

John Locke noted that "new opinions are always suspected, and usually opposed, without any other reason but because they are not already common."[6] Thus, *The Unfinished Gospel*, perhaps in a manner not unlike Wegener's book, may encounter resistance, in part, because it is different. It may find opposition in the scholarly community because it argues that several widely accepted assumptions cannot stand in the light of rational critique. It may also meet criticism from certain sects of Christianity, since it shows that common ideas about the first century church and the nature of the gospels must be revised.

On a personal note, it would be naive to presume that readers would approach a book such as this without curiosity about, and concern for, the religious and philosophical orientation of its author. Indeed the most frequent question asked of me during the two years the manuscript was being written was *"Do you believe Jesus was the Son of God?"* The question is not unwarranted, for it is legitimate that the reader should wonder whether this or any work on religious themes may have been influenced by hidden ideological agendas.

To address this concern I will close with a brief statement of personal faith. This book has been composed with the conviction that spiritual realities exist which may be perceived in some limited way by the human mind. However, the full nature of the spiritual universe is beyond the ability of the finite human mind to grasp. We may catch glimpses of the eternal without fully comprehending. It is ours to seek without ever truly finding, until in death we move to a higher plane of awareness. As the apostle Paul said, "For now we see in a mirror dimly, but then face to face. Now I know in part; then I shall understand fully" (1 Cor. 13:12).

Humankind was created with the ability to reason. Thus if a rational God created us, we may assume that he intended us to use our

---

[6] An Essay Concerning Human Understanding, 1690, Dedicatory epistle

rational faculties to survive, to live, and to explore our universe. We have been created with the ability and the desire to seek the truth in all things. Thus if God is a God of truth, we may proceed boldly and confidently in the spirit of Thomas Jefferson:

> Shake off all the fears of servile prejudices, under which weak minds are servilely crouched. Fix reason firmly in her seat, and call on her tribunal for every fact, every opinion. Question with boldness even the existence of God, because, if there be one, he must more approve of the homage of reason than that of blind faith.[7]

The Unfinished Gospel sheds new light on some of the formative influences which shaped the gospels. It presents new evidence of how the ideas of the primitive church evolved and changed during the course of the first century. It traces the earliest traditions backward in time, rooting them in a vision of the historical Jesus which is comprehensible by the modern mind. Finally, it offers a carefully reasoned speculation about the nature of the historical event which came to be known as the resurrection, and interprets this event in the light of reason. In so doing, it reinterprets Christianity so that its traditions are in harmony with modern perceptions of reality.

It is natural and proper that we should ask these questions, for it is our nature to seek the truth. Faith will always remain an impulse of the will rather than a consequence of well-reasoned argument. However, we as rational creatures cannot ultimately be fulfilled except by an intuitive faith which harmonizes with reason. Though there is risk to our preconceived notions and myths, if God is a God of truth, he will honor our quest, and we may be confident that our search for truth is, in fact, a search for God.

Lake Sherwood, California
April, 1994

---

[7] To Peter Carr, August 10, 1785

❖   *1*   ❖

The Quest for the Historical Jesus

Who was Jesus of Nazareth?   How did he view his own mission?   Which of the teachings of Jesus recorded in the gospels originated with him, and which were developed and attributed to him by his followers afterward? Since the dawn of the age of reason, New Testament scholars, historians, and archaeologists have been trying to answer these questions.   The study is known as the quest for the historical Jesus.

In addition to being an inquiry into Jesus' teachings and self-perception, the quest has also raised questions regarding the historical reliability of the gospels. Was Jesus really crucified by the Romans, and if so, why? How are the miracle stories to be interpreted? What were the historical events behind the greatest of miracles--that of the resurrection?   Indeed, what infused the Jesus movement with such power that it launched the beginning of Christianity? Underlying all these questions is the fundamental concern--how can Christian faith be reconciled with modern reason?

The Origin of the Quest

The quest for the historical Jesus began in the 18th century when serious students of the New Testament noticed that the four gospels, Matthew, Mark, Luke, and John, contain different perceptions of Jesus. They present divergent accounts of what he taught and how he interacted with people. Not only are the gospel accounts different, but they are sometimes in conflict with one another. For instance, the

Gospel of John says Jesus boldly and frequently proclaimed himself to be the Messiah. The Gospel of Mark says he did not; it says Jesus gave strict orders to his followers not to discuss his messianic status. In order to resolve the confusion, researchers have tried to separate the most historically probable traditions from those which appear to be theologically motivated by the first century church.

The quest has swung like a pendulum over the years. Prior to World War I, most researchers were optimistic that the historical elements of the gospels could be isolated from the theological interpretations of the authors. They assumed that once the historical elements were pulled together, a clear portrait of Jesus would appear.

The task turned out to be more complex and elusive than early scholars had hoped. As the quest developed in the 20th century, it became apparent that the gospels were not literal histories or biographies in the sense we understand these terms today. Instead, the gospels were collections of stories about Jesus which had been developed and attributed to Jesus by the early Jesus movement.[1] The authors had not assembled their gospels for the purpose of recording objective historical events. Rather, their purpose was to document certain traditions of the movement in order to support the evangelical mission of the church. The author of John's Gospel wrote:

> Now Jesus did many other signs in the presence of the disciples, which are not written in this book; but these are written that you may believe that Jesus is the Christ, the Son of God, and that believing you may have life in his name. (John 20:30-31)

Here the author tells us that his foremost objective is to produce a document which will bring readers to faith. So it may be interpreted primarily as an evangelical work rather than simply an historical record. Further, the author says he has selected certain stories from the various traditions of Jesus which he believes will be the most effective for his purpose. He uses them to convey his vision of who Jesus was so readers might be brought to faith.

---

[1] Scholars use the term "Jesus movement" instead of "Christianity" to emphasize the fact that the institutionalized world religion we know today as Christianity did not exist in the first century.

The other three gospels, Matthew, Mark, and Luke, were composed by persons who selected other stories and created different portraits of Jesus which were more in line with their beliefs. Not only do these gospels tell a variety of stories which do not appear in John, but even those which are similar to stories found in John are told in a different manner.

In the first century, rendering an event or saying with historical precision was less pertinent to writers and their audiences than it is for our culture; the important aspect for the authors of these stories was the greater truth which they were alleged to have contained. This becomes obvious when we consider how the authors of Matthew and Luke, in using the Gospel of Mark as a source document for their own writings, appear to have edited and rephrased the stories in Mark to clarify the text or to put their own interpretation on it. For these writers, literal accuracy was subordinated to the greater evangelical objective--to proclaim what they understood to be the meaning of the life, death, and resurrection of Jesus. So the problem is apparent: What in the gospels is rooted in historical fact, and what is the result of evangelically motivated interpretation?

After World War I, Rudolf Bultmann and the school that developed in his wake convinced most researchers that virtually all of the gospel material was developed by the early Jesus movement in order to effectively proclaim the new faith. It was supposed that since the gospels had not been composed as literal histories of Jesus' ministry, there was no way to know whether *any* of the gospel stories had historical foundation. Under these circumstances, they argued, the quest for the historical Jesus was a hopeless venture. Thus, in the middle decades of this century the quest came to a virtual halt.

More recently the quest has been reopened. Most now believe that the gospels contain similar sketches of a ministry of Jesus which, after all, must have *some* historical origin, although it is still believed that much of what we find in the gospels is the product of theological concerns of the authors rather than actual recorded history. However, scholars are once again sifting through the texts to isolate the earliest traditions which may go back to the authentic ministry of Jesus.

The Gospels as Evolved Literary Works

The authors of Matthew, Mark, Luke, and John, did not simply sit down and write their gospels out of thin air.[2] Rather, the gospel writers may more accurately be seen as editors who compiled collections of oral and written traditions about Jesus. Some of these may have been in circulation for many decades. Indeed, the author of Luke begins his gospel by telling us precisely this:

> Inasmuch as many have undertaken to compile a narrative of the things which have been accomplished among us, just as they were delivered to us by those who were eyewitnesses and ministers of the word, it seemed good to me also, having followed all things closely for some time past, to write an orderly account for you, most excellent Theophilus, that you may know the truth concerning the things of which you have been informed. (Luke 1:1-4)

Here the author says he has decided to compile his own set of traditions so that Theophilus may know the truth. The implication is that the author believes a number of stories have been circulating about Jesus which are not in accord with his beliefs--other narratives have been written which have not gotten the story quite right. So the author of Luke has done his own research and compiled a collection of stories which have been handed down from "eyewitnesses and ministers," and which he believes represent the truth.

Though Matthew and Mark do not explicitly say they have collected earlier traditions, it is evident from their similar method of arranging and editing the various stories that they followed the same procedure. So the gospels are each a collection of earlier traditions

---

[2] The four gospels are written anonymously. The attributions, Matthew, Mark, Luke, and John, were assigned later by the church.   According to church tradition, Matthew and John were two of the original twelve apostles, although the possibility of authorship by these apostles is usually dismissed since the gospels are presumed to have been composed late in the first century, and beyond the life expectancy of Jesus' contemporaries. Mark is alleged to have been a follower of the apostle Peter, and Luke a companion of Paul. However, nothing more is known of these two figures. Since all four attributions are questionable, this book will defer to the gospel convention of anonymous authorship.

which have been arranged and interpreted by the authors. In essence they are literary works which evolved over time.

Furthermore, from the array of ancient manuscripts which have been recovered we know that the gospels themselves, once written, were subject to revision, correction, and enhancement by subsequent editors and scribes as they copied the manuscripts. With regard to the gospels of John and Mark, what we appear to have in the NT is enhanced versions of these texts which may be second or third editions of the originals.

For example, the story of The Woman Caught in Adultery (John 7:53 - 8:11) is not found in the earliest and best manuscripts of John, yet it appears in later ones. Scholars infer from this that the story was not part of the original gospel, but was added by editors at a later time. Similarly, the resurrection appearances of Jesus found in Mark 16:9-20 are missing from the earliest manuscripts of Mark, and are clearly an addition by later editors.

Sometimes, even though there is no manuscript discrepancy, the hand of a subsequent editor is evident. For instance, the Gospel of John appears originally to have ended with the final verse of John 20. The last chapter, John 21, looks to most observers as though it is an epilogue or appendix added later by a different author. Though all complete manuscripts of John which have been recovered contain John 21, the oldest is dated to about 200 CE,[3] or about 100 years after the presumed composition date of the gospel. So in this case, the manuscript evidence is inconclusive about what the original composition may have included.

In general, since most ancient manuscripts date from 200 CE onward, the discrepancies between them can provide positive evidence where changes were made to the documents over time, but it is less certain how closely the earliest surviving manuscripts match the original compositions. Thus, an addition such as John 21 appears to have occurred early enough to be reflected in all extant manuscripts.

---

[3] CE = Common (or Christian) Era. BCE = Before Common (or Christian) Era. These are the equivalents of A.D. (anno domini) and B.C. (Before Christ) respectively. Hence "70 A.D." is the same year as "70 CE." It has become common in scholarly literature to reference dates using CE and BCE.

The theory that John 21 is a later addition does not derive from manuscript evidence, but from the observations that John 20 contains an appropriate conclusion to the gospel, and the content of John 21 is incongruous in many ways with the rest of the gospel.

To note a degree of uncertainty regarding how closely the earliest manuscripts match the original compositions is not to raise a specter which should be blown out of proportion. Over 5,000 full and partial manuscripts of the NT documents have been recovered, making them by far the best attested writings from the ancient world. Furthermore, though John and Mark in particular show signs of editing, the fact that the four gospels contain numerous inconsistencies between them is good evidence that they were not extensively revised to bring them into an artificial harmony. Thus, it is apparent that the early church treated them with some degree of respect for their integrity as originally composed.

The Gospels as Products of Conversations

Not only are the gospels collections of assorted traditions which have had an evolutionary literary history, but they may be seen as products of ongoing conversations as well. The authors of the gospels arranged and edited the stories in part to address concerns and issues of the audiences for which they were writing. In this regard, we might imagine that reading the gospels is similar to listening to one end of a telephone call; from the snippets of conversation we overhear from a person speaking on the phone, we can usually piece together much of what the other party has said, even though we do not hear it directly.

We may read the gospels with the same sensitivity. For example, at one point the Gospel of John says of John the Baptist, *"He confessed, he did not deny, but confessed, 'I am not the Christ'"* (John 1:20). The theme that John the Baptist is not to be mistaken as the Christ is repeated several times in this gospel.[4]

---

[4] John 1:20; 1:25; 3:28; 10:41 Note that John the Baptist is not to be confused with John the apostle, to whom the gospel is attributed. John the Baptist was not a follower of Jesus; rather he conducted a ministry independent of Jesus, and was arrested and executed sometime prior to the death of Jesus.

Here we can sense something of an ongoing conversation which was part of the background for the author of John. The author's insistence that the Baptist emphatically denied he was the Christ probably implies that some of the intended readers of the gospel were promoting John the Baptist as the Christ. The gospel appears to have been written in the midst of an ongoing debate between the followers of Jesus and the followers of John the Baptist as to which was the genuine Christ, or Messiah.[5] If there were not, the recurrent theme in this gospel makes little sense.

The scenes which show John the Baptist denying he was the Christ do not appear in Matthew, Mark, or Luke, the "synoptic" gospels.[6] The important thing to infer from this is that this debate was most likely resolved or moot for the audiences the synoptic writers were addressing. Conversely, it must have been an important question for the audience of the Fourth Gospel[7] *at the time the gospel was written.* Whether it was truly a historical debate during the life of Jesus is difficult to say. The theme has been included into John's gospel to make a theological and confessional statement of vital interest to his contemporary readership.

So in this manner, as we read the gospels we can make it a point to imagine what must have been occurring at the time for the authors to have written in the manner that they did. This reconstruction of the historical social setting is a key activity of NT scholars, for we can learn a great deal more about the origins of Christianity by understanding the issues which helped shape and motivate the NT writers.

---

[5] The English word "Christ" is translated from the Greek *christos,* meaning *"anointed one."* The English word "Messiah" is translated from the Greek *Messias,* which in turn is a translation of the Hebrew word *masiah,* which denotes an anointed person. So "Christ" and "Messiah" are equivalent terms.

[6] Due to their similarity of narrative structure and theological orientation, Matthew, Mark, and Luke are frequently referred to as the *synoptic* gospels. The word refers to the fact that they can easily be compared side by side, or seen together *syn-optically.*

[7] The four gospels are often referred to by their sequence in the New Testament. Hence, Matthew, Mark, Luke, and John are the First, Second, Third, and Fourth Gospels respectively. This terminology can be confusing since it does not reflect the chronological order in which the gospels were composed. Most scholars believe Mark was the earliest, yet it is still referred to as the Second Gospel due to its place in the NT canon.

Isolating the Earliest Traditions

The quest for the historical Jesus has consisted of numerous attempts to isolate the most reliable and historical of the gospel traditions from those which appear to be products of the primitive church's theological expression or concern. Several techniques have been used to identify and isolate traditions which may have greater historical authenticity. They include a study of the languages of the texts, an inquiry into known historical events which seem to be reflected in the writings, and a relative comparison of the gospel texts to see if later writers may have used earlier gospels as source documents. Also, a growing body of knowledge from the field of archaeology continues to shed more light on the social and religious milieu of Palestine in Jesus' time. With this new information researchers can better weigh the plausibility of the gospel accounts based on coherence within their historical context.

One of the techniques which has been used to analyze the gospels involves a comparison between the Greek texts and an Aramaic translation of them. It is widely assumed that Jesus' native tongue was Aramaic, a Semitic language related to Hebrew. Aramaic was the common spoken language among Jews of first century Palestine, and Hebrew was the sacred language of the Jewish scriptures. One might compare it to modern Italy, where Italian is the common spoken language, and Latin is the sacred language of the Roman Catholic Church.

It would have been natural for Jesus to conduct his ministry in Aramaic; yet none of the ancient manuscripts recovered for the NT documents are written in Aramaic. Most are written in Greek, which was the language of the gentile world to which the Jesus movement was spreading at the time the gospels and letters of the NT were written.[8] Scholars believe that all of the books of the NT were originally composed in Greek.[9]

---

[8] Manuscripts have been recovered which are written in languages such as Coptic, which were prevalent in North Africa. They have been determined to be translations from Greek texts.

[9] From time to time the argument is advanced that the Gospel of John was originally composed as an Aramaic text, though most scholars do not hold this view today. The Aramaic nuances in the text which suggest the theory are most often explained by

Therefore, one technique scholars have used to judge the authenticity of Jesus' sayings is to determine how well they translate from the Greek texts into an Aramaic original. If a saying translates easily into Aramaic, it is thought to have a higher probability of having originated with Jesus. If a saying's wording or syntax is difficult or impossible to translate into Aramaic, it may be suspected as a later attribution to Jesus by his followers rather than something he actually said. Analyses such as these have netted some interesting observations. However, the most important task in isolating the earliest traditions is the dating and sequencing of the gospels and their sources.

Dating the Gospel Materials

Which of the gospels is the earliest? In what order were they composed? The determination of the correct chronological sequence of the gospels as well as the sources their authors relied upon is a vital first step in the quest for the historical Jesus. It is presumed that since an early gospel would have been composed closer to the actual events, its historical integrity may be higher. Conversely, the later gospel writers would have had more time to be influenced by growing legends and evolving theological outlooks. So a correct temporal sequencing of the materials may give us not only a better view of the historical Jesus as recorded in the earliest traditions, but a study of the later works may also indicate how the beliefs of the Jesus movement evolved during the first century. Both of these aspects of the study are important to understanding the historical origins of Christianity.

One can readily see that dating the gospel materials is much more complex than it first appears. Establishing a date for the final compilation of each gospel as we have it today is only the beginning. Within each gospel there are traditions which researchers attempt to identify as earlier or later than the gospel in which it appears. Sometimes this is easy--John 21 (in its present canonical form) is certainly a later addition and was composed subsequent to the writing

---

supposing a writer whose native tongue was Aramaic, but who had an adequate command of Greek as a second language. Such a writer could have written the relatively simple Greek text of John.

of John itself. However, often the evidence is not so clear. Though the story of the Woman Caught in Adultery was added to John by a later editor, the story could have been a separate tradition which predated John and circulated independently prior to its inclusion in the gospel.

Though the ultimate goal is to identify the earliest traditions embedded in the gospels, we must first arrange the gospels themselves in their proper chronological order. Unfortunately, even this has not been without difficulty.

Relative Dating of the Gospels

If we were able to compare the gospels to one another and arrange them in their most probable chronological sequence it would be a major step toward dating them accurately. Researchers have tried to do this by determining which authors may have used other gospels as source documents for their own work. If there is evidence that the author of Matthew used Mark for instance, it would demonstrate that Mark was the earlier of the two gospels.

A large majority of scholars today believes that the authors of Matthew and Luke used the Gospel of Mark as a reference. If so, this would establish that Mark was the earliest of the three synoptics. However, this is a subjective process. Often the evidence of literary interdependence can be read in both directions. In many instances where it appears as though Matthew copied from Mark, one might also argue that Mark was the later writer, and that it was Mark who copied from Matthew. So while a literary interdependence between Matthew and Mark is accepted by virtually all researchers, it is the *direction of dependence* which is critical to sequencing the gospels, and it is the direction which is often subject to debate. Similarly such an interdependence is accepted between Luke and Mark, although again the direction of dependence is debated. However, since both Matthew and Luke are substantially longer documents with a greater array of traditions and teachings, most scholars are inclined to accept that Mark was the earliest of the three.

Literary Dependence Between John and Mark

When we turn to John and Mark, we find a different story. There is a remarkable literary correlation between these two gospels which cannot easily be dismissed as coincidental. The overall framework of the two gospels is similar; some common stories appear in the same order; and several incidental details agree in John and Mark which do not appear in Matthew or Luke. Many contemporary researchers, therefore, believe the author of John must have been intimately familiar with the Gospel of Mark.

On the other hand, Mark contains several important traditions which do not appear in John. Notably the Great Commandments, the tradition that Jesus taught in parables, and the institution of the Eucharist[10] at the Last Supper, all appear in Mark, but are missing from John. Why would the author of John set aside such significant traditions as irrelevant to the story of Jesus if he had been aware of them?

Furthermore, when stories appear in both John and Mark, such as the Feeding of the Five Thousand, or the Anointing at Bethany, Mark's versions often appear to be more refined as compared to John's accounts; in these stories Mark puts Jesus in a better light. It is difficult to imagine, if the author of John did indeed use Mark, that he would edit Mark's comparatively attractive stories in such a remedial style.[11]

So just as there is evidence to suggest the author of John used Mark as a source, there are equally compelling reasons to conclude that he could not have been aware of Mark. In short, the comparison between John and Mark allows for no solution which accounts for all the textual data. Since the issue can be argued convincingly both ways, a slim majority of scholars believe the author of John could not have known Mark, and a large minority argue that he must have.

---

[10] The Christian sacrament of the Eucharist is the taking of the bread and wine as symbolic ingestion of the body and blood of Christ. Protestants believe the bread and wine to be symbols only; Roman Catholics believe that through the miracle of the transubstantiation of the elements, the bread and wine become the actual body and blood of Christ upon ingestion. The tradition that Jesus instituted the sacrament of the Eucharist as the Last Supper appears in all three Synoptic Gospels.

[11] We will examine the differences between the common accounts in John and Mark in Chapter Six.

Dating the Gospels with Known Historical Events

Another method used to date the gospels is to identify the social, political, or religious issues reflected in them, and then attempt to relate them to a particular historical event which can be dated independently. A prime example of this is J. Louis Martyn's analysis of the phrase "put out of the synagogue" which is found three times in the Gospel of John,[12] and which refers to the penalty befalling those who profess Jesus as the Messiah. From these references we know that the author of John is aware that believers risk being eliminated from the synagogue for proclaiming a faith in Jesus.

Martyn suggests that this situation relates to an excommunication of Christians from the synagogues resulting from a formal rabbinical benediction against heretics, known as the *birkat ha-minim*. This benediction is thought by many to have been instituted around 85 to 90 CE. If Martyn is correct in associating the Johannine[13] theme of Christians being put out of the synagogues with a formal benediction against heretics, it would imply that the Gospel of John was composed subsequent to this time frame.[14]

However, this kind of analysis is an inexact science which leans heavily on intuition instead of fact. In the case of Martyn's thesis, detractors have argued that (a) it is not clear when the *birkat ha-minim* was instituted, (b) it is not clear that it was levied at Christians per se, (c) it is not clear that it called for excommunication, and (d) it is not clear that John's reference to believers being put out of the synagogue is the consequence of this formal benediction or an earlier informal hostility. Since there is doubt at so many turns, critics would argue that the occasion of the *birkat ha-minim* cannot be used to reliably date the Gospel of John.[15]

---

[12] John 9:22; 12:42; 16:2

[13] The term *Johannine* means of or pertaining to the writings attributed to John. These would include the Gospel of John as well as the epistles 1, 2, and 3 John. Similarly, *Petrine* refers to the thought and writings of Peter, and *Pauline*, the writings of Paul.

[14] Martyn's argument can be found in his book *History and Theology in the Fourth Gospel*, Abingdon Press, Nashville, 1979, pp. 37-62

[15] This issue will be examined in Chapter Four.

In this case Martyn has identified the *possibility* that the Johannine references to being put out of the synagogue reflect the formal benediction, but there is no certain proof. Most scholars believe Martyn is probably correct, but few would argue that the issue is decisive. The observation leaves the door open for dissenting opinion.

The Fall of Jerusalem

Perhaps the most significant historical with regard to the dating of the gospels was the siege and destruction of Jerusalem by the Romans in 70 CE. Scholars have examined the gospel texts for passages which might indicate an author's awareness of the fall of Jerusalem. If such an awareness can be demonstrated, it is usually taken as an indication that the text was composed subsequent to 70 CE. Though this seems like it should be a rather straightforward analysis, it often ends up being inconclusive as well.

For example, many point to Jesus' statement in John 2:19 in which he says, "Destroy this temple, and in three days I will raise it up." Does this indicate the author was aware of the destruction of the temple in 70 CE, or may we only assume he was aware of the impending possibility of the event? If the former, then the edition of the gospel we have must have been composed subsequent to that date. If the evidence is uncertain, which in this case it is, then the passage offers no concrete evidence to date it subsequent to the events of 70 CE.

Many would date the Gospel of Mark just after 70 CE based on the reference to the destruction of the temple found in Mark 13. However, the passage is an uncertain reference, just as it is in John--it may reflect only the anticipation of the destruction of temple rather than knowledge of the event. In fact there is no good evidence by which to date the Gospel of Mark, and the assumption that it is to be dated around 70 CE is really little more than a guess. Since most would date Luke and Matthew in the decade of the 80s, and since Mark appears to have been used as a source document for the authors of Luke and Matthew, the placement of Mark around 70 CE is a comfortable one.

References to the destruction of the temple appear to be more definite in the gospels of Luke and Matthew. Both gospels contain the same vision of the Temple's destruction found in Mark 13.[16] Furthermore, Luke contains a detailed vision of the siege and destruction of the city, and the mass murder of its inhabitants. It is an accurate depiction of the actual event.[17] These references make most scholars comfortable with dating Matthew and Luke subsequent to 70 CE.

In general it is fair to say the attempt to date the gospels by linking them with known historical events has been of modest value. There are few textual links to historical events to begin with, and those which do exist are often subject to debate.

The Discovery of the Lost Gospel "Q"

To develop a reliable reconstruction of the historical Jesus the earliest gospel traditions must be identified and isolated from mythical and legendary overlays which are presumed to have been added to the gospel story over time. Certainly the correct dating and sequencing of the four NT gospels is a vital element of the study. However, in recent decades two other influential "discoveries" have altered the path of the quest for the historical Jesus. One is the proposal that, in addition to the Gospel of Mark, the authors of Matthew and Luke used another source document which is commonly referred to today as Q. The other is the discovery in 1945 of a full manuscript of the Gospel of Thomas, which is not a NT document, but which many scholars now believe should be granted equal status as a source for historical Jesus research.

The Q theory originated in 1838 when Christian Hermann Weisse proposed that the authors of Matthew and Luke must have each used the same source documents when they wrote their gospels. One was the Gospel of Mark, and the other was identified only as an unknown second source which consisted primarily of a collection of sayings of Jesus. Its author is not known, and since it has just been "discovered" by modern scholars, it never had a name that we are aware of. Its technical name in the academic world is the Synoptic

---

[16] Matt. 24:1-2; Luke 21:5-6
[17] Luke 19:41-44; 21:20

Sayings Source, but it is most frequently referred to simply as "Q" (from the German word *Quelle*, meaning *source*).

Why did Weisse propose a lost sayings document?

The Q theory is a solution to what scholars refer to as the "synoptic problem." The three gospels Matthew, Mark, and Luke, are known as the *synoptic* gospels since they are similar in narrative structure and content, and can be easily compared together side-by-side, *synoptically*. Each of the synoptic gospels contains material that also appears in one or both of the other synoptics. The synoptic problem can be reduced to one simple question: How did these textual duplications occur? The synoptic authors seem to have copied from one another, but the question is the order in which they were written; which authors used which of the other synoptic gospels as sources?

Matthew and Luke are each much longer than Mark. They both contain a significant amount of material which also appears in Mark. In addition they each have quite a few other traditions which do not. Weisse proposed that Matthew and Luke must each have used Mark as a source. This would account for the frequent duplication of material between all three. The texts which appear in all three gospels are collectively known as the *triple tradition*. Figure 1.1 is an illustration of a story which is part of the triple tradition. Most researchers believe Matthew and Luke each took the story from Mark and rendered it in his own words.

In addition to the material common to all three synoptics, there is a significant collection of traditions which appears in both Matthew and Luke, but which is absent from Mark. There are quite a few passages which fall into this category, and collectively they are referred to as the *double tradition*. Figure 1.2 is an example of double tradition material. In this instance the texts are duplicated word for word in both gospels. This is not an infrequent occurrence in the double tradition. In other instances the wording is not identical but similar, and yet in others there are significant variations. Yet the problem is clear: How did Luke and Matthew end up with so many common passages if they did not copy them from Mark?

Figure 1.1: The Healing of Simon Peter's Mother-in-law[18]

Mark 1:29-31	Luke 4:38-39	Matt. 8:14-15
And immediately he left the synagogue, and entered the house of Simon and Andrew, with James and John. Now Simon's mother-in-law lay sick with a fever, and immediately they told him of her. And he came and took her by the hand and lifted her up, and the fever left her; and she served them.	And he arose and left the synagogue and entered Simon's house. Now Simon's mother-in-law was ill with a high fever, and they besought him for her. And he stood over her and rebuked the fever, and it left her; and immediately she arose and served them.	And when Jesus entered Peter's house, he saw his mother-in-law lying sick with a fever; he touched her hand, and the fever left her, and she rose and served them.

Figure 1.2: Jesus' Lament over Jerusalem

Luke 13:34	Matt. 23:37
34 "O Jerusalem, Jerusalem, killing the prophets and stoning those who are sent to you! How often would I have gathered your children together as a hen gathers her brood under her wings, and you would not!	37 "O Jerusalem, Jerusalem, killing the prophets and stoning those who are sent to you! How often would I have gathered your children together as a hen gathers her brood under her wings, and you would not!

The Q theory offers a possible solution. Weisse proposed that Matthew and Luke each used a source document other than Mark which contained a variety of sayings that did not appear in Mark. This is the hypothetical sayings document Q. The material which is common only to Luke and Matthew is assumed to have been drawn from this document.

The Two-Document Hypothesis and the Q Gospel

Today Weisse's theory is more formally known as the Two-Document hypothesis or the Two-Source hypothesis. Though Weisse

---

[18] The gospels indicate that Simon was given the name *Peter* by Jesus. Hence Simon and Peter are the same individual.

had envisioned the Q document to be only a miscellaneous collection of sayings, the theory has evolved into a more formidable concept today--some contemporary scholars believe Weisse set researchers on the path to the discovery of a lost gospel.

During the last few decades the notion that this lost gospel can be largely recovered has caught the imagination of many NT scholars. Some herald the discovery as a new breakthrough in understanding the origins of Christianity. They say it gives us a much clearer picture of the historical Jesus than we have ever had in the past. The lost gospel is alleged to give us a new window through which we can see the beliefs of the first people that followed Jesus.

How is this possible? Quite simply, scholars say that most if not all of this "lost gospel" is embedded in the texts of Matthew and Luke. When the double tradition material is isolated from the larger texts of Matthew and Luke, scholars claim they see an early document from which a whole new perspective of Christian origins comes into view.

Implications of the Discovery

The Q theory has already had a substantial impact on historical Jesus research. Some scholars are busy trying to reconstruct the community which produced the Q gospel, and have tried to define what this community might have believed about Jesus. Burton Mack recently published a book entitled *The Lost Gospel--The Book of Q and Christian Origins*. In it he states:

> The remarkable thing about the people of Q is that they were not Christians. They did not think of Jesus as a messiah or the Christ. They did not take his teachings as an indictment of Judaism. They did not regard his death as a divine, tragic, or saving event. And they did not imagine that he had been raised from the dead to rule over a transformed world. Instead, they thought of him as a teacher whose teachings made it possible to live with verve in troubled times. Thus they did not gather to worship in his name, honor him as a god, or cultivate his memory through hymns, prayers, and rituals.[19]

---

[19] Mack, Burton, *The Lost Gospel: The Book of Q and Christian Origins*, Harper-Collins, 1993, p. 4

In essence Mack's conclusion is that Q gives us a glimpse of a primitive pre-Christian history in the first decades after Jesus' death. His radical view of a pre-Christian people of Q is based on the premise that there is no crucifixion/resurrection material in the double tradition. Hence it is presumed not to have existed in the original Q document, and therefore not been part of the beliefs of the people of Q. The implication of Mack's interpretation is that the preponderance of NT narrative testimony regarding the life of Jesus is a religious invention which bears little resemblance to the historical Jesus:

> Q reveals what Jesus people thought about Jesus before there was a Christian congregation of the type reflected in the letters of Paul, and before the idea of a narrative gospel was even dared. When that thought did occur, it was Q that the authors of the narrative gospels used as a foundation upon which to build their own novel myths of origin.
> Q is the best record we have for the first forty years of the Jesus movements.[20]

Of course such findings would have a significant long term impact on Christianity. The question is whether any of these musings have any real merit. It is a question we will turn to later in this book.

The Gospel of Thomas

The Gospel of Thomas is a recent discovery in biblical research. The first and only complete text of the Gospel of Thomas was discovered in Egypt in 1945 and was first published in 1959. The manuscript was a Coptic translation of the original Greek text. In addition to this text, three Greek fragments have been found as well.

The Gospel of Thomas is exclusively a collection of sayings of Jesus. It contains 114 random sayings of Jesus with no apparent organization, although they might all be characterized as wisdom sayings. Over half of these sayings have direct parallels in the NT gospels. Others contain elements of NT sayings mixed with elements of

---

[20] Mack, Ibid., p. 245

another tradition. Some are entirely foreign to NT thought. The following are a sample of sayings from Thomas[21]:

(20) The followers said to Jesus, "Tell us what heaven's kingdom is like." He said to them, "It is like a mustard seed. It is the smallest of all seeds, but when it falls on prepared soil, it produces a large plant and becomes a shelter for birds of heaven."

(31) Jesus said, "A prophet is not acceptable in the prophet's own town; a doctor does not heal those who know the doctor."

(44) Jesus said, "Whoever blasphemes against the father will be forgiven, and whoever blasphemes against the son will be forgiven, but whoever blasphemes against the holy spirit will not be forgiven, either on earth or in heaven."

(54) Jesus said, "Fortunate are the poor, for yours is heaven's kingdom."

(69) Jesus said, "One who knows all but is lacking in oneself is utterly lacking."

(77) Jesus said, "I am the light that is over all things. I am all: From me all has come forth, and to me all has reached. Split a piece of wood; I am there. Lift up the stone, and you will find me there."

(100) They showed Jesus a gold coin and said to him, "Caesar's people demand taxes from us." He said to them, "Give Caesar the things that are Caesar's, give God the things that are God's, and give me what is mine."

(114) Simon Peter said to them, "Mary should leave us, for females are not worthy of life." Jesus said, "Look, I shall guide her to make her male, so that she too may become a living spirit resembling you males. For every female who makes herself male will enter heaven's kingdom."

Of these sayings, the first four (20, 31, 44, and 54) have direct counterparts in the synoptic gospels. Also, 100 is similar to a synoptic saying, with the exception of the final phrase *and give me what is*

---

[21] Meyer, Marvin, *The Gospel of Thomas*, HarperCollins, 1992

mine. However, the remaining sayings, 69, 77, and 114, are entirely foreign to the thought in the canonical gospels.

The Gospel of Thomas is an independent record of Jesus' sayings derived from a different sect of the Jesus movement. Notably, it contains no narrative structure. It tells us nothing of the birth or life of Jesus, nor does it mention his trial, crucifixion, and resurrection. Some have deduced from this that the Thomas sect of the Jesus movement must have had no concept of the death of Jesus as a sacrificial event related to salvation or redemption.

Scholars have been unable to date the Gospel of Thomas with certainty. However, since several Thomas sayings which have parallels in the canonical gospels seem to be more primitive than their canonical counterparts, some researchers are comfortable with a date in the second half of the first century. However, independent attestation of its existence does not appear until 200 CE, when the earliest of the three Greek fragments is dated, and 225 - 235 CE, when Hippolytus, a church writer, first made reference to it. Accordingly, the circumstances and date of its composition are subject to speculation.

The Influence of Thomas on Q Interpretation

The Gospel of Thomas constitutes new evidence which must be factored into historical Jesus research. The discovery of Thomas establishes that a literary genre existed during the first or second century which highlighted the sayings of Jesus while ignoring issues surrounding his substitutionary and atoning death. The implication is that the sect or community which circulated Thomas was more interested in the teachings of Jesus than his crucifixion or resurrection. Some even conclude from this that the Thomas sect was not aware of these traditions.

The discovery of the Gospel of Thomas has provided the primary impetus to revisualize the Q material. Perhaps Q, rather than being an informal collection of sayings, should instead be thought of as a formal gospel, not unlike Thomas, which circulated during the first century, and which represented the beliefs and teachings of a particular community or sect of the primitive Jesus movement. Researchers have developed speculations along these lines. Perhaps, they suggest, since the double tradition in Matthew and Luke does not include any references to Jesus' crucifixion or resurrection, the Q gospel is evidence of another primitive community which was more interested in the teachings of Jesus than doctrines about his atoning death and resurrection. Since the precedent has been established by the Gospel of Thomas, there is no reason to presume Q could not have represented another community with a similar focus.

Contemporary research has gained momentum in this direction. John Dominic Crossan, in his grand work *The Historical Jesus*, refers to Q as the Q Gospel.[22] Arland Jacobson has published a work entitled *The First Gospel, An Introduction to Q.*[23] Already noted is Burton Mack's book *The Lost Gospel: The Book of Q and Christian Origins.* The modern classic work on Q is John Kloppenborg's *The Formation of Q.*[24] Each of these has (to varying degrees) advanced the notion that Q is a lost book of Jesus traditions which reflects beliefs of a very primitive sect of the Jesus movement. So the idea that Q may be viewed as a formal gospel with its own developmental history and tradition has gained a wider following in recent years. Accordingly, historical Jesus research has begun to consider what the Q Gospel and the Gospel of Thomas may reveal about primitive beliefs in circulation in the decades immediately following Jesus' death.

Currently underway is the International Q Project, headed by James M. Robinson in Claremont, CA. Its principal objective is to reconstruct the original Greek text of Q. Ongoing results are being printed in the Journal of Biblical Literature, but the full text will eventually be published. That publication will generate a momentous increase in Q research.

---

[22] Crossan, John Dominic, *The Historical Jesus: The Life of a Mediterranean Jewish Peasant*, HarperCollins, 1991

[23] Jacobson, *The First Gospel: An Introduction to Q*, Polebridge Press, 1992,

[24] Kloppenborg, John S., *The Formation of Q*, Fortress Press, 1987

Critics of the Q Theory

Proponents of the new Q Gospel theory are not without their critics. Many scholars who would agree that some type of common source must have been used by Matthew and Luke to generate the double tradition would stop short of characterizing it as a lost gospel. They would argue that nothing definitive can be known about the scope and circumstances of origin of this source, and the tendency to think of it as a lost gospel is misguided. In particular, the notion that a unique pre-Christian community of Q people might be discerned from the data at hand is considered a "wholesome return of conjecture on such a trifling investment of fact."[25]

Certainly a more moderate approach which would incorporate the Q findings might be that the Q source circulated as one of several documents in the primitive Jesus movement, and that other documents existed which addressed the narrative elements of Jesus' life, including his death and resurrection. Thus, any evidence which might suggest these traditions did not exist in Q cannot be used to infer that the community which circulated Q was not aware of them.

William Farmer has led a significant minority campaign to advance an alternative solution to the synoptic problem which eliminates the need to assume Q ever existed at all.[26] Farmer argues that the Q theorists have assumed an erroneous chronological sequence of the gospels. He believes Matthew was the first of the three synoptics to be composed, and that Luke followed Matthew. The double tradition, according to Farmer, is to be explained simply by assuming the author of Luke used Matthew as a source and copied Matthew's text directly into his own gospel. There are serious problems with Farmer's position, and not many scholars hold his views. Yet, in defense of his alternative solution, he points out numerous shortcomings of the Q theory which cannot be dismissed as groundless.

Though Farmer's alternative sequencing of the gospels has difficulties, he poses the question which threatens the entire edifice of

---

[25] Phrase borrowed from Mark Twain, *Life on the Mississippi*, Ch. XVII

[26] Farmer, William R., *The Synoptic Problem: A Critical Analysis*, Mercer University Press, 1976

Q theory: If the author of Luke used Matthew, or the author of Matthew used Luke, then the common material between them is to be explained by the second writer copying from the first. If this were the case, there is no need to postulate the existence of a lost gospel. Therefore, the entire Q hypothesis depends upon a reasonable demonstration that the authors of Luke and Matthew could not have been aware of each other's work.

This may be the Achilles' heel of the Q theory. For though a reasonable argument can be sustained that the author of Luke could not have been aware of Matthew, no substantive argument exists to demonstrate that the author of Matthew could not have used Luke. Since the quest for the historical Jesus has focused so heavily upon Q as a window into the primitive Jesus movement, the failure to address this issue is surprising. Yet in most of the latest Q literature, the question is not discussed. We will examine the issue in Chapter Eight.

The Consensus Opinion

A number of issues have been raised thus far. What was the historical sequence of the gospels? Which contain the earliest and most reliable traditions which may go back to the historical Jesus? Does the new Q theory represent a true discovery of a lost gospel which is a trustworthy window into primitive Jesus traditions? For each of these questions an array of answers have been given, and for every majority opinion there is a minority position. However, though there is disagreement on virtually every issue, there is clearly a prevailing opinion among scholars on most aspects of the debate.

Most believe that Mark is the earliest of the four canonical gospels, and that it should be dated around 70 CE. Most believe that Matthew and Luke were compiled sometime in the decade of the 80s CE, and most would place John in the 90s. The Q theory is widely held by most scholars in some form, although most do not draw Mack's radical inferences from it. The Q material is usually assumed to be earlier than Mark, and perhaps as early as the 50s CE.

The Jesus Seminar and the Seven Pillars of Scholarly Wisdom

The Jesus Seminar is an association of prominent biblical scholars who have taken up the task of identifying what they believe to be the authentic words and deeds of Jesus. In 1993, the Jesus Seminar published a work entitled *The Five Gospels*,[27] in reference to Matthew, Mark, Luke, John, and Thomas. This work focuses on the sayings of Jesus in these gospels, and ranks them according to the probability of having been spoken by Jesus.

The work of the Jesus Seminar has drawn criticism from Christians who object to the Seminar's results. Burton Mack writes:

> Part of the problem is that the Jesus Seminar has not been able to explain to the public how it arrives at its conclusions. When it has tried, the frightful lack of basic knowledge about the formation of the New Testament among average Christians has blocked the conversation.[28]

In this book, we will attempt to bridge the gap between the theories of the scholars and the knowledge level of the lay reader who is interested in understanding how the Jesus Seminar arrived at its conclusions. As a side note, the reader should not infer from Mack's comment that there is no criticism of the Jesus Seminar from the academic community. To the contrary, many scholars who are well aware of the issues take exception to the Seminar's methods and results.

The Seminar derived the probabilities that Jesus' sayings originated with him by a democratic vote of the association. Each participating scholar categorized the sayings of Jesus into four groups. The four categories represented (1) sayings which undoubtedly originated with Jesus, (2) sayings which probably originated with Jesus in some similar form, (3) sayings which did not originate with Jesus, but which reflect ideas close to his own, and (4) sayings which did not originate with Jesus and which were derived from a different tradition. Point values were assigned to each category, and a weighted average probability for each saying was calculated based on the number of times it was assigned to each category by the Fellowship.

---

[27] The Jesus Seminar, *The Five Gospels*, Polebridge Press, 1993
[28] Mack , Ibid., p. 193

Having assigned probabilities to each saying, they were statistically ranked from most probable to least probable. The admonition to turn the other cheek (Matt. 5:39; Luke 6:29a) was ranked first, with a probability of 92%. Several were given a 0% probability, such as "every tree which does not bear good fruit is cut down and thrown into the fire" (Matt 7:19). Those sayings which scored a high probability, when isolated together as a subgroup of sayings, are thought to be a good starting point for reconstructing the original message of Jesus.

There are several problems with this methodology. The use of statistical rankings and discrete categories implies that there is an objective basis for categorizing the sayings. Clearly there is not. While certain guidelines may be used to infuse the process with a degree of objectivity, and indeed the Jesus Seminar employed such guidelines, ultimately the decisions of the individual Fellows are based upon their own assumptions regarding the dating and interrelationships of the texts. If these assumptions do not hold, the decisions based upon them will not be valid either.

The introduction to *The Five Gospels* indicates that the work has been performed using a specific set of assumptions, which are identified as the Seven Pillars of Scholarly Wisdom. These constitute fundamental assumptions underlying the work of the Jesus Seminar.[29] The first pillar is the recognition that there is a distinction between the historical Jesus and the Christ of faith. The creeds and beliefs of the Jesus movement served to interpret the life and teachings of Jesus such that the actual life of Jesus was overlaid with a legendary and mythical interpretation. Few would dispute the reasonableness of this assumption, for the effort to distinguish between the historical Jesus and the Christ of faith is the definition of the quest for the historical Jesus itself.

The second pillar states that the historical Jesus is to be found within the traditions of the synoptic gospels. The Gospel of John is not relevant in the study, for it is a spiritualized work with little historical value. This assumption, while widely held among scholars today, is subject to challenge. Several traditions in the Fourth Gospel seem to have greater historical credibility than their synoptic counterparts. On

---

[29] See *The Five Gospels*, pp. 2-5 for full discussion.

frequent occasions the author appears to have command of historical details which are simply missing from the synoptic gospels. So to discard the entire gospel based on its spiritual orientation is to set aside data which may indeed be relevant to historical Jesus research.

The third pillar is the recognition that Mark is the earliest of the three synoptic gospels, and forms the foundation for both Matthew and Luke. Though there is a minority of scholars who would dispute this claim, the large majority are willing to assume this as fact. The evidence in this book will support this assumption.

The fourth pillar is the discovery of Q as a hypothetical source for the double tradition. Since Q was used by both Matthew and Luke, it is assumed to be an older writing which was closer to the historical Jesus. Though this is also widely accepted as fact, two inferences from the Q theory are subject to challenge. First, there is no firm evidence that Q circulated as an independent document prior to the composition of Matthew and Luke. Second, there is no way to determine with certainty the relative date of the traditions reflected in the Q material. All we know with certainty is that the Q traditions existed by the time Matthew and Luke were composed. The statistical analysis in this book will offer evidence that the Q material was not as early as is commonly supposed. The implication is that a reliance upon Q traditions as a window into the primitive Jesus movement may be misguided.

The Jesus Seminar's fifth pillar of wisdom relates to the recognition that the visions of the end of the world which are so prominent in the synoptic gospels do not go back to the historical Jesus. All of the material regarding the day of judgment and the second coming are presumed to be later overlays of legend which were added by the first century Jesus movement. The statistical analysis to be presented here will show that this assumption is also well founded.

The sixth pillar states that the authentic sayings of Jesus circulated in an oral form in the early decades, and only later were they written down. Accordingly, teachings which appear to have originated in oral transmission are alleged to have a greater potential for historical authenticity. Further, sayings which are presumed to have originated in oral tradition are those which are "short, provocative, and memorable." These are characteristics of aphorisms which, along with parables, are assumed to have constituted the earliest Jesus traditions.

Now there is a problem with this assumption. It predefines the character and nature of Jesus' teaching style before determining who the historical Jesus actually was. Once we presume that Jesus had a particular message, and used a unique teaching style, the gospel sayings which fit the message and style will automatically be granted a higher probability of having originated with Jesus. Hence the assumption largely predetermines the outcome.

However, there is no logical ground for assuming *apriori* that Jesus' teaching style was primarily aphoristic or parabolic in nature, for such a conclusion has not been independently arrived at. Further, there is no reason to equate short, provocative, memorable sayings with historical authenticity, since any saying attributed to Jesus at a later time may have had an origin in oral transmission, and may have been short, provocative, and memorable. So to make judgments regarding historical authenticity using oral origin as a criterion is not likely to shed any meaningful light on the subject, and may potentially be misleading.

The final pillar of wisdom recognizes a shift in the burden of proof from proving that the various gospel traditions are not historical, to proving that they are. Once it was assumed that all accounts in the gospels were historical, and it lay with the historian to demonstrate that certain elements may not have been. Today of course, the scholarly approach is reversed. It assumes the gospels are theologically motivated works, and that the various traditions within them must be demonstrated as historical. Though this was once a radical idea, it is an assumption which amounts to common sense in contemporary historical inquiry.

In short, the Jesus Seminar has produced work based on a series of assumptions which may or may not be accurate. Certainly, assumptions as fundamental as the priority of the Q material or the irrelevance of the Gospel of John will prejudice the outcome of the study before it is out of the starting gate. When the Gospel of John is set aside as irrelevant to the inquiry, and the hypothetical Q Gospel is held to be an important, and perhaps crucial primitive source, the probabilities regarding what Jesus may or may not have said are largely predefined. Thus, a close examination of these "pillars of wisdom" is the key to verifying whether the conclusions of the Jesus Seminar may be considered trustworthy.

The Johannine Dilemma

One of the key assumptions made not only by the Jesus Seminar, but by almost all scholars involved in historical Jesus research, is that the Gospel of John is irrelevant to the study. Yet it cannot be dismissed with such ease. For it is a work steeped in paradox which threatens to defy all common sense analysis. Upon close examination, virtually every aspect of John's thought is accompanied by an unexplained void.

For instance, it is common to characterize John as a mythologized gospel, since it is the only one of the four which depicts Jesus as a preexistent heavenly being--the man who came down from heaven. While this is true, John is also the gospel which contains the fewest supernatural stories which could have been used to illustrate its divine characterization of Jesus. In John, there are no demons and no temptations of Jesus by Satan. There is no virginal conception of Mary, and angels do not appear from on high to startle human observers. There is no transfiguration of Jesus upon the mountain, nor any appearance of Moses and Elijah. Earthquakes and eclipses of the sun do not occur upon Jesus' death, and the temple curtain is not torn in two. The saints are not raised from the tombs to walk the streets of Jerusalem. There is no ascension of Jesus into heaven after his resurrection.

These and other stories of a mythical nature appear throughout the synoptic gospels. If John is such a mythological work (and with respect to its characterization of Jesus it indeed may be considered as such), where is the rest of this mythological tradition which could so effectively illustrate the story of the divine man from heaven?

This is only the beginning of the paradox. John is often described as a deep theological reflection on the nature of Jesus which must have taken many decades to develop. However, though there is a profound vision of Jesus as a heavenly being, the moral content of his teaching as compared to the synoptic tradition is limited.

In John, we find no Golden Rule, and no admonitions to love one's neighbor, to turn the other cheek, or to answer evil with good. There is no charge to love one's enemies, or to pray in private, or to sell all one has and give to the poor. There is no caution about laying up treasures on earth rather than in heaven. Indeed, the moral teachings of Jesus which are documented throughout the synoptic gospels are almost absent from John. Where, we may wonder, is the profound moral vision that one might expect to accompany an evolved and deeply spiritual interpretation of Jesus?

Yet another paradox exists in the visions of the end of the world. John is presumed to have been written in the 90s CE, at a time when apocalyptic fever seems to have been prominent. Matthew (most would presume) had already written his dark vision of the end of the world, foretelling violent persecution of the faithful, God's destruction of the world, and the final judgment.[30] Similarly the Revelation to John (or The Apocalypse), another tremendous image of the violent end of the world, was written in the 90s. We may wonder, then, how it came to be that the Gospel of John, presumably written during the same period of time, shows no awareness of an impending violent cataclysm--such a concept is simply absent from the text.

Another peculiar element missing from the Gospel of John is any awareness of the church as an institutionalized entity. By the end of the first century, the concept of clergy vs. laity had already appeared, at least in some churches.[31] Titles such as bishop, deacon, and presbyter were in use, and the notion of Apostolic Succession had already appeared. Rules and procedures regarding the sacrament of the Eucharist had developed.

Now it is not known to what degree the various Christian communities had assumed formal organizational structures by the end of the first century. However, the odd aspect of John is that evidence of organizational structure is missing entirely. The words *church* and *apostle* do not appear anywhere in John, as they do in the synoptics.

---

[30] Matthew 24, 25

[31] The First Epistle of Clement, the fourth Bishop of Rome, written to the church at Corinth in about 96 CE, provides an extraordinary view of the degree to which the churches in Rome and Corinth had developed as institutional entities.

There is no hierarchy among disciples; the Lord's Prayer is not recorded in John, nor is the sacrament of the Eucharist. There are no complex liturgical formulas. How can these missing elements be explained?

Finally, though the Jesus movement had spread throughout the Roman Empire by the end of the first century, there appears to be no awareness in John of a deliberate mission to the gentile world. Indeed, John is the only gospel which does not contain the word *gentile*.

In pointing out that John does not contain all of these elements, it is not suggested that a late first century writing would be expected to contain all of them. Any given topic may be explained away as inconsequential to the objectives of the author or irrelevant to the concerns of the community for which he was writing. Perhaps the Johannine community, unlike other Christian communities, had no belief in an apocalyptic end of the world. Perhaps they felt Jesus' moral teachings were to be subordinated to larger issues at hand; perhaps they had no concept of apostles, bishops, deacons, and presbyters, or a separation of clergy and laity; perhaps they had not yet adopted the Eucharist as a formal sacrament.

In this manner the evidence can be dismissed one category at a time without further explanation. However, it is the collective absence of so much of what constituted the expression of the late first century church that raises the question. How is it that such a lengthy treatise on the person of Jesus avoids all traces of so much that had become integral to Christian thought and expression?

For researchers on the quest for the historical Jesus, the Gospel of John presents an enormous dilemma which has yet to be satisfactorily resolved. It is a dilemma which is often simply ignored. Frequently the Fourth Gospel is dismissed as a theological work with little historical value. Geza Vermes, in his recent work *The Religion of Jesus the Jew*, makes the point definite:

> Research has to be restricted to Mark, Matthew, and Luke and to exclude John because, despite the occasional historical detail it contains, its Jesus portrait is so evolved theologically as to be wholly unsuitable for historical investigation.[32]

---

[32] Vermes, Geza, *The Religion of Jesus the Jew*, Augsburg Fortress Press, 1993, p. 4

Yet to dismiss the Gospel of John as "wholly unsuitable for historical investigation" without coming to terms with its paradoxical nature is to set aside potentially vital data in the historical quest. All four gospels are theological reflections on the life of Jesus, John no more so that the others. The difference is that many of John's attributions seem to have obliterated the historical language of Jesus. For example, the pronouncement of the arrival of the kingdom of God which is so prominent in the synoptic gospels is virtually absent from John. Further, many of Jesus' sayings in John sound very much like theological attributions rather than something he actually may have said. For instance, consider Jesus' prayer to the Father in John 17, in which he says, "and now Father, glorify thou me in thy own presence with the glory which I had with thee before the world was made." (17:5)

Nevertheless, John constitutes evidence unexplained and unaccounted for, and it is contrary to that found in the synoptic traditions. Until someone demonstrates with firm evidence that the Fourth Gospel is irrelevant to historical inquiry, its contradictions to the synoptic traditions must somehow be factored into the research in order for the results to be valid. Any portrait of the historical Jesus which starts by discarding the puzzling evidence from the Gospel of John is potentially a house built upon the sand.

Current Status of the Quest

The quest for the historical Jesus continues. At its core is the ongoing debate about the dates, the historical viability, and the literary interrelationships between the canonical and non-canonical writings which have survived from the first and early second centuries. Somewhere between the lines of these highly interpreted and theologically motivated documents, the true historical Jesus is to be located. Many scholars remain committed to the effort.

However, due in part to the array of theories regarding the dating and relative historical value of the documents, scholars have created a variety of portraits of Jesus which conflict with one another. This cannot help but lead many scholars to conclude again, as they did earlier in this century, that the quest itself is hopeless. The problem is acknowledged by Crossan in the prologue to *The Historical Jesus*:

> Historical Jesus research is becoming something of a scholarly bad joke. There were always historians who said it could not be done because of historical problems. There were always theologians who said it should not be done because of theological objections. And there were always scholars who said the former when they meant the latter. Those, however, were negative indignities. What is happening now is rather a positive one. It is the number of competent and even eminent scholars producing pictures of Jesus at wide variance with one another.[33]

Crossan goes on to summarize seven different images of Jesus that have been proposed by scholars in recent years:

> There is Jesus as a political revolutionary by S. G. F. Brandon (1967), as a magician by Morton Smith (1978), as a Galilean charismatic by Geza Vermes (1981, 1984), as a Galilean rabbi by Bruce Chilton (1984), as a Hillelite or proto-Pharisee by Harvey Falk (1985), as an Essene by Harvey Falk (1985), and as an eschatological prophet by E. P. Sanders (1985).[34]

To this list must be added Burton Mack's characterization of Jesus as a cynic sage. In short, every conceivable characterization of Jesus has at one time or another been advanced by someone. We are unlikely to embark upon a new quest for the historical Jesus and end up with an answer that no one has yet imagined. The question then is which of the characterizations of Jesus already proposed is closest to the truth, and how may we determine this reliably?

Such a diverse set of results clearly derives from the fact that many theories about the gospels in vogue today are often inherently paradoxical, and leave as many unanswered questions as they do explanations in their wake. In essence, they do not explain all the evidence. When the underlying theories do not account for all the facts, the result is predictable. It is natural that each scholar will have an inclination to see Jesus in a certain light. For each, some of the

---

[33] Crossan, Ibid., p. xxvii
[34] Crossan, Ibid., p. xxvii-xxviii

inconclusive documentary evidence will have more intuitive appeal than other. Hence a solution that is satisfying for one scholar with be met with negative critique by another; a different portrait of Jesus may be drawn from each researcher's preferred subset of data.

The Assumptions are the Problem

Historical Jesus research is undermined before it begins when the paradoxical nature of its underlying assumptions is disregarded. To set aside the Gospel of John as non-historical without accounting for its ironic silence on so many issues is to ignore data which may be vital after all. Similarly, as we will see, the theory of Q, while explaining much about synoptic relationships, leaves an array of facts unexplained as well. To build a portrait of Jesus largely based on the assumption that Q is a "lost gospel" without reconciling the theory's inherent difficulties is to effectively exclude data which may be crucial.

Alternatives to the Q theory have been largely unsuccessful. Farmer's solution to the synoptic problem, though it succeeds in explaining most of what the Q theory does not, in the process it leaves an even larger bag of unexplained data out on the porch. It is for this reason that most scholars default to the Q theory. Most researchers who opt for some form of the Q theory do not do so because it ties everything together in one neat ball, but rather because it seems to leave a smaller assortment of messy loose ends than competing theories. Yet as long as the edifice of historical Jesus research is built upon theories which explain only portions of the data, the quest cannot yield anything but a variety of contrasting portraits of Jesus.

A New Approach

Imagine that the quest for the historical Jesus is like climbing a mountain, and that the answers we seek do not come into view until we get to the peak. Many have tried to scale this mountain, and several different routes to the top have been attempted. Rudolf Bultmann claimed earlier in the century that the summit could not be achieved, that it would forever remain hidden in the clouds and shrouded in mystery. More recently, scholars armed with a new trail map known as Q have tried to make the climb once more. However, they have often come back with reports that are inconsistent, or that do not explain all of the evidence available to us. For Q reveals a trail which ends before the peak is achieved. One suspects that scholars following the Q map stopped short of the peak where the map ended, and settled for describing the vista they saw from their resting place.

This book will present an entirely new map to the top of the mountain. It blazes a new trail which begins and ends in a very unlikely place--the Gospel of John. Chapter Two will begin the quest by exploring an unusual feature of John. This gospel contains an unprecedented attack on the character and credibility of the apostle Peter. In fact, the gospel was written, in large part, to show that Peter was a betrayer of the Jesus movement, just as Judas Iscariot was. This is not a well recognized feature of John, but a close examination of the literary devices used by the author will show that he was highly motivated to convince his audience that Peter could not be trusted as a leader of the movement.

The chapter will then show that John 21, which is an appendix to the original gospel, was added later by someone who was interested in negating the unsavory attack on Peter which exists in the gospel itself. The hostility toward Peter in the gospel, and the attempt to mitigate it in the appendix, presents us with a fascinating glimpse of a struggle between two different factions of the Jesus movement who were each attempting to discredit the other, and define what they believed was the true legacy of Jesus.

Thus, the origin of John 21 becomes a critical piece of the puzzle. Who wrote it, and how did it come to be appended to the gospel? Why did those who circulated the original Gospel of John allow the appendix to be added? The last part of Chapter Two explores the clues which might reveal the answers to these questions.

Based on this inquiry, Chapter Three presents a new observation in NT studies. It is that the text upon which John 21 is based was most likely the missing ending to the Gospel of Mark. Scholars are in wide agreement that the Gospel of Mark originally ended at 16:8, where the earliest and best manuscripts terminate. However, this ending shows the women on Easter morning fleeing from the empty tomb in fear. The gospel ends without any resurrection appearances to the disciples, and it makes the gospel appear to be unfinished. Why would the author have chosen to end his gospel at such an unlikely place? Though scholars have made great attempts to explain this abrupt ending, Chapter Three reveals that the gospel did in fact have a more traditional ending after all. Furthermore, it can be largely reconstructed from John 21.

Chapter Three ends with a reflection on the nature of John and Mark once they are reconstructed as originally composed. Once John 21 is deleted from the Gospel of John, and the stories it contains added to Mark 16:8, something remarkable appears. It looks as though the Gospel of Mark was originally composed as a rebuttal of the Gospel of John. Yet how could this be? Mark is presumed to have been composed around 70 CE, and John in the 90s. If these dates are correct, then Mark could not have been a response to John. The problem forces us to reconsider the evidence for the dating of the gospels.

Chapter Four will examine the evidence scholars rely upon to date John in the 90s. It will be shown that this evidence is inconclusive, and nothing certain has really been established about the composition date of this important gospel.

Chapter Five explores the positive evidence that John could be a very primitive work. This chapter will open the door to the possibility that many of the traditions which are missing from John are missing because it was composed before these traditions emerged as part of the expression of the primitive church. Though the proposal that John may have been the earliest of the four gospels has been made several times by scholars during the course of this century, the academic community has not generally accepted the traditional arguments in favor of this thesis. However, with a new understanding of the hostility between the Johannine community and Peter, and the striking literary relationship between John 21 and the missing ending of Mark, a new and more convincing argument can be constructed which shows that John was indeed the earliest gospel.

This finding establishes the grounds for a further examination of the relationship between John and Mark. Chapter Six demonstrates that the author of Mark did in fact write in response to John, and that many of the ideas presented in Mark were written as correctives to John. Notably, Mark's prominent theme of the Messianic Secret was developed in response to John's characterization of Jesus as one who boldly and frequently proclaimed himself to be the Messiah. Yet this is only one of a number of examples of the discord between the Johannine and Markan traditions that are taken up in Chapter Six.

At this point in the book, two of the Jesus Seminar's seven pillars of wisdom will have been called into serious doubt--the claim that John is historically irrelevant to the quest for Jesus, and the claim that Mark is the earliest of the narrative gospels. Furthermore, the results of the study through the end of Chapter Six will leave us with an interesting observation. We will have identified three independent, or semi-independent, traditions of Jesus which are early--the Gospel of John, the Gospel of Mark, and the letters of Paul. These three traditions have two important things in common. First, they all focus on the death and resurrection of Jesus as the supreme event by which the meaning of Jesus' career is to be defined. Second, none of the three have any significant awareness of the traditions manifested in Q. Hence, a significant discrepancy exists between the evidence from these traditions and the evidence from Q. If Q was truly a primitive record, with origins in the ministry of the historical Jesus, how did the Q traditions escape the notice of John, Mark, and Paul?

The dilemma forces us to reconsider how the primitive church's ideas about Jesus may have grown and evolved during the first century. When we interpret John as the first gospel, Mark as the second, and Luke and Matthew as later documents, is it possible to discern a pattern of development through the four? Chapter Seven undertakes this study, and shows that there is a remarkable statistical progression of thought from John to Mark to Luke, and finally to Matthew. The statistical patterns are virtually duplicated as we look at the growth in moral vision, the growth in supernatural mythologies, and the growth in the urgency and prominence of eschatological reflection (ideas about the end of the world and the second coming of Jesus). The statistical patterns provide independent evidence that the gospels must have been produced in the chronological sequence John-

Mark-Luke-Matthew, and that each gospel represents a snapshot of Christian thought at several stages of development.

These findings are in conflict with the academic vision of Q as separate and primitive tradition. The problem must be confronted directly: What is the evidence for the existence of the Q gospel? Are scholars correct in seeing a primitive gospel in the double tradition? Chapter Eight examines the evidence, and uncovers a serious flaw in the logical presuppositions underlying the Q theory. The chapter shows that it is extremely remote that the duplication of texts in Matthew and Luke could be the result of the two authors' common use of the same source. Thus, the chapter challenges the viability of the Q theory, and suggests that Q, as a single source document, probably never existed. With this conclusion, a third vital pillar underlying the studies of the Jesus Seminar is shown to be unreliable.

With the undermining of the Q theory, we near the end of our quest. Since Q may be dismissed as a significant factor, and since Luke and Matthew will have been shown to be late and mythologized traditions, the results of our study will lead us back into the gospels of John and Mark as the earliest surviving records of the life and ministry of Jesus. Between the lines of these two gospels the historical Jesus is to be found. We will discover, perhaps not surprisingly, that Rudolf Bultmann was not entirely wrong--there are mists at the peak which obscure our vision. Our ability to discover the historical Jesus is hampered by the ideological conflict out of which the gospels of John and Mark were formed.

Yet at the same time, a clear and coherent sketch of Jesus will emerge from John and Mark. We cannot know fully, but we can know truly several important elements of the life and purpose of Jesus. Further, we can begin to discern the historical reality of the event which would define Jesus for all time--his resurrection from the dead. In the pages of the Gospel of John we will find fascinating clues as to what really may have happened that day. At the top of the mountain, the historical Jesus is recognized and the resurrection story becomes rational. It is a place where faith and reason may be reconciled.

❖ 2 ❖

Peter and the Beloved Disciple

The Gospel of John is commonly regarded as the most spiritual gospel among the four in the NT. It is frequently interpreted as a deep theological reflection on the divine nature of Jesus which was composed late in the first century, and most commentaries on John focus on its unique theological and spiritual characteristics. Thus the fact that John is also extraordinary antagonistic toward Peter is often overlooked. This chapter will show that John's Gospel contains an urgent warning about Peter which was as vital to the author's purpose as his theological reflection on the nature of Jesus. His message was bold and deliberate: the apostle Peter was a betrayer of Jesus, and was not to be trusted as a leader of the movement.

Such a claim may strike some readers as hyperbolic if not completely absurd. In Christian tradition, Peter is revered and loved as the leading apostle among the twelve. He is a prominent figure in all four NT gospels. He was a great Christian martyr, crucified by the Romans during the decade of the 60s CE. To Roman Catholics, Peter was the first Pope of the church. Furthermore, John 21 contains a scene in which the risen Jesus commissions Peter to tend the flock. So to suggest that the author of John intended to sully the character of Peter and cast him as a betrayer of the cause will be difficult to imagine. Even scholars who believe the gospels individually tend to reflect pro-Petrine or anti-Petrine bias may think it excessive to suggest John intended to denounce Peter as a betrayer of the Jesus movement. Yet upon close examination of the passages in which Peter appears in John, such an inference seems inescapable.

John 21

The true extent of the animosity toward Peter in the Gospel of John has gone unrecognized due in large part to the appendix--John 21. In John 21 we find a scene in which the resurrected Lord converses with Peter, forgives him for his earlier denials, and restores him to a position of grace. In this scene, Jesus encourages Peter to feed his sheep--to actively nourish and propagate the movement. If this appendix is a legitimate part of the Johannine tradition, then it may be improper to interpret the gospel as excessively hostile toward Peter. The question is whether John 21 truly has a genuine Johannine origin.

We will take a closer look at John 21 and its relationship to the gospel later in this chapter. For the present, only a few observations need be made before we turn to a study of Peter in John. First, scholars are divided regarding the origin of John 21. Many have attempted to demonstrate that this appendix is an integral part of Johannine tradition, and that it shows an affinity with Johannine thought. Some have even argued that it was written by the author of the gospel; others have suggested it was added by a disciple of the author.

However, other researchers have pointed to elements in John 21 such as the sons of Zebedee (21:2), and the fishing motif, as being foreign to the gospel. Further, the storyline of John 21 is not compatible with the end of John 20, for there is no explanation as to why the disciples would return to their fishing boats in Galilee after seeing the risen Lord in Jerusalem. This has caused many to suggest that John 21 looks as though it was originally composed at a different time, and for a different purpose, than as an appendix to the gospel.

The purpose of John 21 is obscure. Many believe it was added to clarify the confusion which arose from the death of the Beloved Disciple, whose death was apparently not expected prior to Jesus' return. Others think it was intended to clarify the dual role of Peter and the Beloved Disciple as leaders of the movement.

Since few have recognized the severity with which the Gospel of John maligns Peter, John 21 is rarely interpreted as an addition by pro-Petrine editors intent upon reversing the negative appraisal of Peter found in the gospel. Yet such an interpretation becomes plausible once we consider the author's treatment of Peter throughout John 1-20.

The appendix cannot be properly interpreted except in its relation to the politics of the gospel. So it is premature to delve into a detailed analysis of John 21 until we have analyzed the gospel's position on Peter. However, for reasons which will become clear later, the original Gospel of John will be assumed to have been complete at the end of John 20, and references in this chapter to the "gospel" or the "Gospel of John" will refer only to the first twenty chapters. John 21 will be considered a separate appendix which was not originally intended by the author or his disciples.

Peter in the Gospel of John

Anyone who reads the Fourth Gospel with attention to its treatment of Peter will agree that he appears as a prominent, although not particularly inspiring figure. A quick review of the scenes in which he appears shows him to be an affable but bumbling, impulsive, and uncomprehending disciple. Though he is often well-intentioned, Peter does not understand Jesus' purpose. It is this widely acknowledged characterization of Peter as ineffective and confused which lead many to conclude that the author may have had an anti-Petrine bias.

However, even those who would acknowledge the gospel's unattractive portrayal of Peter will object that it is a tremendous leap to conclude that the author intended to cast him as a betrayer of the movement. Is there really any evidence to support such an extreme conclusion? Indeed there is. It will become clear that the author intended to draw sinister implications from Peter's perpetual state of confusion. This is evident from the structure of the first three scenes in which Peter engages in dialogue. Peter does not have a speaking role until John 6. In this passage, Jesus has just finished giving a disturbing teaching which repelled not only his larger audience, but many of his own followers as well:

[Jesus said,] "It is the spirit that gives life, the flesh is of no avail; the words that I have spoken to you are spirit and life. But there are some of you that do not believe." **For Jesus knew from the first who those were that did not believe, and who it was that would betray him.** And he said, "This is why I told you that no one can come to me unless it is granted him by the Father."

After this many of his disciples drew back and no longer went about with him. Jesus said to the twelve, "Do you also wish to go away?" <u>Simon</u> Peter answered him, "Lord, to whom shall we go? You have the words of eternal life; and we have believed, and have come to know, that you are the Holy One of God." Jesus answered them, **"Did I not choose you, the twelve, and one of you is a devil?" He spoke of Judas <u>the son of Simon Iscariot</u>, for he, one of the twelve, was to betray him.** (John 6:63-71)

This episode, generally referred to as Peter's Confession of Faith, is attested in all four gospels (Mark 8:27-30; Luke 9:18-21; Matt. 16:13-20), and is universally interpreted as consistent with Peter's special leadership role in the primitive movement. However, the rendering of the story in John is different from the corresponding accounts in the synoptic gospels, as we will see shortly.

The first important element to note is that Peter's appearance is sandwiched between two reflections upon the fact that Jesus is soon to be betrayed. This sequence of themes is not accidental. The technique the author uses here is known as *intercalation*. Intercalation is the bracketing of one idea or story with two parts of another. The author's purpose in juxtaposing the two stories or themes is to allow one to interpret the other. Intercalation was a common technique among first century writers, and it appears frequently in John and Mark.[1] The author of John makes repeated use of it in his portrayal of Peter.

---

[1] Intercalation is widely recognized as a literary technique found in Mark. It is less recognized in John. Prime examples of intercalation in Mark include the healing of the woman with the 12 years flow of blood, which is sandwiched by two halves of the story of the raising of Jairus' 12 year-old daughter (Mark 5:21-43), and the Cleansing of the Temple which is bracketed between two elements of the Cursing of the Fig Tree (Mark 11:12-25). In the first bracketed story, the healing of the woman's hemorrhage is the consequence and result of her faith--it is not simply a magic act performed by Jesus. This is to inform the interpretation of the raising of Jairus' daughter, an act which again is not to be interpreted as a random miracle of Jesus' but rather an event which transpires as a direct result of the faith of Jairus. In this intercalated sequence, the author has made a strong statement that faith precedes healing. In the second set

Note that the author draws attention to the fact that Judas Iscariot's father's name was *Simon*. This is not an irrelevant detail, nor is it accidental. The same ironic juxtaposing of Simon Iscariot and Simon Peter occurs twice more in this gospel. In both it is within the context of a similar bracketed sequence in which the appearance of Peter is preceded and followed by reflections of Jesus' imminent betrayal. This will be interpreted momentarily.

In the passage above, the author has been careful to indicate that the twelve have collectively come to believe; it is not just Peter alone. Peter speaks on behalf of the twelve in declaring that they *all* know that Jesus is the "Holy One of God." Thus, Jesus' response is not to Peter, but to the twelve. There is no indication in this passage that Peter has gained a unique insight which the other disciples do not have.

Another singular element in this passage is Jesus' abrupt response which does not seem to follow from Peter's positive recognition of him. C.K. Barrett attempts to explain it:

> . . . Peter's confession of faith, which is true so far as it goes . . . must not be allowed to suggest that the maker of it is in any sense conferring a benefit upon Jesus. The Twelve have not chosen him; he has chosen them.[2]

In essence, then, Jesus' response diminishes the import of Peter's statement of faith as an individual revelation. Any one of the twelve disciples was capable of making the confession of faith. The faith of the twelve is expected since Jesus has chosen them.

To see how unique John's account is relative to the synoptic gospels, we may compare it with Matthew's version of the same event. Matthew tells us that Peter's confession of faith derives from a unique revelation which he alone has been privileged to receive. Accordingly, his confession is not followed by an abrupt response from Jesus, but rather by a tremendous positive affirmation:

---

of stories, the fig tree is cursed, the temple is cleansed, then the fig tree is found withered. The author intends for the fig tree story to interpret the cleansing of the temple. The implication here is that the cleansing amounts to a cursing of the temple, an institution from which no further fruit will be derived.

[2] Barrett, C.K., *The Gospel According to St. John*, Second Edition, Westminster Press, 1978, p. 307

[Jesus] said to them, "But who do you say that I am?" Simon Peter replied, "You are the Christ, the Son of the living God." And Jesus answered him, "Blessed are you Simon Bar-jona! [Bar-jona = son of John] For flesh and blood has not revealed this to you, but my Father who is in heaven. And I tell you, you are Peter, and on this rock I will build my church, and the powers of death shall not prevail against it. I will give you the keys to the kingdom of heaven, and whatever you bind on earth shall be bound in heaven, and whatever you loose on earth shall be loosed in heaven. Then he strictly charged the disciples to tell no one that he was the Christ." (Matt. 16:15-20)

There can be little doubt from this passage that the author of Matthew supports Peter as the rightful heir to leadership of the movement. Peter's confession of faith is treated as a revelation by Jesus, and since Peter alone is the recipient of this special revelation, it is heralded by Jesus as a sign that Peter shall be the foundation of the church. Matthew has given us a version of Peter's confession which anticipates his future leadership role in the church, as confirmed by the first chapters of Acts and Paul's letters (Gal 1:18; 2:7-9). On the other hand John diminishes the confession since Jesus has chosen the twelve. There is no hint in John's version that Peter will have any leadership role in the future.

Peter's second appearance is in John 13:

Now before the feast of the Passover, when Jesus knew that his hour had come to depart out of this world to the Father, having loved his own who were in the world, he loved them to the end. **And during supper, when the devil had already put it into the heart of Judas Iscariot, Simon's son, to betray him,** Jesus, knowing that the Father had given all things into his hands, and that he had come from God and was going to God, rose from supper, laid aside his garments, and girded himself with a towel. Then he poured water into a basin, and began to wash the disci-ple's feet, and to wipe them with the towel with which he was girded. He came to Simon Peter; and Peter said to him, "Lord do you wash my feet?" Jesus answered him, "What I am doing you do not know now, but afterward you will understand." Peter said to him, "You shall never wash my feet." Jesus answered him, "If I do not wash you, you have no part in me." Simon Peter said to him, "Lord, not my feet only but also my hands and my head!" Jesus said to him, "He who has bathed does not need to wash, except for his feet, but he is clean all over; and you are clean, **but not every one of you." For he knew who was to betray him; that was why he said, "You are not all clean."** (John 13:1-11)

In this second episode the appearance of Peter is once again sandwiched between two separate reflections on the fact that Jesus is about to be betrayed. We also find the second of three notes that Judas is the son of Simon. By framing the appearances of Peter around the betrayal theme, the author intentionally associates Peter with Judas. Further, by repeating the detail that Simon is the father of the betrayer, the connection is being drawn so that it is unmistakable. In this scene, Peter is portrayed as exuberant and well-intentioned, but ignorant of the meaning of Jesus' symbolic act. Peter's incomprehension of Jesus' purpose is a feature which will appear several more times.

Moving along to the third dialogue which includes Peter, we find that he is once again bracketed by the betrayal theme:

> **When Jesus had thus spoken, he was troubled in spirit, and testified, "Truly, truly, I say to you, one of you will betray me."** The disciples looked at one another, uncertain of whom he spoke. One of his disciples, whom Jesus loved, was lying close to the breast of Jesus; so Simon Peter beckoned to him and said, "Tell us who it is of whom he speaks." So lying thus, close to the breast of Jesus, he said to him, "Lord, who is it?" Jesus answered him, It is he to whom I shall give this morsel when I have dipped it." **So when he had dipped the morsel, he gave it to Judas, the <u>son of Simon Iscariot</u>. Then after the morsel, Satan entered into him.** (John 13:21-27)

Since this is the third appearance of Peter within the context of the betrayal theme it is clear that the author has intentionally constructed an association of Peter with Judas. The third occurrence of the detail regarding Judas' father Simon confirms this.[3] The question for us is to determine why the author has done so.

From what we have seen so far in the text, two literary objectives are possible. The first is that the author wishes to contrast Peter as an example of faith with Judas as a symbol of failure. The second

---

[3] There is another passage in which Judas appears where Peter is not present. This is the story of the Anointing at Bethany (John 12:1-8). In this passage, Judas is identified simply as *Judas Iscariot, one of his disciples (he who was to betray him)*. The absence in this passage of a reference to his father Simon indicates that it is not required to identify Judas, and that the repeated references in the Peter passages are to strengthen the link between Peter and Judas.

possibility is that the author wishes the reader to *associate* Peter with the betrayer Judas, in order to color Peter as a second betrayer of Jesus.

The problem with the first possibility is that the character of Peter as developed so far is not a great model of faith. He has spoken only three times. In the first dialogue, his confession of faith is dismissed as expected due to the fact that Jesus has chosen the twelve. In the second, Peter does not comprehend the meaning of Jesus' act. In the third dialogue, Peter is befuddled, and is asking the Beloved Disciple to intervene and discover from Jesus who the betrayer is. These are not complimentary images of Peter. Furthermore, Peter's performance gets less attractive as the gospel proceeds. We will soon see that Peter attacks someone with a sword against Jesus' wishes, and that he ultimately denies Jesus and abandons him. It is difficult to make the case that the author created in Peter a model of faith to be interpreted as a positive contrast to Judas.

The second interpretation is that the author associates Peter and Judas so the reader will infer that each of them in his unique way has betrayed the cause of Jesus. Judas stands against Jesus through a sinister act of the will; Peter unintentionally stands against Jesus in his dangerous misunderstanding of Jesus' will and purpose. Though Peter does not mean to, his thorough misapprehension of Jesus' mission is just as devastating as if he had intended to betray the cause.

There are three more scenes in the Gospel of John in which the statements or actions of Peter continue to develop this theme. Here is the next passage in which Peter speaks:

> Simon Peter said to him, "Lord, where are you going?" Jesus answered, "Where I am going you cannot follow me now; but you shall follow afterward." Peter said to him, "Lord, why cannot I follow you now? I will lay down my life for you." Jesus answered, "Will you lay down your life for me? Truly, truly, I say to you, the cock will not crow, till you have denied me three times. (John 13:36-38)

In this passage, Jesus predicts that Peter will deny him three times before the evening is over. It now becomes clear that the author has carefully foreshadowed the three denials of Peter with the three bracketed Judas/Peter/Judas sequences. The author has constructed this gospel to lead to this event, which stands as a singular and momentous failure of Peter. The author is consistent in his repetition of established themes. Peter is represented once again as having good intentions, but he appears not to know what he is saying. Jesus' rebuke exposes Peter's promise of allegiance as frivolous.

As a side note, it is worth emphasizing that the passage seems to ridicule the notion that Peter will lay down his life for Jesus. Since Peter was crucified as a martyr in the mid-60s CE, and since this gospel is often presumed to have been composed in the 90s, one may wonder what conceivable motive the author may have had to malign the character of a martyr--even to the extent of belittling his willingness to die for the cause? Further, why would the church accept such a trivialization of the death of Peter in one of its gospels? These inconsistencies require an explanation. We will return to them in our consideration of John 21 at the end of this chapter.

To return to the previous passage, note that the author has told us that it is Peter alone who commits to lay down his life, and it is he alone who fails to stand by Jesus as the events of Jesus' arrest and trial unfold. This stands in remarkable contrast to the synoptic traditions. For example, in the gospel of Mark we find the same prediction of Peter's denial, but the author has framed it in such a manner that Peter's failure is not unique; it is only representative of the failure of all the disciples:

> And Jesus said to them, "You will all fall away; for it is written, 'I will strike the shepherd, and the sheep will be scattered.' But after I am raised up, I will go before you to Galilee." Peter said to him, "Even though they all fall away, I will not." And Jesus said to him, "Truly I say to you, this very night, before the cock crows twice, you will deny me three times." But he said vehemently, "If I must die with you, I will not deny you." And they all said the same. (Mark 14:27-31)

Here the author of Mark makes the point that *all* the disciples will abandon Jesus. Further, and more importantly, it is *prophesied* that this should occur. Peter's good intentions will not stand against an event which has been preordained by God. The author adds the final comment that all the disciples committed themselves to stand by Jesus, just as Peter did.

As the story unfolds, the disciples all scatter as foretold. By associating Peter's failure with that of the disciples at large, and by indicating that their abandonment of Jesus was preordained by God, the author has presented Peter's denials in such a manner that the reader may interpret them in a more sympathetic light.[4]

Compared to the sympathetic account in Mark, John isolates the failure and abandonment of Jesus to Peter alone, and further builds the case for the indictment of Peter as the unfaithful disciple. Peter makes bold proclamations, but does not stick by them. For the author, Peter is a character of weak will, and one who is not to be respected or trusted. Further, the author has not yet completed his unsavory portrait.

Peter and Judas appear together one more time in the scene where Jesus is betrayed and arrested. This is a carefully structured scene which is presented below in sequential indentations to highlight the latent structure. Note that the passage begins and ends with the reference to the band of soldiers and officers of the Jews. This is the outer bracket of the scene. Within this outer bracket there is a secondary bracket which reflects upon the inevitability of the betrayal, both by Judas and by Peter. Then two identical mini-scenes are presented, the first highlighting the presence of Judas as the betrayer, and the second highlighting the presence of Peter as one who acts against Jesus' will and purpose. The notations *A, B, C,* and *D* are inserted to illustrate the deliberate duplication of structure which serves to associate Peter and Judas:

---

[4] Church tradition holds that the author of Mark was a follower of Peter, and composed his gospel for the purpose of documenting the teachings of Peter. Many scholars discount this tradition today. Some have argued that the Gospel of Mark is an anti-Petrine work for reasons to be discussed later. The thesis of this book is compatible with the church tradition that Mark was a sympathetic follower of Peter. Evidence in favor of this view will be presented in Chapter Three.

So Judas, procuring a band of soldiers and some officers from the chief priests and the Pharisees, went there with lanterns and torches and weapons.

> Then Jesus, knowing all that was to befall him, came forward and said,

> (A) "Whom do you seek?"

> (B) They answered him, "Jesus of Nazareth."

> (C) Jesus answered, "I am he."

> (D) Judas, who betrayed him, was standing with them. When he said to them, "I am he," they drew back and fell to the ground. Again he asked them,

> (A) "Whom do you seek?"

> (B) And they said, "Jesus of Nazareth."

> (C) Jesus answered, "I told you that I am he; so, if you seek me, let these men go." This was to fulfill the word which he had spoken, "Of those whom thou gavest me I lost not one."

> (D) Then Simon Peter, having a sword, drew it and struck the high priest's slave and cut off his right ear. The slave's name was Malchus. Jesus said to Peter, "Put your sword into its sheath;

> shall I not drink the cup which the Father has given me?"

So the band of soldiers and their captain and the officers of the Jews seized Jesus and bound him. (John 18:3-12)

Notice that the passage opens with a reference to Judas as the one who procured the soldiers and led them to Jesus. The reader knows Judas is present. The reader also is well informed that Judas was the one who betrayed Jesus. So the second reference to Judas' presence and his status as the betrayer (*Judas, who betrayed him, was standing there*) is redundant. However, the author has inserted this redundancy to complete the literary parallel between Judas and Peter.

Thus far in the gospel the betrayal has been predicted, and both Judas and Peter have appeared together in each prediction. Here the betrayal is no longer an imminent event; it is actualized in this scene. Judas acts deliberately to turn Jesus over to the authorities. Similarly, Peter performs a violent act which is contrary to Jesus' will, even as Jesus is pleading for the soldiers to let his disciples go free. The author shows that Peter's ignorant impetuosity is at odds with Jesus' purpose. Jesus wishes to fulfill his destiny, and Peter resorts to violence in order to prevent it. Jesus' reprimand of Peter, "Put your sword into its sheath; shall I not drink the cup my Father has given me?" may be paraphrased, *are you to stand in the way of my destiny?*

Notably, only John among the four gospels tells of Jesus' request of the soldiers to let his disciples go, and only John depicts the sword-wielding disciple as being at cross purposes with this particular objective. Mark, Matthew, and Luke report the incident of the sword attack, but the disciple with the sword remains anonymous; only the Gospel of John identifies him as Peter.

The Denials of Peter

The final sequence of events in which Peter speaks show the denials of Peter and the interrogation of Jesus by the high priest. This passage, John 18:15-27, is longer than the previous texts we have seen. However, the author has carefully structured it as a final indictment of Peter. The bold and italicized type draw attention to the literary devices the author has used to condemn Peter:

Simon Peter followed Jesus, and so did another disciple. As this disciple was known to the high priest, he entered the court of the high priest along with Jesus, while Peter stood outside at the door. So the other disciple, who was known to the high priest, went out and spoke to the maid who kept the door, and brought Peter in. *The maid who kept the door said to Peter, "Are you not also one of this man's disciples?" He said, "I am not."* Now the servants and officers had made a charcoal fire, because it was cold, and they were standing and warming themselves; **Peter also was with them, standing and warming himself.**

The high priest then questioned Jesus about his disciples and his teachings. Jesus answered him, "I have spoken openly to the world; I have always taught in synagogues and in the temple, where all the Jews come together; I have said nothing secretly. **Why do you ask me? Ask those who have heard me, what I said to them; they know what I said."** When he had said this, one of the officers standing by struck Jesus with his hand, saying, "Is that how you answer the high priest?" Jesus answered him, "If I have spoken wrongly, bear witness to the wrong; but if I have spoken rightly, why do you strike me?" Annas then sent him bound to Caiaphas, the high priest.

Now Simon Peter was standing and warming himself. *They said to him, "Are you not one of his disciples?" He denied it and said, "I am not."* One of the servants of the high priest, a kinsman of the man whose ear Peter had cut off, asked, "Did I not see you in the garden with him." Peter again denied it; and at once the cock crowed. (John 18:15-27)

Several observations may be made in this passage. First, Peter is accompanied by another disciple, who is usually assumed to be the unnamed "disciple whom Jesus loved." The text implies that this disciple is known to be a follower of Jesus by the high priest and by the maid. This interpretation is made necessary by the fact that this other disciple enters the court with Jesus, making no apparent attempt to hide his association with him. Further, he has just spoken with the maid, and the maid then asks Peter, "Are not you *also* one of this man's disciples?" So the author has made it clear that Peter's denial stands in contrast to the faithfulness of this other disciple who does not hide his allegiance to Jesus.

Notice further how the author has carefully double bracketed the event of Jesus' interrogation with the activities of Peter. The passage takes the following form:

A. Peter denies Jesus

   B. *Peter warms himself by the fire*

   C. Jesus requests testimony of witnesses

   D. *Peter warms himself by the fire.*

E. Peter denies Jesus.

During the interrogation, Jesus appeals to the high priest to *"ask those who have heard me, what I said to them; they know what I said."* This appeal appears only in John. That Jesus' plea is bracketed by Peter's denial is irony in the extreme. Jesus can only rely on those who heard him to tell his story, while Peter stands warming himself by the fire and denies his association with him. Through the double bracketing of the hostile interrogation of Jesus between reflections on the activities of Peter, the author has leveled a final indictment against Peter. Peter seeks his own comfort and warmth by the fire while Jesus is being mistreated; Peter denies his knowledge of Jesus while Jesus is in need of his testimony.

At the end of the passage, the author underscores his judgment of Peter by recalling Peter's act of violence in the garden. His third opportunity to deny Jesus is set up by a relative of the man whose ear had been severed by Peter. After this, the cock crows, and Peter disappears from the scene without further comment. There is no indication in John that Peter recognizes his failure. The cock crows, and Peter simply disappears. By contrast, the three synoptic gospels report that upon realizing what he had done, Peter was overcome with grief:

> Then [Peter] began to invoke a curse on himself and to swear, "I do not know the man." And immediately the cock crowed. And Peter remembered the saying of Jesus, "Before the cock crows you will deny me three times." And he went out and wept bitterly. (Matt. 26:74-75; see also Mark 14:72; Luke 22:61-62)

Thus in presenting the remorseful and grieving Peter, the synoptic authors once again encourage the reader to interpret Peter's failure with sympathy.

70

This completes the review of the dialogues which include Peter in the Gospel of John, at least through the end of John 20, where the gospel originally ended. There is one last reference to Peter after Jesus' death where he is seen running to the empty tomb with the other figure known as the disciple whom Jesus loved. Peter arrives first, but it is the Beloved Disciple who understands what has happened and believes. By the author's silence regarding Peter, the gospel implies that Peter is still befuddled (John 20:1-10).

The original Gospel of John ends with the last verse of John 20. There are three resurrection appearances of Jesus in John 20, and Peter is not mentioned in any of them. This is a notable omission since Christian tradition otherwise gives Peter a prominent place. Mark 16:7 anticipates a meeting between Peter and Jesus; Luke 24:34 reports a prompt appearance of Jesus to Peter; and Paul writes that Jesus was raised on the third day and appeared to Cephas (Peter), then to the twelve (1 Cor. 15:5).

The deliberate attack upon Peter's character which is sustained throughout the gospel, and which is culminated in Peter's absence from the resurrection accounts in John 20, suggests that the author of John 1-20 intended for the denials of Peter to stand as the great and final sign of Peter's unworthiness. They were to be the last act of a disciple who could not be trusted. They were to remain unresolved and unforgiven in the gospel as originally composed. Throughout John, Peter exists in the shadow of Judas. For the author, Peter's bewilderment, unthinking spontaneity, and lack of character make a dangerous combination. For reasons which will become clear, he intended for his readers to see Peter as the unwitting second betrayer of Jesus.

The Mystery of John 21

John 21 is the last chapter in the canonical text of the Gospel of John. Most scholars view it as an appendix which was added under unknown circumstances, and it has remained one of the mysterious anomalies of the NT texts. Scholars have frequently debated its origin and nature, yet no consensus exists on even the most basic questions. Who wrote John 21? Was it the author of the gospel, or a subsequent editor? If it was added to the gospel at a later time, who added it and why? Was John 21 originally composed as a single literary unit, or is it a collection of several miscellaneous traditions which have been patched together?

Many scholars hold that John 21 is an authentic addition to the gospel which developed out of the traditions of the Johannine community. Some have even argued that the appendix was written by the author of the gospel. Others believe John 21 could not have been written by the author of the gospel, and the idea that it reflects authentic Johannine traditions is questionable. Therefore, the first question is whether or not John 21 is truly an authentic part of Johannine tradition.

Related to the question of its origin is the question of its purpose. Everyone acknowledges that John 21 indicates Peter is to be forgiven for his denials of Jesus. Most would also infer from the commands to feed the sheep that Jesus has given Peter a key role in the leadership of his movement. Furthermore, reflections upon Peter's martyrdom and the subsequent death of the Beloved Disciple appear in 21:18-23. From this many have suggested that the text was written to address concerns of the early church arising from the deaths of these two persons.

John 21 as a Political Correction to the Gospel

We have seen that the Gospel of John was, in part, a vehicle designed to undermine the credibility of Peter as a leader of the movement. Since John 21 shows that Jesus and Peter are reconciled, and that Peter is now to assume leadership responsibility for the movement, it is discontinuous and unexpected as a finale to the gospel. The facts suggest an obvious scenario: the Gospel of John was subsequently appended by pro-Petrine editors to reverse the gospel's condemnation of Peter and to affirm him as a true and legitimate leader of the movement.

The implication here is that both the gospel and the appendix were written by persons embroiled in a political conflict between two sects of the Jesus movement, and the role of Peter was at the center of the controversy. Since John 21 reverses the political message of the gospel, we may take a closer look at this unusual chapter to see if it can truly be considered a genuine record of Johannine tradition as so many scholars have believed, or conversely, whether it may have been written by editors influenced by the synoptic tradition.

Evidence for Johannine Authenticity

There are a large number of scholars, primarily those on the conservative end of the spectrum, who are interested in defending the integrity of John 21 as a harmonious addition to the gospel. They argue that John 21 is not a separate appendix, but rather an epilogue which is integral to the entire work. They argue that John 21 must be understood as an accurate reflection of traditions within the Johannine community. If the author of the gospel did not write John 21, then at least we may presume his followers accurately recorded beliefs consistent with those of the author and the Johannine community at large.

Such an argument is usually motivated by a desire to protect the integrity of the gospel and its appendix as inspired scripture. For if it is admitted that the gospel has been altered by editors from another tradition, such a finding implies that the doctrine of the inspiration of scripture must at least be revisited.[5] To avoid this difficult question a series of arguments demonstrating the harmony between John 21 and the gospel have been marshaled.

Scholars who believe John 21 reflects an authentic Johannine tradition base their conclusions primarily on similarities of linguistic style between the gospel and John 21, as well as the common use of a number of uniquely Johannine words and names. For example in 21:1 the scene is identified as the *Sea of Tiberias*, which is another name for the *Sea of Galilee*. This alternative name for the Sea of Galilee is not mentioned anywhere in the NT other than the Gospel of John. So its use in John 21 has the effect of relating the text to the gospel tradition.

---

5 The Church teaches that the gospel writers composed them under the inspiration of the Holy Spirit, and therefore the gospels are to be considered the inspired Word of God. For some, the idea that subsequent editors altered the documents is incompatible with the doctrine of inspiration. However, the question is already on the table, since one must question in what manner the Fourth Gospel's maligning of Peter is to be considered inspired.

Furthermore, in 21:2 there is a list of disciples who are present on the scene. The reference to Peter as "Simon Peter" throughout John 21 is typical Johannine style; the synoptic gospels commonly refer to him either as Simon or as Peter. Only twice does the double name appear in the synoptic gospels (Luke 5:8; Matt. 16:16). Nathanael is also named in 21:2. This person is known only from the Gospel of John, for he does not appear at all in the synoptic gospels. Nathanael does not even appear in the lists of the twelve disciples which are reported in Matthew, Mark, and Luke. Verse 21:2 also names "Thomas, called the Twin" among the disciples present. While this character does not play any role in the synoptic gospels, Thomas does appear in the synoptic lists of the twelve. However, it is only in the Gospel of John that Thomas is referred to as *the Twin*. Later in the text, in 21:7, the Beloved Disciple appears. This character is strictly Johannine, as there is no other reference anywhere in the NT to a "disciple whom Jesus loved" other than within the Gospel of John.

So there are a number of obvious textual references which are immediately suggestive of authorship by someone steeped in Johannine tradition, if not by the author of the gospel himself. There are other indicators which are less obvious and which require a knowledge of Greek grammar and syntax. For example, the Greek word *anthrakia*, translated "charcoal fire" in v. 9, appears in only one other place in the NT--John 18:18. In addition to specific words, there are numerous similarities in linguistic style and grammatical structure between the gospel and the appendix which contribute to the impression of Johannine authenticity.

Commentators who argue for the authenticity of John 21 as a Johannine writing also frequently point to the fact that there is no ancient manuscript evidence which indicates the gospel ever circulated without John 21. Yet as noted earlier, this observation is not informative. The earliest complete manuscripts of John have been dated to about 200 CE. The fact that surviving manuscripts from the third century on contain the appendix does not tell us whether the original composition contained the appendix. It merely indicates that if John 21 was added after the fact, it was done early enough to be reflected in all surviving manuscripts.

However, given all of the unique Johannine elements in John 21, some scholars have argued that John 21 must have been composed by the author of John 1-20. Many other scholars believe it is an addition by a disciple of the author, and one who lived in the same community--perhaps one who had taken oral dictation from the author. Either way a large contingent of scholars believes there is adequate evidence to conclude that John 21 is an authentic reflection of Johannine tradition. As Raymond Brown wrote:

> From the start it should be clear that in thought and expression ch. 21 belongs to the Johannine group of writings; and had it been preserved separately in the NT, all would have recognized its close affinities to the Gospel.[6]

Evidence Against Johannine Authenticity

Though there is quite a bit of data to indicate John 21 is an integral part of Johannine tradition, there is also a notable amount of evidence which argues against this conclusion. Of course, the political disharmony of the appendix with the gospel is a strong indication that it was not composed by the author of John, or subsequent Johannine editors in the same political camp. However, in addition to this there are numerous textual clues of non-Johannine, and most probably synoptic origin.

The first clue is that the Gospel of John is complete at the end of John 20. There is no literary or theological need to show one more resurrection appearance. For if the readership is not convinced by the gospel's message through John 20, there is no incremental information in John 21 by which the reader may become convinced. In other words, John 21 is not relevant to the evangelical purpose of the gospel. If anything, it diminishes the powerful literary climax of John 20.

The second clue is directly related to the first: the storyline of John 21 is discontinuous from the gospel. At the end of John 20, Jesus has appeared to the disciples twice in the upper room, and they have recognized that Jesus has risen from the dead. Immediately following

---

[6] Brown, Raymond E., *The Gospel According to John*, Doubleday, 1970, p. 1079

this, John 21 tells us that the disciples have returned to Galilee and decided to take up their previous occupation as fishermen. That they would have done so after seeing the resurrected Lord in Jerusalem makes no literary sense. So the discontinuity of the storyline indicates this chapter was most likely written for a different original purpose than as an extension of the Gospel of John.

Third, John 21 presents the disciples as commercial fishermen. There is no mention of the fact that any of the disciples were fishermen in John 1-20. The fishing motif is strictly a synoptic tradition, and one which originated with Mark. So it is suspicious that a Johannine writer would introduce it without comment in the appendix.

Fourth, the premise that they have taken up their occupation in Galilee implies that these disciples currently lived in Galilee, which is consistent with the traditions found in Mark and Matthew. Yet in John 20, after Peter and the Beloved Disciple visit the empty tomb in Jerusalem, the author says they "went back to their homes." (20:10) Since they were to see Jesus later that same day in Jerusalem, the text forces the interpretation that these two disciples lived in the vicinity of Jerusalem. This is another clue that John 20 and John 21 originated out of different traditions.

Fifth, there are twenty-eight Greek words which appear in John 21 which do not appear anywhere in the gospel itself. Many of these are situation specific, such as the words translated *beach, net,* and *breakfast.* Some have suggested that this indicates nothing more than the subject matter requiring their usage had not occurred previously. Yet the point is that the subject matter itself, primarily the fishing scenario from which many of these unique words derive, is not Johannine in character or origin.

In addition, some of the unique words in John 21 are not situation specific. For example, 21:20 says "Peter *turned . . .*" The verb used here, *epistrephein,* "to turn," does not appear in John 1-20. It is however a verb used by the synoptic writers; it appears twice each in Mark and Matthew, and five times in Luke.

Also, there are several Greek words which are translated "fish" in the NT: the two most common are *ichthys* and *opsarion.* Matthew, Mark, and Luke use *ichthys* exclusively. John 1-20 contains two occurrences of the word "fish" and the Greek word used in both cases is *opsarion* (John 6:9,11). In John 21, both *ichthys* and *opsarion* appear three times each. The Greek texts of 21:6, 8, and 11 contain the word *ichthys*, and in 21:9, 10, and 13 the author used the word *opsarion*.

John A. T. Robinson notes, "it is perhaps worth observing that the distinctive name for cooked fish *(opsarion)*, in which the [fishing] trade would have been conducted, occurs five times in the Gospel of John, but nowhere else in the New Testament."[7] However, if *opsarion* is a distinctive term in the fishing trade for "cooked fish," then it is properly used in 21:9 and 21:13, but it has been misused in 21:10, where Jesus says, "Bring some of the fish *(opsarion)* that you have just caught." Peter then goes aboard and hauls the net ashore full of fish which most certainly have not yet been cooked.

Furthermore, in this same verse, the word "some" is translated from the Greek *apo*, a usage which does not appear in John 1-20. Raymond Brown comments:

> The partitive use of *apo* is found only here in John, as contrasted with fifty-one uses of partitive *ek*. At the same time, the noun governed by the preposition, *opsarion*, is peculiarly Johannine in the NT. This one phrase, then, is a practical example of how difficult it is to decide whether or not the style of the chapter is Johannine.[8]

In this one verse we find the partitive use of one word, *apo*, which does not occur anywhere else in John, and another word, *opsarion*, which appears only in John, but which is misused in this verse. The implication is that a different author may have composed the text and may not have been entirely familiar with the proper use of the distinctive trade term *opsarion*.

A sixth indicator that John 21 was influenced by non-Johannine sources is found in 21:2. Even though 21:2 names several disciples according to typical Johannine tradition (Simon Peter, Thomas called the Twin, Nathanael), the verse also names the *sons of Zebedee* as

---

[7] Robinson, John A. T., *The Priority of John*, 1985, p. 117. Robinson's point is that the use of a trade term by the author implies an awareness of historical detail which contributes to the impression that the work was composed by one close to the events.

[8] Brown, Ibid., p. 1073

present on the scene. Now James and John, the two sons of Zebedee, are prominent figures in the synoptic gospels, but they are entirely absent from John 1-20. That they suddenly appear in the appendix without introduction or comment is suggestive that the author/editor has been influenced by the synoptic tradition.

In summary, what we find in John 21 is a stylistic muddle. There are clearly a number of textual indicators which point to authentic origin within the Johannine community. However, the text is discontinuous in storyline from the Gospel of John, and it also contains numerous clues that indicate synoptic origin or influence.

Accordingly, various scholars have argued a number of positions, including (a) the author of the gospel also wrote John 21 (Carson), (b) the author of John 21 was a disciple of the author of the gospel (Brown), (c) the author of Luke wrote John 21 (Boismard), and (d) John 21 is a collection of several synoptic traditions which were added by an editor to harmonize John with the synoptics (Loisy). What should be clear is that John 21 is a melting pot of Johannine and synoptic linguistic styles and traditions, and contains enough of both to sustain arguments for a wide variety of proposals. Further, since the debate has been focused on linguistic styles, the fact that it negates a tremendous attack on Peter has been overlooked. Once we introduce the political factor, the mystery of John 21 begins to resolve itself.

John 21 and the Second Betrayer Theme

Since we have discovered that John 1-20 denigrates Peter while John 21 affirms him, we cannot understand the relationship between the gospel and the appendix without focusing on the political struggle within the movement which was the reason for their having been written. For the author of John to have constructed such an elaborate assault upon Peter's credibility suggests that he must have had a significant motivation to do so; such an attack cannot have developed in isolation; the gospel was written by someone who hoped to confirm or persuade his audience of the unsavory character of Peter.

The conflict suggests the author saw Peter as a political and/or ideological adversary who had challenged either the beliefs of the Johannine community, or the right to leadership of those in control of the community. Further, since John 21 specifically affirms Peter's authority to lead the movement, we may infer that the author of the gospel had written in the hope of denying Peter this authority. By associating Peter with Judas, by portraying him as routinely misunderstanding Jesus' purpose, and by detailing the account of his triple denial of Jesus, the Gospel of John shows Peter to be unfit for leadership in the movement.

It is precisely this conclusion which is reversed in John 21. For in this appendix, contrary to all foreshadowing, Jesus reconciles Peter to himself and gives him the assignment of acting as a new shepherd of the movement (21:15-17). Further, we find that Peter will glorify God through the ultimate act of martyrdom (21:18-19). This is in contrast to the belittlement of Peter's willingness to die, which was noted earlier. Since John 21 reverses the gospel's attack on Peter's reputation, it is logical to suppose John 21 was written by a pro-Petrine editor rather than someone sympathetic with the Johannine community's beliefs.

The vital issue for both the author of the gospel and the editors who attached the appendix is whether Peter is to be considered a legitimate and authorized leader of the Jesus movement. Not only do we detect here a question of legitimacy, but one of hierarchy as well. Is Peter the supreme authority among the apostles of Jesus? Is he the rock upon which Jesus intended to build his church? The Gospel of John says no--he is confused and untrustworthy. John 21 says yes--he is the new shepherd of the flock.

The political evidence is overwhelmingly against the notion that John 21 is an authentic Johannine tradition. Indeed it could not have been composed by the author of the gospel or anyone sympathetic to his cause unless we are to imagine that the author and his followers had a radical change of heart after the gospel was written. Further, if such a change of heart had occurred, we may wonder why the entire Gospel of John would not have been withdrawn.

The Clash between Peter and the Beloved Disciple

We may now turn to a related question. Since the author of John went to such length to notify his readers that Peter was *not* to be trusted as a leader of the movement, does it give us a corresponding indication of who the rightful leader should be? The only candidate in the Gospel of John is the "disciple whom Jesus loved," a designation which by itself indicates at minimum a favored status. Does the gospel tells us that the Beloved Disciple is the one Jesus intended to take over the movement? Remarkably, there is evidence that it does.

Notably, the "disciple whom Jesus loved" is first identified by this title at the Last Supper, the night before Jesus' death (John 13:21-27). In this passage the Beloved Disciple is said to have been "lying close to the breast of Jesus." This translation is from the Revised Standard Version, Second Edition, 1971. However, the literal Greek translation of this phrase says that the disciple "was reclining on Jesus' bosom." The image of the Beloved Disciple resting upon Jesus' bosom is noted in 13:23, and repeated again in 13:25 so that the reader cannot miss the reference. It is clearly important to the author that the reader understand in specific terms that the Beloved Disciple was "lying close to the breast of Jesus," or "reclining on his bosom."

Virtually all commentators on John recognize this as a scene of warmth and intimacy between Jesus and the Beloved Disciple, although few understand it as anything more. Yet W.H. Brownlee makes a vital connection between this reference to lying close to the breast of Jesus and another established and relevant tradition:

> The description of the Beloved Disciple as reclining in the bosom of Jesus means far more than a relationship of affection and intimacy, as is shown by [The Book of] Jubilees 22:26 where 'Jacob slept in the bosom of Abraham.' This occurred when the older patriarch was about to die, but he first conferred his final blessing (along with much moral exhortation) on his grandson. *Lying in the testator's bosom seems to designate one as true son and heir.*
>
> In Luke 16:19-23 it is Lazarus the poor beggar who lies in the patriarch's bosom. It was just like Jesus to show in this way that the social outcast rather than the rich man is the true son of Abraham.

Jubilees 22:26 is in the context of Abraham's final blessing and testamentary exhortation. It is on a like occasion that the Beloved Disciple lies on Jesus' breast. *This means that he and all true disciples (whom he symbolizes) inherit the task, the Spirit, and the peace which Jesus has bequeathed.* Similarly, the divine Logos as God's only begotten is one 'in the bosom of the Father' (John 1:18), for he is the heir of all things, to whom all that the Father has belongs (John 16:15).[9] (emphasis added)

When the author depicts the Beloved Disciple as lying close to the breast of Jesus, he intends for his readers to see that the Beloved Disciple, on the night before Jesus dies, *assumes the posture of heir to Jesus' ministry.* Jesus has bequeathed the responsibilities of his work and his movement to the Beloved Disciple; this disciple is to be the new shepherd of the flock.

In this quotation, Brownlee indicates his belief that the figure of the Beloved Disciple is a symbol for all true disciples. Though "the Beloved Disciple as symbol" has been argued by Bultmann and others, most scholars today see the Beloved Disciple as an unnamed individual rather than as a symbol. Given the political implications of the present analysis, the identification of the Beloved Disciple as a specific individual is the only reasonable option.

In short, not only does the Gospel of John tell us that Peter is unfit and untrustworthy, but also that the Beloved Disciple is the one whom Jesus designated as the rightful heir to lead the new movement. This interpretation is confirmed later in the scene at the cross where Jesus bequeaths the responsibility for the care of his mother to the Beloved Disciple:

When Jesus saw his mother, and the disciple whom he loved standing near, he said to his mother, "Woman, behold, your son!" Then he said to the disciple, "Behold, your mother!" And from that hour the disciple took her to his own home. (John 19:26-27)

Here we may infer that Mary's husband is no longer alive, and Jesus as the eldest son is the legal head of the family. Just before his death, he indicates that the Beloved Disciple is to take his place. The

---

[9] Brownlee as quoted by J.A.T. Robinson, Ibid., p. 98

statement "Woman, behold, your son" is not a plea of Jesus for his mother to look at him in his crucified state; rather it is a request that she regard the Beloved Disciple as a son who is to take Jesus' place as her guardian and head of the family.

Therefore, for all of its theological reflection and evangelical purpose, we may conclude that the Gospel of John must also have been an inflammatory political document within the first century church. Not only does it reflect hostility between the followers of Peter and the Beloved Disciple, but the gospel itself may be presumed to have added fuel to the fire. In the Petrine community, the Fourth Gospel would have been perceived as a gauntlet thrown down. John 21 is firm evidence that pro-Petrine believers thought a response was warranted. Behind the scenes we may sense an acute power struggle between the followers of Peter and the followers of the Beloved Disciple.

A Further Note on John 21

Once we see that the image of one lying close to another's breast, or in one's bosom, is reflective of a relationship between testator and inheritor, we may return to John 21 with a greater ability to understand the closing verses. The chapter through 21:19 has shown a reconciliation of Peter with Jesus, a forgiveness of Peter by Jesus for his denials, the establishment of Peter as the new shepherd of the flock, and a prediction that Peter will glorify God through his own crucifixion. Following this we find two telling verses:

> Peter turned and saw following them the disciple whom Jesus loved, who had lain close to his breast at the supper and had said, "Lord, who is it that is going to betray you?" When Peter saw him, he said to Jesus, "Lord, what about this man?" (John 21:20-21)

Why has the editor gone to such length to describe the Beloved Disciple, who within the context of the gospel is well known at this point? Even within John 21, the Beloved Disciple has already been identified without these reminders of who he was (21:7). So the extensive identification of the Beloved Disciple in these verses appears at first to be superfluous.

However, from what we have just seen, this elaborate identification takes on tremendous meaning. The author of John 21 has turned the tables on the author of the gospel; he says Peter is the rightful heir to leadership of the movement, so he now asks *what about the man who had lain close to the breast of Jesus*--what are we to make of his claim that he is *the true leader of the movement?*

Furthermore, the author of John 21 puts a different spin on the question at the Last Supper. In John 13, after Jesus announces that someone will betray him, it is Peter who ironically asks of the Beloved Disciple, "Tell us who it is of whom he speaks." (13:24) Prompted by Peter's inquiry, the Beloved Disciple asks Jesus, "Lord, who is it?" (13:25) Within the context of the gospel, the irony of Peter's question is that it is Peter himself who is going to betray Jesus.[10]

However, in John 21, Peter is the new shepherd, and Peter is the one to be crucified as a martyr. Peter is the authorized leader of the movement. For the pro-Petrine editor of John 21, *it is the author of the Gospel of John who is to be considered the real betrayer* for having besmirched the character of Peter and led the flock away from the teachings of Peter. So he identifies the Beloved Disciple as the one who initiated the question--it was this disciple *"who had lain close to his breast at the supper and had said, 'Lord who is it that is going to betray you?'"* In repeating this question and showing it as having been initiated by the Beloved Disciple rather than Peter, the editor turns the irony of the statement against the Beloved Disciple. If anyone is a betrayer here, it is this man who so vigorously attacked Peter.

Lord, what about this man? Jesus responds:

> "If it is my will that he remain until I come, what is that to you. Follow me." The saying spread abroad among the brethren that this disciple was not to die; yet Jesus did not say to him that he was not to die, but "If it is my will that he remain until I come, what is that to you." (21:22-23).

---

[10] Irony is widely recognized by scholars as a frequent literary technique in the Gospel of John. Robert Kysar: "Irony is an important feature in this gospel. The author is fond of setting up situations in which the reader knows something important that some of the actors/speakers in the narrative do not know. In that situation the actors are made to say something of far greater significance than they know." (Anchor Bible Dictionary, Vol. III, p. 916). Hence to interpret Peter's question *Lord who is it that is going to betray you?* as an ironic reflection on Peter himself is consistent with the author's use of irony throughout the gospel.

Within the context of this story, Jesus has just suffered cruci-fixion and has been resurrected to the glory of God. It has just been announced that Peter will follow in his footsteps, ending his life as a martyr crucified for the sake of the movement; this is how Peter will glorify God (21:19). In contrast, Jesus indicates that the death of the Beloved Disciple will be inconsequential.

The thrust of the message in John 21 is that the future of the Beloved Disciple is irrelevant to the work that Jesus and Peter have yet to do. In contrast to the fact that Jesus and Peter both die the death of martyrs, the Beloved Disciple will not; in fact he may not even die at all before Jesus returns. The counterpoint diminishes the Beloved Disciple, as he will not be required to give his life as Peter does.

Implications

The Fourth Gospel cannot be fully understood except within the context of the struggle for leadership between the Beloved Disciple and Peter. In Chapter One we noted how the gospels may be read as if listening to one part of a telephone conversation. Remarkably, between John 1-20 and John 21, both parties to the conversation are audible. We see in the Fourth Gospel an intense competition between the Beloved Disciple and Peter which constitutes a primary reason for the gospel's existence. The author of John sensed a competitive threat from Peter, and composed the gospel in large part to answer the threat.

Since the members of the Johannine community were already dedicated followers of the Beloved Disciple, it makes little sense to imagine that the harsh castigation of Peter was written for their benefit. Why would the author preach to his own choir? Therefore, we may infer that one of the author's objectives was to convince Peter's followers to reject the teachings of Peter and join the Johannine community. Thus an important target audience for the Fourth Gospel was the Petrine community.

With this as background, several puzzling references in John may make more sense. For example, consider the shepherd vs. the hireling passage of John 10:

> I am the good shepherd. The good shepherd lays down his life for the
> sheep. He who is a hireling and not a shepherd, whose own the sheep
> are not, sees the wolf coming and leaves the sheep and flees; and the
> wolf snatches them and scatters them. He flees because he is a hireling
> and cares nothing for the sheep. I am the good shepherd; I know my
> own and my own know me, as the Father knows me and I know the
> Father; and I lay down my life for the sheep. And I have other sheep,
> that are not of this fold; I must bring them also, and they will heed my
> voice. So there shall be one flock, one shepherd. (John 10:11-16)

In this passage it is reasonable to assume that both the author
and his audience knew who the hireling was. Given the animosity
toward Peter, and the recurring implication that Peter is not to be
trusted, we may suppose the author has depicted Peter as the hireling.
It is Peter's flock which has been led astray, and to whom the author
has issued a plea to leave Peter and join the Johannine community, so
that there may be one flock, one shepherd.

This interpretation is consistent with the rebuttal of John 21, in
which we find that Peter is designated as the true shepherd--the one
whom Jesus gives command and authority to feed the sheep (21:15-17).
The use of the shepherd motif may have originated from a common
recognition that the author had characterized Peter as the hireling in
this story. Further, the commands of Jesus for Peter to tend the flock
are followed immediately by a reflection upon the fact that Peter will
lay down his life for the sheep (21:18-19), which negates the allegation
that the hireling was unwilling to sacrifice himself for the sheep.

As an aside, church tradition holds that Peter was crucified
during the Neronian persecution in Rome in 64/65 CE. John 21
confirms that Peter was crucified as a martyr (John 21:18-19). So it is
worth noting that even though the author of John is intensely aware of
Peter as a formidable competitive threat, there is not the slightest hint
in John 1-20 of an awareness that Peter has suffered martyrdom.
Silence on the issue would be puzzling enough, but we find more than
mere silence in John. If the hireling in the story above was intended to
refer to Peter, it belittles the idea that Peter would be willing to die for
the cause. The charge is consistent with the passage wherein Peter's
claim of willingness to die for Jesus is met with the abrupt response,

"Will you lay down your life for me? Truly, truly, I say to you, the cock will not crow, till you have denied me three times" (John 13:38).

Where does this trivialization of Peter's martyrdom come from? It is not intuitively probable that a gospel written two to three decades after Peter's crucifixion, and especially one intended to win over the followers of Peter, would make light of Peter's willingness to die a martyr. Not only is there a serious moral issue here, but as a practical matter it would have been extremely poor salesmanship. We may add this to the long list of paradoxes which characterize the Fourth Gospel.

The findings introduce yet another paradox relative to conventional NT scholarship. As noted previously, there is a significant body of traditions about Jesus and his teachings which do not appear in John, but are well documented in the synoptic gospels. Scholars have often suggested that this may be explained by presuming the Johannine community was isolated from the other sects of the Jesus movement, and that its own traditions had developed separately. This would account for a host of missing traditions as well as the absence of numerous key words which had become part of the expression of faith.

The evidence here suggests an opposite conclusion: the Johannine community was not isolated at all. Rather, it was embroiled in a hostile confrontation with Peter and the makers of the synoptic tradition. The Fourth Gospel was composed in part to draw Peter's followers away from their false teacher and to join the true community of believers. This scenario implies that the author of John must have been intimately aware of the teachings of Peter in order to have judged them false or misguided.

At the same time we may suppose the Petrine faction was just as anxious to defend the integrity of Peter and his teachings as the author of John was to discredit them. In their active defense of Peter it would be unusual if they did not attempt to call the "wayward sheep" of the Johannine community back into their Petrine fold. Such a competitive threat to the Johannine community and its leaders would likely have motivated the aggressive denunciation of Peter found in John.

If we can draw one final inference from the texts, it would be that pro-Petrine forces appear to have eventually gained ascendancy over the Johannine community, and that these two communities must have merged. Petrine ascendancy is implied by John 21's existence; the gospel which survived is one which was controlled by Petrine editors. The merging of the communities is implied by the existence of the gospel itself. For if the Johannine community had dissolved or gone its own way, why would Petrine leaders have continued to circulate the Gospel of John? Why would they not have simply destroyed it?

The addition of John 21 implies an accommodation of Johannine thought by the Petrine community's leadership. John 21 not only legitimizes Peter for the Johannine believers, but legitimizes the gospel for the Petrine believers. Thus a truce and reconciliation must at some point have been forged between the two. Yet the traces of conflict remain embedded in the Fourth Gospel. Between its lines we can read a remarkable story of political and ideological struggle to gain control of the movement and ultimately to define the legacy of Jesus.

❖ 3 ❖

The Unfinished Gospel

The Gospel of John is not the only gospel of the four to end in an odd manner; the Gospel of Mark also has a peculiar conclusion. However, its problem is the opposite of John's. For as John has an extra conclusion, Mark is missing a conventional ending altogether. The earliest and best manuscripts of the Gospel of Mark end on a rather abrupt note. On the morning of the third day after Jesus' death, several women go to the tomb, only to find the tomb open and a young man dressed in a white robe sitting there:

> And he said to them, "Do not be amazed; you seek Jesus of Nazareth, who was crucified. He has risen, he is not here; see the place where they laid him. But go, tell his disciples and Peter that he is going before you to Galilee; there you will see him, as he told you." And they went out and fled from the tomb; for trembling and astonishment had come upon them; and they said nothing to anyone, for they were afraid. (Mark 16:6-8)

With the women fleeing in fear, the manuscripts end. Jesus does not appear to anyone--none of the disciples witnesses him in his resurrected state. The additional canonical text of Mark 16:9-20, which reports several resurrection appearances, only appears in later manuscripts, and is universally considered to be an addition by the church to provide a more traditional closure to the story.

In the original Greek text the sudden truncation is even more glaring, for the text ends in mid-sentence with the conjunction *gar*, normally translated *for*. Bruce Metzger comments on this unexpected ending:

> . . . from a stylistic point of view, to terminate a Greek sentence with the word *gar* is most unusual and exceedingly rare--only a relatively few examples have been found throughout all the vast range of Greek literary works, and no instance has been found where *gar* stands at the end of a book.[1]

This abrupt ending to the Second Gospel has been the source of much speculation and theory. What could have caused the author to end the work on such a note? Was there an original conclusion to the gospel that is now missing, one that has been replaced with the appendix we see in 16:9-20? If so, what happened to the original ending? The manuscript evidence does not help us. Several later ancient manuscripts add one additional verse to 16:8 to provide a brief, but more conclusive ending to the gospel:

> But they reported briefly to Peter and those with him all that they had been told. And after this, Jesus himself sent out by means of them, from east to west, the sacred and imperishable proclamation of eternal salvation.

One manuscript adds these two sentences, and then continues with 16:9-20. In most of the manuscripts which contain 16:9-20, this text follows immediately after 16:8. In addition, one manuscript adds additional material after v. 14.

Faced with this confusion, researchers have suggested different explanations. Most scholars today believe the author actually intended to end the gospel at 16:8, and that there is no missing ending. Others have suggested the original ending was accidentally lost very early after its composition, and that subsequent editors added the final verses to finish the story. Still others theorize the original ending was intentionally destroyed because it contained material incompatible with the interests of the church. Some say the author may have died before the work was finished.

There is one implication which is certain. If there was an original ending which was lost or intentionally deleted, this must have

---

[1] Metzger, Bruce M., *The Text of the New Testament*, Third Edition, Oxford University Press, 1992, p. 228

occurred soon after the gospel was first written. Since it is impossible to conceive of the ending being lost from several different manuscripts at precisely the same place in the text, we may assume it was lost from the original autograph before it was copied and distributed. If the ending was intentionally deleted, though it would have been possible to alter a few copies in circulation, it would have become more difficult to edit all copies once the document was widely distributed.

How may we explain the sudden truncation of the text soon after it was published? Two of the suggestions noted above have immediate objections. First, if the original ending was lost or mutilated, would not the author or a close associate have been able to reconstruct it? Can we really imagine those who published this formidable work on the life of Jesus simply mislaid the key final chapter, and elected to distribute what they had without the report that the disciples had seen the resurrected Lord? If the author had written a conclusion, it is unlikely the gospel would have been circulated without it due to carelessness.

The second improbable explanation is that the author died before the work was finished. This scenario encounters similar objections. Would not church leaders or other close associates have finished it before its release for general circulation? Why would the church have thought the publication of an unfinished gospel would be of benefit? Since most scholars presume it would have been finished by someone prior to its distribution, the untimely death of the author is not a compelling explanation either.

If we can set aside the loss or accidental mutilation of the autograph and the premature death of the author as unlikely explanations, two possibilities remain. First, the author never wrote a conventional ending and intended for his work to be complete at 16:8. Second, the original ending was intentionally deleted after the fact.

Was the Final Chapter Intentionally Destroyed?

The proposal that the ending was destroyed because it contained material contrary to the church's interest is typically dismissed, usually without an argument. James Brooks sets it aside with one statement in his commentary on Mark:

It is unlikely in the extreme that there would have been anything objectionable in the ending.[2]

R.L. Fox gives the same short appraisal:

> The sinister view, that the original ending was cut out because it said something awkward, is not compelling: the rest of Mark's Gospel is too straightforward.[3]

The suggestion that the ending was cut to eliminate inappropriate material prompts us to imagine what could have been so troublesome that removing it was warranted. Since it is not immediately obvious what the objectionable subject matter could have been, many conclude that there most likely was not any. However, such a conclusion does not logically follow. Though it is unlikely the author would have introduced an inappropriate theological concept, there is no reason to presume he could not have created a politically uncomfortable scenario between the competing factions of the Jesus movement. We have already seen that the Gospel of John was edited to negate its hostile rhetoric toward Peter. If John was altered for political reasons, it is not unreasonable to suspect that Mark may have been as well. Though this represents a legitimate potential solution, it is not often admitted as such. We will return to this prospect after examining the evidence for the leading contemporary theory.

The Prevailing Theory: Mark was complete at 16:8

Having dismissed the possibilities that an original ending was lost, that the author died, or that the ending was intentionally destroyed, most scholars hold the view that the author of Mark must have deliberately ended the work at 16:8 for whatever reason he had in mind. The theory has been bolstered by supporting observations which

---

[2] Brooks, James A., *The New American Commentary Series, Mark*, Broadman Press, 1991, p. 274

[3] Fox, Robin Lane, *The Unauthorized Version*, Knopf, 1992, p. 144. Fox's use of the word "sinister" is unfortunate, for it implies that those who may have edited the manuscript would have done so out of an intent to deceive. Though this is a possibility, there is no justification for leaping to such a conclusion.

presume to show that such an ending would have been in stylistic harmony with other elements of the gospel. Some have cited (a) the equally abrupt beginning of the gospel, (b) the repeated use of the last phrase *for they were afraid*, and (c) the recurrent theme of the Messianic Secret as evidence that the abrupt ending is consistent with the author's style and message. We will consider each of these in turn.

1. *Does the abrupt ending have a literary symmetry with the abbreviated opening of the gospel?* The argument that the non-ending harmonizes with the beginning of the gospel must be considered in two aspects. First, the opening phrase is an incomplete sentence, and second, Jesus' encounter with John the Baptist is condensed. Are these opening elements in harmony with the truncated ending?

The gospel begins with an announcement which functions somewhat like a title:

The beginning of the gospel of Jesus Christ, the Son of God. (Mark 1:1a)

It has sometimes been inferred that the gospel's non-ending is consistent with its abbreviated opening. For by ending the gospel without resurrection appearances, the author is sometimes thought to be making a theological statement that the gospel of Jesus *cannot* be finished, that it continues in the lives of Jesus' followers. Thus when the author says that this is the beginning of the gospel of Jesus Christ, he is not referring to the beginning of the document. Rather, everything contained in the Gospel of Mark is merely the beginning of the gospel of Jesus Christ. The gospel story will remain unfinished, and will continue on as the kingdom of God is revealed upon earth.

Though such an interpretation is possible, it is not the only plausible reading of the text. We may suspect that at the time Mark was composed others were already developing genealogies and infancy narratives, and beginning the story of Jesus with his miraculous birth. Or perhaps, as in John, some were teaching that "In the beginning was the Word, and the Word was with God and the Word was God; and the Word became flesh and dwelt among us (John 1:1,14a), arguing that Jesus was preexistent and divine, and his story had begun long before.

93

Thus the author of Mark may have intended his opening line to indicate that these were inappropriate places to start the story of Jesus-- that the gospel of Jesus rightfully begins with his baptism by John the Baptist. Furthermore, it may not be wrong to default to the literal meaning--that the author simply meant this is the beginning of a document which will tell the story of Jesus Christ.

If the gospel had originally contained resurrection appearances, we would feel comfortable with one of these alternative interpretations. Even as it stands, one of them may more accurately describe the author's intent. Therefore, the stylistic connection between the concise opening line and the truncated ending is tenuous and perhaps non-existent. It is feeble evidence for the notion that the author intended to leave the gospel unfinished.

Related to the incomplete sentence which introduces the gospel is the concise treatment of John the Baptist. The episode which introduces the Baptist as the forerunner to Jesus and depicts Jesus' baptism by him is told in only ten verses (Mark 1:2-11). Does the epitomized treatment of John the Baptist harmonize with the non-ending? Three comments may be made. First, though the other gospels contain reflections upon Jesus' birth or preexistence, the story of John the Baptist is the point at which all four gospels begin the story of Jesus' ministry. Therefore, from a literary perspective, Mark's beginning, even though brief, is a legitimate and natural embarkation point for the gospel. One cannot argue persuasively that the women fleeing in fear from the empty tomb is an equally natural conclusion.

Second, if the gospel had a more conventional ending, surely no one would suggest that the brief story of John the Baptist was in literary conflict with it. Rather, most would assume that the author simply epitomized the story of John the Baptist, using it as a starting point with which he assumed his readers were familiar. Hence, there is nothing about the condensed prologue which suggests that an incomplete ending would be appropriate.

Third, the gospel does not anticipate a spiritualized allusion to the resurrection, nor does it foreshadow one which is not directly experienced or confirmed by the disciples. Instead it twice predicts a specific resurrection appearance to the disciples in Galilee.[4] Therefore, to argue that an ending without a resurrection appearance is in literary accord with the condensed prologue is to ignore the fact that it is in dissonance with the foreshadowing in the text itself. In short, the allegation that there is a literary symmetry between the epitomized opening and the truncated ending is tenuous. The observation contributes little weight to the theory that the author intended to end at 16:8.

2. Does the phrase "for they were afraid" carry significance as an end to the gospel? The second common argument from textual analysis focuses on the author's use of the phrase *for they were afraid*. This (or a similar) phrase occurs several times in Mark prior to 16:8. It is typical for the author to follow the depiction of an event which has startled those present with the note that they were afraid. The following passages illustrate:

> The herdsmen fled, and told it in the city and in the country. And people came to see what it was that had happened. And they came to Jesus, and saw the demoniac sitting there, clothed and in his right mind, the man who had had the legion; and they were afraid. And those who had seen it told what had happened to the demoniac and to the swine. And they began to beg Jesus to depart from their neighborhood (Mark 5:14-17)

> For [Peter] did not know what to say, for they were exceedingly afraid. (Mark 9:6)

> . . . for he was teaching his disciples, saying to them, "The Son of man will be delivered into the hands of men, and they will kill him; and when he is killed, after three days he will rise." But they did not understand the saying, and they were afraid to ask him. (Mark 9:31-32)

> And they were on the road, going up to Jerusalem, and Jesus was walking ahead of them; and they were amazed, and those who followed were afraid. (Mark 10:32a)

It is suggested that to end the gospel on the note that the women reacted with fear after confronting the empty tomb would be in keeping

---

[4] Mark 14:28; 16:7

with the author's reflections upon the fear of witnesses to miraculous events throughout the gospel. While this is true as far as it goes, it sheds no light on the author's intended conclusion. If the author had composed a more conventional ending which followed after 16:8, the note that the women fled in fear from the tomb would appear to be just one more case of the author's tendency to note such reactions. There would be nothing unusual about its appearance at this point in the text, so a reflection upon the women's fear in 16:8 says nothing about whether the text originally continued beyond this point.

A related question is whether the author typically uses the note of fear on the part of witnesses to end a logical sequence. Clearly, it does end the story of the women's visit to the empty tomb (16:1-8). If the gospel were to continue beyond this point, a change of scene is warranted by the closure implied in 16:8. If we were to compose an ideal continuation, the next scene would depict the disciples in a state of unawareness of the empty tomb. Thus in this case the phrase *for they were afraid* is the end of the story of the women's visit to the tomb.

There are other examples in the gospel where the author ends a logical sequence by noting the reaction of the witnesses. After Jesus says he will be killed and subsequently raised, the author says the disciples "did not understand the saying and they were afraid to ask him" (9:32). After Jesus answers the double-edged question regarding payment of taxes to Caesar, the author indicates the witnesses "were amazed at him" (12:17). With evidence such as this it has been argued that the final *for they were afraid* is a typical conclusion for Mark.

However, a close look at the instances of fearful response by those who have witnessed miracles yields no pattern which would indicate the author used it as a formula to close a story. The woman with the hemorrhage approaches Jesus with fear and trembling, and it is her fear which leads to Jesus' response (5:25-34). The people who hear of Jesus' healing of the demoniac are fearful, and out of fear they ask Jesus to depart their neighborhood (5:1-20). The disciples are terrified at the sight of Jesus walking on the water (6:50). Finally, the disciples are "exceedingly afraid" in the midst of the transfiguration (9:2-10). In each of these instances, the fearful reactions are integral to the progress of the storyline; they are not the culmination of it. There is no correlation in Mark between the notation that persons were fearful and the close of a story or logical sequence. Thus there is no reason to conclude that the phrase *for they were afraid* in 16:8 is an appropriate end to the gospel based on the author's prior usage of it.

Now the fact that the women's visit to the tomb appears to be a complete literary unit *does* indicate something of importance. It implies that if there was a conclusion now missing, it is probably not missing due to accidental loss or mutilation. Since the manuscript ends at the precise point of a logical break in the text, it lends credence to any solution which presupposes rational intent--either the author deliberately ended the gospel at 16:8, or editors severed the original conclusion from the manuscript at this point. The fact that 16:8 completes a logical sequence lends equal credence to both solutions, and tips the scales further away from accidental loss.

3. *Does the Messianic Secret harmonize with the non-ending?* A third argument in support of the no-resurrection-appearance ending is that it is compatible with the theme of the Messianic Secret. The Messianic Secret is a theme which appears frequently throughout the first half of the Gospel of Mark. The motif consists primarily of references that Jesus does not want to be identified as the Messiah or as a miracle worker. The first example of this occurs during an exorcism:

> And immediately there was in their synagogue a man with an unclean spirit; and he cried out, "What have you to do with us, Jesus of Nazareth? Have you come to destroy us? I know who you are, the Holy One of God." But Jesus rebuked him, saying, "Be silent, and come out of him!" And the unclean spirit, convulsing him and crying with a loud voice, came out of him (Mark 1:23-26).

In addition to silencing demons, Jesus commands that some of his miracles are not to be publicized. The prime example of this occurs after the raising of Jairus' daughter:

> Taking her by the hand he said to her, "Tal'itha cu'mi"; which means, "Little girl, I say to you, arise." And immediately the girl got up and walked (she was twelve years of age), and they were immediately overcome with amazement. And he strictly charged them that no one should know this . . . (Mark 5:41-43a)

Jesus also commands the disciples not to publicize his identity:

> . . . and on the way he asked his disciples, "Who do men say that I am?" And they told him, "John the Baptist; and others say, Eli'jah; and others one of the prophets." And he asked them, "But who do you say that I am?" Peter answered him, "You are the Christ." And he charged them to tell no one about him (Mark 8:27b-30).

The final command that the disciples should keep quiet about a particular event follows the transfiguration, which occurs very near the half way point in the text of the gospel:

> And as they were coming down the mountain, he charged them to tell no one what they had seen, until the Son of man should have risen from the dead. So they kept the matter to themselves . . . (Mark 9:9-10a)

The origin and purpose of the Messianic Secret has intrigued scholars for some time. Why does the author seem to cloak the mission of Jesus in secrecy and mystery? This is a question we will explore in Chapter Six. Meanwhile, the question is whether the Messianic Secret is in harmony with the abrupt and mysterious ending of the gospel. May we reasonably interpret the Messianic Secret motif as supporting the idea that the author wanted to leave the entire story of Jesus shrouded in mystery?

It is difficult to derive such an inference. For upon close scrutiny one wonders how these two elements can be logically related. The most fundamental difference between them is that the reader is explicitly aware of the Messianic Secret; the reader knows from the text that Jairus' daughter was raised, and that Peter identified Jesus as the Christ, and that the transfiguration occurred. The author never leaves the reader in the dark about who Jesus was or what he did. Conversely, an ending without resurrection appearances causes the reader to wonder what happened. So in this regard it is not at all compatible with the Messianic Secret motif.

Not only is the reader fully aware of the secrecy theme as it develops, but the theme is not left to stand unresolved in the text. It is clear from the gospel itself that the commands of Jesus not to reveal who he was were to be understood as temporary. Jesus tells his disciples not to discuss the transfiguration "until the Son of man should have risen from the dead."

The episode of the transfiguration (9:2-10) contains the last explicit command to the disciples not to discuss what they had seen. Soon afterward, the gospel shifts into a new motif of Messianic Proclamation. Jesus teaches his disciples what it means to bear the name of Christ (9:33-50). Jesus gives bold teachings about the cost of discipleship and the commitment required to inherit eternal life (10:17-31). He is referred to as the Son of David twice by the blind beggar (10:47-48); these are the first occurrences of this messianic title being used of Jesus in the gospel. Jesus effects his triumphal entry into Jerusalem where he is hailed as the expected Son of David, and the one to usher in the new kingdom (11:1-10). He claims the authority to drive the money-changers from the temple (11:15-17). Finally, during the interrogation of Jesus by the high priest, the gospel's momentum toward identifying Jesus as the Messiah reaches its climax:

> Again the high priest asked him, "Are you the Christ, the Son of the Blessed?" And Jesus said, "I am; and you will see the Son of man seated at the right hand of Power, and coming with the clouds of heaven (Mark 14:61b-62).

With this declaration, the unveiling of Jesus as *Messiah* is complete. Upon his death, even a Roman centurion is able to recognize and confess, "Truly, this was the Son of God" (15:39). The last half of the gospel contains a literary resolution of the Messianic Secret. There is no longer any secret, and no mystery. For the author, Jesus was indeed the Messiah, and there is to be no reservation in boldly proclaiming him as such. The Messianic Secret is a dramatic element which is introduced in the first half of the gospel and resolved in the second. The author did not intend for the Messianic Secret to be interpreted as an unresolved theme.

In what manner, then, may we understand the unresolved ending as thematically consistent with the Messianic Secret? Since the author's momentum in the gospel shifts so decidedly toward a proclamation of the triumphant Messiahship of Jesus, it would seem contrary to the author's design to have left the resurrection story unfinished and the prophecy of his appearance in Galilee unfulfilled. If one may argue that the mysterious non-ending is in accord with the Messianic Secret, one may just as persuasively argue that it is contrary to the theme of bold and decisive proclamation which dominates the climax of the work.

Therefore, the alleged link between the Messianic Secret and the truncated ending is difficult to sustain, and the suggestion of a stylistic link between the two is questionable. So to invoke the Messianic Secret as supporting evidence that the original gospel ended at 16:8 is to underscore how tenuous the theory really is.

In summary, the textual evidence offered in support of the prevailing theory carries little weight. The abbreviated opening of the gospel does not harmonize with a radically terminated storyline, nor does it imply that such an ending would make literary sense. The last phrase *for they were afraid* only indicates the text was probably terminated by rational design rather than by accident. Finally the Messianic Secret has little demonstrable relevance to the question at hand.

Though there is little solid evidence to support the theory, many researchers have embraced it. The problem which follows it is to explain why the author decided to end the gospel so severely. At face value it does not make much intuitive sense to suggest that Mark intended to end his story proclaiming the good news of Jesus Christ with the women fleeing in fear and confusion from the empty tomb, and the disciples unaware of his resurrection. In spite of this, commentators on the Gospel of Mark have attempted to explain why he may have done so. A sample follows:

C.S. Mann, The Anchor Bible Commentary, Mark:

Mark's gospel was, in our view, specifically designed to elicit the response: "But surely there were resurrection appearances?" The message of Mark was that there were indeed resurrection appearances, but first the community must share with the trembling women all the feelings of fear, know those fears to be in the final analysis groundless, and only then can they hear the voice the women heard--just as he told you.[5]

---

[5] Mann, C.S., *Mark*, Doubleday, 1986, p. 663

James Brooks, The New American Commentary, Mark:

... Mark had a definite purpose in his ending. He apparently wanted an open ending to indicate that the story was not complete but was continuing beyond the time he wrote. He wanted the readers/hearers to continue the story in their own lives ... [6]

Lamar Williamson, Jr., Mark, Interpretation Commentary Series:

The crucifixion had seemed to end the story but did not. The resurrection does not really do so, either. Resurrection-with-appearances would bring closure to the narrative, a closure which characterizes the other three gospels. Mark's ending is no end; only the reader can bring closure.

In one sense, this unfinished story puts the ball in the reader's court. It puts us to work; we must decide how the story should come out.

In a deeper sense, however, Jesus remains in control of the ball. No ending proposed by our decisions can contain him, any more than the tomb with its great stone could ... [7]

These three commentators have placed pastoral interpretations on the unfinished gospel by proposing the abrupt ending was intended to encourage readers to meditate upon the meaning of the gospel for the purpose of transforming it into active response. Mann postulates that the community for which the gospel was written was terrorized by impending persecution and ready to flee. He suggests the termination of the gospel on the note of the women's fear was intended to force the community to consider an appropriate response in the face of fear. Williamson adds that the unfinished gospel is a theological reflection upon the story of Jesus which is still in the making.

Such philosophical and psychological interpretations are typical of attempts to infuse the unfinished gospel with meaning. While they are intriguing, and perhaps even ingenious, they are not grounded in the text itself. Rather, they are speculations about why the author might have been led to do so.

---

[6] Brooks, Ibid., p. 275

[7] Williamson, Jr., Lamar, *The Interpretation Commentary Series, Mark*, John Knox Press, 1983, p. 285-6

There is no doubt that the author of Mark made extensive use of symbolic and mechanical literary devices to impart significance to his text. Several of them are important and will be explored later. However, the absence of resurrection appearances is a large step beyond mere symbolism. Further, it is a step with which the early church itself was clearly uncomfortable; 16:9-20, which the church added later, contains the resurrection appearances needed to rectify the problem. So even though many contemporary scholars see profound meaning in Mark's non-ending, the early church apparently did not.

In short, modern theory on the meaning of the unfinished gospel is founded on the *incompleteness* of the text; scholars have attempted to derive meaning from what is not there rather than from what is. Accordingly, such speculations have more of a sermon-like quality than anything grounded in academic research. In the final analysis, the ability to imbue the gospel's incompleteness with meaning has no rational bearing on how the text was originally composed.

On balance the theory that Mark ended the gospel at 16:8 is intuitively improbable. The textual evidence is sparse, and the meanings assigned to it by its proponents are obscure and often irrelevant to the question. Not only does it not offer a compelling solution to the problem, it serves to divert attention from an equally if not more probable explanation: those who controlled the publication of the gospel, for reasons yet to be explored, intentionally removed the original conclusion of the Gospel of Mark.

The Missing Ending of Mark

The suggestion that the conclusion of Mark was intentionally removed by editors raises the uncomfortable possibility that such editing was done out of a motive to deceive. This may be the most pressing reason why many are unwilling to admit it as a solution. Yet such an inference is not necessarily warranted. We may just as easily suppose that it was deleted in an effort to make the document conform to the divergent beliefs of sects trying to reconcile their differences, in much the same way that John 21 may have been added for this purpose. Thus to automatically infer sinister intent is not justified.

Perhaps another reason for ignoring this solution is that it suggests a potential dead end in research. If the ending was deleted, must we not then rely on pure speculation about what it may have contained and why it was removed? What would be the point of such fanciful conjecture? Yet this also is a hasty conclusion; the author of Mark was fond of theological symbols and other literary devices. Mark is a highly structured work which contains a good amount of foreshadowing as well as several definite predictions as to what will occur after Jesus' resurrection. So once we focus on these symbols, literary devices, and predictions, it is possible to construct in rather specific terms the ideal literary conclusion. Perhaps such a reconstruction may yield a clue as to why it would have been deleted. Most would consider this a speculative waste of effort. Yet the result does indeed suggest a stunning solution to the mystery.

The first step in constructing the ideal conclusion is to isolate the predictions in the gospel which bear upon it. Three of these are obvious. The gospel tells us that the first resurrection appearance of Jesus to the disciples will occur in Galilee. It also tells us specifically that Peter will be present at this appearance. Finally, it tells us that the text beyond 16:8 would include a scene in which the disciples are unaware of the empty tomb. Each of these will be considered in turn.

1. *The first resurrection appearance will be in Galilee.* Sean Freyne has demonstrated in his book *Galilee, Jesus, and the Gospels*, that one of the great symbols of the Gospel of Mark is that of Galilee as an antithetical location to Jerusalem.[8] Throughout the gospel, Galilee is the stage upon which Jesus conducts his ministry, and it is where he is anticipated to appear after his resurrection. The following passages illustrate Mark's development of Galilee as the place where the kingdom of God is revealed on earth:

In those days Jesus came from Nazareth of Galilee (1:9).

Now after John was arrested, Jesus came into Galilee, preaching the Gospel of God (1:14).

---

[8] Freyne, Sean, *Galilee, Jesus, and the Gospels: Literary Approaches and Historical Investigations*, Fortress Press, 1988

> And passing along by the Sea of Galilee, he saw Simon and Andrew the brother of Simon casting a net in the sea; for they were fishermen. And Jesus said to them, "Follow me and I will make you become fishers of men." (1:16-17)

> And at once his fame spread everywhere throughout all the surrounding region of Galilee. (1:28).

> And he went throughout all Galilee, preaching in their synagogues and casting out demons. (1:39)

As Galilee is the symbolic center of the new kingdom of God, conversely the author develops Jerusalem as the place where those who oppose Jesus abide. While Jesus conducts his ministry in Galilee, his adversaries, the Pharisees and scribes, come from Jerusalem to challenge him:

> And the scribes who came down from Jerusalem said, "He is possessed by Beelzebul, and by the prince of demons he casts out demons." (3:22)

> Now when the Pharisees gathered together to him, with some of the scribes, who had come down from Jerusalem, they saw that some of his disciples ate with hands defiled, that is, unwashed. (7:1-2)

As Jesus approaches Jerusalem for the first time, he identifies it as the place where he will be executed:

> And they were on the road, going up to Jerusalem, and Jesus was walking ahead of them; and they were amazed, and those who followed were afraid. And taking the twelve again, he began to tell them what was to happen to him, saying, "Behold, we are going up to Jerusalem; and the Son of man will be delivered to the chief priests and the scribes, and they will condemn him to death, and deliver him to the Gentiles; and they will mock him, and spit upon him, and scourge him, and kill him; and after three days he will rise." (10:32-34)

On the evening before his crucifixion, Jesus and his disciples are in Jerusalem. Jesus predicts his resurrection, but he makes it clear he will not appear to them in Jerusalem, but rather in Galilee:

> You will all fall away; for it is written, "I will strike the shepherd, and the sheep will be scattered." But after I am raised up, I will go before you to Galilee. (14:27-28)

This prediction is confirmed by the young man at the tomb, just prior to the abrupt end of the Gospel. When the women discover the empty tomb, the young man announces Jesus' resurrection, then says:

> But go, tell his disciples and Peter that he is going before you to Galilee; there you will see him as he told you. (16:7)

Therefore Mark establishes Galilee as the symbolic alternative to Jerusalem, the Holy City, where until now God has dwelt. Jesus has established the kingdom of God on the periphery of Jewish society, in the region of Galilee, to overthrow the authority of the temple cult in Jerusalem. Hence, the ideal ending to Mark would present the *first* resurrection appearance of Jesus to his disciples in Galilee. No other scenario would fit either the symbolism of the gospel or the specific predictions that he is to "go before the disciples" and appear there.

2. *Peter and Jesus will be reconciled during the first appearance of Jesus.* A second element in the ideal ending is that this first resurrection appearance of Jesus will include Peter. Recall the young man's instructions to the women at the tomb -- "tell his disciples *and Peter* that he is going before you to Galilee"(16:7). With this unusual detail, the author has foreshadowed a meeting between Jesus and Peter. This is actually the second time the gospel anticipates a meeting between Jesus and Peter in Galilee after the resurrection. The first is this:

> And Jesus said to them, "You will all fall away; for it is written 'I will strike the shepherd, and the sheep will be scattered.' But after I am raised up, *I will go before you to Galilee.*" Peter said to him, "Even though they all fall away, I will not." And Jesus said to him, "Truly, I say to you, this very night, before the cock crows twice, you will deny me three times." (14:27-30)

Here the prediction of the Galilean appearance and the denial by Peter are placed together in the same context. Jesus is clearly aware of

both impending events. Though Peter is to deny Jesus, he is anticipated to be one of those present in Galilee. So from the admonition to
the women at the tomb *tell the disciples and Peter* we may reasonably
infer that Jesus intends to resolve the conflict created by Peter's denials.
Such an outcome would be in harmony with the foreshadowing.

The notion of a reconciliation of the tension created by Peter's
denials is supported by several observations. First, Peter is presented as
the leading disciple throughout the gospel, and a meeting between
Jesus and Peter in which Peter was upbraided or condemned would not
be in keeping with the character of either Jesus or Peter as developed in
this gospel. Second, the fact that it was foreordained that the *all the
sheep would scatter* and abandon Jesus signifies that Peter's denial was
not something he alone should be condemned for. Third, Mark shows
Peter grieving over his failure once he realizes what he as done (14:72).
Such a reaction foreshadows forgiveness rather than condemnation.
Therefore the most harmonious resolution of the gospel would show a
meeting of reconciliation between Jesus and Peter during the first
resurrection appearance in Galilee.

**3. When Jesus appears, the disciples will have been unaware of
the empty tomb.** Note that the last verse in the surviving text says the
women fled from the tomb and *"said nothing to anyone, for they were
afraid"* (16:8). This note is in conflict with the tradition in the other
three gospels. In John, Mary runs to tell the disciples once she
discovers the tomb empty (John 20:2). Matthew and Luke both indicate
the women returned from the tomb and immediately told the disciples
(Matt 28:8; Luke 24:9). Though many assume the women would have
told the disciples had Mark's story continued, 16:8 prevents this
speculation from being used to reconstruct the ending. It is unlikely
that the author would have written this line, and then shown the
women reporting what they had discovered to the disciples in the next
scene. From the silence of the women we may infer that, in the next
scene, we would find that the disciples are as yet unaware of the
women's discovery.

Furthermore, the gospel has set the stage for a scene change to
Galilee. Jesus has been crucified and buried. The tomb is found empty

but the women flee and tell no one. The gospel has clearly predicted a resolution in Galilee. Though it is possible that the next scene would show the disciples gathered in Jerusalem, the storyline does not require it, nor suggest it. There is no reason why they would reassemble; they are "scattered sheep" and nothing that they are aware of has occurred to bring them together again. Since the gospel twice indicates that Jesus will go before the disciples to Galilee, the inference is that the disciples will have returned to Galilee unaware of the empty tomb. Though such an inference is not mandated by the text, it is the most coherent continuation of the storyline.

In summary, the author has predicted a first resurrection appearance of Jesus to his disciples in Galilee, and a meeting with Peter wherein Jesus reconciles with him after his denial episode. Further-more, in the scene following 16:8 the disciples will be unaware of the empty tomb, and it is reasonable to expect that the setting of this scene would be Galilee.

Many will have recognized by now that all of these elements occur in the mysterious appendix of the Fourth Gospel--John 21. Since John 21 bears such a remarkable affinity with the ideal literary ending of Mark, it is not unreasonable to ask if John 21 could have originally been composed as the final chapter of Mark. Furthermore, we may wonder whether this text was deleted from Mark, edited, and added to John at the same time and for the same purpose. Is there any evidence which would support these possibilities?

In Chapter Two we found that John 21 was most likely added by pro-Petrine editors to negate the Fourth Gospel's hostility toward Peter. John 21 was also discovered to contain a mixture of Johannine and synoptic traditions. We will return to this odd blend of traditions shortly, but first it must be demonstrated that the key elements which define the ideal end of Mark do indeed exist in John 21.

The Original Text of John 21 as a First Appearance of Jesus

At face value, John 21 claims to be reporting Jesus' third appear-ance to the disciples (21:14). The question is whether there are any clues which would imply that the story was written as a first appearance, then edited to represent it as a third appearance; the answer is *yes*.

The first clue is the premise of the story itself. In John 21 the disciples have returned to Galilee and decided to take up their previous occupations as fishermen. This scenario makes little sense if they have already witnessed the resurrection of Jesus in Jerusalem as reported in John 20. From this discontinuity we may infer that John 21 was originally composed for a different purpose than as an appendix to John.

Further, the premise is that the disciples have again taken up their occupation as fishermen. That is, they have gone back to what they were doing prior to the time they met Jesus at the beginning of Mark. While this makes no sense after the resurrection appearances in John 20, it is entirely coherent as a continuation of Mark 16:8. They logically take up their prior occupations because they assume Jesus is dead and the ministry is ended. Now let us look at how the story unfolds in John 21:

> Just as day was breaking, Jesus stood on the beach; yet the disciples did not know that it was Jesus. Jesus said to them, "Children, have you any fish?" They answered him, "No." He said to them, "Cast the net on the right side of the boat, and you will find some." So they cast it, and now they were not able to haul it in, for the quantity of fish. That disciple whom Jesus loved said, "It is the Lord!" (John 21:4-6)

Here Jesus appears on the beach, but the disciples do not know that it is Jesus. Not until an apparently miraculous catch of fish occurs do they recognize this person as Jesus. So the storyline continues to support the theory that they have not yet seen Jesus alive, for they do not expect to see him.

Upon recognizing Jesus, Peter swims to shore, and the others follow in the boat. They meet Jesus on the shore as he is preparing breakfast:

> Jesus said to them, "Come and have breakfast." Now none of the disciples dared ask him, "Who are you?" They knew it was the Lord. (21:12)

Note that the author's editorial comment makes no sense if the disciples had already met the risen Lord; if they had already seen him twice in Jerusalem, their confusion in this passage about who he is simply does not fit. The author who wrote these words originally did so on the premise that this was the disciples' first encounter with Jesus after the crucifixion. The text continues:

> 13 Jesus came and took the bread and gave it to them, and so with the fish. 14 This *was now the third time that Jesus was revealed to the disciples after he was raised from the dead.* 15 When they had finished breakfast, Jesus said to Peter, "Simon, son of John, do you love me more than these?" (John 21:13-15a, emphasis added)

Now 21:14, the italicized text, appears to be an editorial insert which attempts to resolve the inherent confusion. On the one hand, the disciples appear to be meeting Jesus for the first time, yet on the other, this text has been appended to John 20, where these same disciples have seen him twice before. The insert is an attempt to tie the appendix to John 20. Note that it breaks the continuity of the story; if it were deleted the story would read comfortably as originally composed.

So there is ample evidence to suggest John 21 was originally composed as an account of the first appearance of Jesus. Several commentators have made this observation:

Raymond Brown:

Most commentators interpret the threefold question about Peter's love for Jesus in [21:]15-17 as a rehabilitation of Peter after his threefold denial, and such a rehabilitation would logically have taken place on the occasion of the first post-resurrection appearance of Jesus to Peter, which is what we seem to have in 21:1-14.[9]

C.K. Barrett:

Moreover, the present narrative looks more like a first than a third appearance . . . The impression is given that the present story does not belong to the carefully composed narrative of Ch. 20 but is a distinct incident drawn from another source . . .[10]

---

[9] Brown, Ibid., p. 1083
[10] Barrett, Ibid., 582-3

Rudolf Bultmann:

> It is apparent that the narrative of 21:1-14 was originally related as the first Easter story; the editorial v. 14 shows that the story was set only subsequently in the place that it now occupies.[11]

Not only does the Gospel of Mark anticipate that the first resurrection appearance of Jesus will be in Galilee, but we find that John 21:1-14 was likely originally composed as a first appearance in Galilee. This is the first of the three elements for which we are looking. The second is a meeting between Jesus and Peter which restores Peter after his denials.

Peter as the New Shepherd

It has always been recognized that the encounter between Jesus and Peter in John 21 is closely related to Peter's triple denial, for as Peter denied Jesus three times, so there is a similar triplet form in Jesus' restoration of Peter. We noted in Chapter Two that this episode was constructed specifically to resolve the damaging story of Peter's denials:

> When they had finished breakfast, Jesus said to Simon Peter, "Simon, son of John, do you love me more than these?" He said to him, "Yes, Lord; you know that I love you." He said to him, "Feed my lambs." A second time he said to him, "Simon, son of John, do you love me?" He said to him, "Yes, Lord; you know that I love you." He said to him, "Tend my sheep." He said to him the third time, "Simon, son of John, do you love me?" Peter was grieved because he said to him the third time, "Do you love me?" And he said to him, "Lord, you know everything; you know that I love you." Jesus said to him, "Feed my sheep." (John 21:15-17)

Note that as a positive outcome of Peter's denials, this story would fit better at the end of Mark than it does at the end of John. Both gospels contain the account of Peter's denials, but it is only Mark which foreshadows this pleasant resolution. However, some may object that

---

[11] Bultmann, Rudolf, *The Gospel of John: A Commentary*, Westminster Press, English Edition, 1971, p. 701

this observation conflicts with the shepherd motif in the passage. Most scholars identify the shepherd motif used in this passage as an echo of the strong Johannine shepherd metaphor established in John 10, in which Jesus says, *"I am the good shepherd. The good shepherd lays down his life for the sheep"* (John 10:11). So this passage is generally regarded as deriving from Johannine tradition. Thus it presumably cannot be accepted as Markan in origin.

This is not the case however. For Mark also establishes the shepherd metaphor, and remarkably, he does so within the conversation which forecasts his first resurrection appearance in Galilee, and Peter's imminent denial of him. Note the three tightly coupled elements of the shepherd metaphor, the appearance in Galilee, and Peter's denial:

> And Jesus said to them, "You will all fall away; for it is written '*I will strike the shepherd, and the sheep will be scattered.*' But after I am raised up, *I will go before you to Galilee.*" Peter said to him, "Even though they all fall away, I will not." And Jesus said to him, "Truly, I say to you, this very night, before the cock crows twice, *you will deny me three times.*" (Mark 14:27-30)

In this passage, Jesus says he will appear in Galilee; John 21 fulfills this prediction. In Mark, Peter denies Jesus three times; John 21 shows the resolution of this failure. In Mark, the shepherd is struck down and the sheep are scattered; in John 21, Jesus indicates Peter is to be the new shepherd, the one to replace the shepherd struck down. The fact that these three concepts are so tightly connected in Mark 14:27-30 and again in John 21:15-17 suggests that the passage in John may have been originally composed as a literary fulfillment of Mark. In particular, the idea that Peter is to be the new shepherd to tend Jesus' sheep is obviously related to Mark's image of the shepherd struck down and the sheep scattered. It is improbable that the literary linking of these three concepts was coincidental.

So two of the three elements anticipated in Mark are clearly present in John 21--the first appearance in Galilee and the restoration of Peter. Does the text of John 21 also indicate that the disciples were unaware of the empty tomb?

The Disciples' Awareness of the Resurrection

While there is no explicit statement in John 21 prior to Jesus' appearance that the disciples were not aware of the empty tomb, the premise of the story seems to suggest it. At the beginning of John 21, we find that the disciples have returned to Galilee and taken up their previous occupation as fishermen. Such a premise is entirely incongruous with the idea that they have witnessed the resurrected Lord, or that they are even aware of the fact that the tomb was empty. Returning to their fishing boats is a response one would expect from disciples who had suffered the shock and defeat of Jesus' tragic end, and who had not yet recognized that the story was to continue. They returned to their former occupation because they believed Jesus was dead and in his grave, and the movement was over.

Their unawareness of the empty tomb is further supported by the author's odd note in 21:12, *"Now none of the disciples dared ask him, 'Who are you?' They knew it was the Lord."* These words seem to have been composed by an author whose premise was that the disciples did not expect to see Jesus since they were unaware of the resurrection.

In short, the three key elements foreshadowed in the Gospel of Mark that are left hanging at Mark 16:8 are fully resolved in John 21.

The Fishing Motif

Jesus' appearance in Galilee and the close relationship between Mark 14:27-30 and John 21:15-17 are not the only literary connections between the Gospel of Mark and John 21. In addition the fishing metaphor, which is used as an opening theme in the first chapter of Mark, is echoed in John 21. Mark establishes the motif in the first chapter:

> And passing along by the Sea of Galilee, he saw Simon and Andrew the brother of Simon casting a net in the sea; for they were fishermen. And Jesus said to them, "Follow me and I will make you become fishers of men." (Mark 1:16-17)

With this theme established in the opening chapter, the story of the miraculous catch of fish in John 21 becomes much more important. The text includes a key detail for interpreting the meaning of the catch:

> Jesus said to them, "Bring some of the fish that you have just caught." So Simon Peter went aboard and hauled the net ashore, full of large fish, a hundred and fifty three of them; and although there were so many, the net was not torn. (John 21:10-11)

The detail that there were one hundred fifty-three fish in the net has intrigued scholars for centuries. Most believe it is symbolic in some way, for the idea that they would count the exact number of fish and record it for posterity seems unlikely. However, the symbolism itself is lost to us. Some have suggested there were one hundred fifty-three disciples following Jesus at the end of his ministry, and this number symbolized the totality of his movement at the time. This is a logical and straightforward guess, and it is as good an answer as any which has been suggested. Others have tried to explore more complex numerological solutions.[12]

Though we do not know the origin of the number 153, it is fair to suggest, as Rudolf Schnackenburg does, that "the quantity of fish is justification for the supposition that the editors saw in it a symbol of universality."[13] The author and his readers most likely recognized it as symbolic of the church at large--a number representing those who would be "caught" by the missionary activity of the disciples. As such it is a metaphoric fulfillment of the opening theme in Mark in which Jesus promises to make the disciples fishers of men.

Should there be any doubt that the "fishers of men" metaphor is to be linked with the miraculous catch of fish, note that these two elements appear in the same text in a story out of Luke:

---

[12] For instance, Augustine pointed out that the numbers from 1 to 17, when added together, equal 153. However, one must admit the symbolic meaning of such a derivation is still quite obscure. Another solution may be derived from the symbolic numbers 3 and 12. Three is a frequent numeric representation of God; twelve symbolizes God's people on earth (twelve tribes of Israel; twelve disciples, etc.). The square of three plus the square of twelve equals 153. Thus 153 may represent God in union with his people.

[13] Schnackenburg, Rudolf, *The Gospel According to St. John*, Crossroad Publishing, 1990, Vol. 3, p. 358.

And he sat down and taught the people from the boat. And when he had ceased speaking, he said to Simon, "Put out into the deep and let down your nets for a catch." And Simon answered, "Master, we toiled all night and took nothing! But at your word I will let down the nets." And when they had done this, they enclosed a great shoal of fish; and as their nets were breaking, they beckoned to their partners in the other boat to come and help them. . . . When Simon Peter saw it, he fell down at Jesus' knees, saying, "Depart from me, for I am a sinful man, O Lord." . . . And Jesus said to Simon, "Do not be afraid; henceforth you will be catching men." (excerpts from Luke 5:3-10)

The "fishers of men" theme from Mark 1 and the miraculous catch of fish from John 21 appear together in a single literary unit in Luke. Thus the evidence is strong that they had a common literary origin. The theme forges a significant link between Mark and John 21.

On the other hand, while the fishing motif in John 21 is an attractive literary fulfillment of the opening Markan theme, John 1-20 contains no reference at all to the disciples as fishermen; the motif is foreign to Johannine tradition. That John 21 introduces the fishing motif without comment is another discontinuity between it and the gospel. So the link between Mark and John 21 is further strengthened by the fact that John 21's fishing motif is foreign to John.

The Bracketing of the Gospel of Mark

There is yet another link between Mark and John 21 which must not be overlooked. It is that the first words spoken by Jesus to a disciple in the Gospel of Mark are "Follow me," directed to Peter in 1:17. The last words of Jesus in John 21 are also "Follow me!" They are also spoken to Peter. Either this is a bizarre coincidence, or there was some literary design at its root.

Let us assume, then, on the strength of the observations so far, that John 21, less its specific Johannine elements, was indeed the last chapter of Mark. If we were to move the text to Mark and append it to 16:8, a remarkable grand pattern manifests itself. We would see that Mark had bracketed the entire ministry of Jesus between the opening and closing passages of the "fishers of men" metaphor. Standing just outside these brackets are the two identical commands of Jesus to Peter: "Follow me!" In its abstract form, the gospel would take the following structure:

> A. Jesus says to Peter, "Follow me!"
>
> B.   *Disciples to be made "fishers of men"*
>
> C. **The Ministry of Jesus**
>
> D.   *Disciples are made "fishers of men"*
>
> E. Jesus says to Peter, "Follow me!"

Once again, such a compelling literary structure cannot be ignored, especially since the techniques of intercalation, bracketing, and framing are so widely recognized by scholars as Markan devices. C. S. Mann has underscored the use of bracketing sections of the gospel as key literary devices:

> It has been pointed out that Mark is fond of enclosing material(s) within similar traditions. Perhaps the most noteworthy example is that portion which presents the three predictions of the Passion within the cures of those who were blind (at 8:22-26 and 10:46-52). Both healings "bracket" the intervening material, and the use of such incidents to interpret that intervening section has been made by many commentators.[14]

Mann notes that the entire gospel is made up of sections of material which have been framed by repeated themes. For example, Segment One opens with the call of the first four disciples (1:16-20) and ends with the selection of the twelve disciples (3:13-19). Segment Two opens with a note on the true family of Jesus (3:20-35) and ends with a reflection on the supposed family of Jesus (6:1-6). Segment Three opens and closes with references to the yeast of Herod (6:7-33 and 8:14-20). In this manner, the entire gospel is composed of six discrete segments which are intentionally framed with interpretive themes.[15]

---

[14] Mann, Ibid., p 175
[15] Mann, Ibid., p. 177-190

Therefore the observation that the entire ministry of Jesus would appear to be double-framed with the fishing motif and the command "Follow me!" is consistent with the more detailed literary structure of the gospel. Indeed, given the author's propensity to intercalate individual stories and bracket each section of his gospel, we may wonder if the lack of a complete frame around the ministry of Jesus is in itself evidence that the original conclusion is missing. For it is clear that the grand opening theme, *"Follow me and I will make you become fishers of men"* has no fulfillment in the gospel. This powerful motif is established and then inexplicably dropped without any further comment or development. However, once John 21 is restored to Mark, the grand frame falls into place and the author's original design becomes apparent.

The interpretation thus placed upon the ministry of Jesus is that it is a call to action. Disciples are to follow; they are to be fishers of men. Action is required of those who wish to become disciples of the Lord. Such an interpretation is in precise harmony with the central teachings in the gospel itself:

> And as he was setting out on his journey, a man ran up and knelt before him, and asked him, "Good Teacher, what must I do to inherit eternal life?" And Jesus said to him, "Why do you call me good? No one is good but God alone. You know the commandments: 'Do not kill, Do not commit adultery, Do not steal, Do not bear false witness, Do not defraud, Honor your father and mother.'" And he said to him, "Teacher, all these I have observed from my youth." And Jesus looking upon him loved him, and said to him, "You lack one thing; go, sell what you have, and give to the poor, and you will have treasure in heaven; and come, follow me." (Mark 10:17-21)

> And he called to him the multitude with his disciples, and said to them, "If any man would come after me, let him deny himself and take up his cross and follow me." (Mark 8:34)

Thus the grand frame *"Follow me, and I will make you become fishers of men"* serves to define the essential message of the Gospel of Mark. The frame does not exist until we restore John 21 to the end of Mark. Having done so, the structure of the gospel is complete and its meaning is enhanced. The literary affinity between Mark and John 21 is so compelling that it cannot be set aside as coincidental.

The Origin of John 21

In Chapter Two we found that John 21 bears distinctive literary clues which link it to John or to Johannine tradition, and that it also contains numerous indicators of synoptic origin; the text appears to be a stylistic melting pot of these two traditions. Thus far in this chapter we have found a number of clues which indicate John 21 may have been the original final chapter of Mark. The findings suggest that John 21 is in substantial form the missing ending of the Second Gospel. It was detached from the Gospel of Mark and appended to John after editors rewrote the text to include Johannine-specific references, thereby making it appear authentically Johannine. This would account for the blend of Johannine and synoptic traditions in the same text.

So two questions remain. Are there signs of such editorial intrusions in the text of John 21 which would support this theory? Further, though we have already identified a political motive to affix the story of John 21 to the Gospel of John, why would the text have been taken from Mark? The balance of this chapter will explore the answers to these two questions.

The Editorial Rewrite of John 21

There are many unusual elements in John 21 which may be explained as the work of editors rewriting an original Markan text. The clues begin with the opening two verses:

> After this Jesus revealed himself again to the disciples by the Sea of Tiberias; and he revealed himself in this way. Simon Peter, Thomas called the Twin, Nathanael of Cana in Galilee, the sons of Zebedee, and two others of his disciples were together. (John 21:1-2)

In this introduction we see an odd list of names: Simon Peter, Thomas called the Twin, Nathanael, the sons of Zebedee, and two others. This list is unique for two reasons. First, nowhere in John are more than two of the twelve disciples named as being together for any purpose. If more than two are together, the group is simply referred to collectively as "the disciples." Second, there is no instance in John where any two of these disciples are cited as being together. They would appear to have no family or business relations. The only thing they have in common is their discipleship of Jesus. So what may we infer about these names?

There is one striking element the first three have in common: each of these three names is in some way *unique* to the Fourth Gospel. "Simon Peter" is a common reference to Peter in the Gospel of John. In Mark he is called either Simon or Peter, but never by the double name. So between Mark and John, the use of the name "Simon Peter" is exclusive to John.

Similarly, Thomas appears in the lists of the twelve disciples in the synoptic gospels, but he is never referred to as "Thomas called the twin" except in John (11:16; 20:24). Hence, this appellation is also exclusive to John. Further, the disciple Thomas is not a developed character in the synoptic gospels; his name appears only once in each of these gospels, and only in the list naming the twelve disciples. Conversely, Thomas appears on three separate occasions in John, and most memorably in his doubting incident in John 20, where he finally meets the resurrected Lord and believes. So the unique association of Thomas with Johannine tradition is clear.

Finally, Nathanael is a disciple who appears in John (1:45-49) but is entirely unknown, at least by this name, in the synoptic gospels. In short, the list of disciples in 21:2 begins with three disciples who have no prior relation to one another, but who share one thing in common: their names as cited are exclusive to the Gospel of John.

Now if this were an original Markan text, it is fair to assume it would have opened with Peter, James, and John (and perhaps Andrew) fishing by the Sea of Galilee. This would have been the ideal fulfillment of the opening theme in Mark, in which these same disciples are called from their nets to become fishers of men. However, the trio Peter, James, and John (with or without Andrew) constitutes a clear Markan signature, for these are the intimate three which appear regularly throughout the Gospel of Mark.

Editors faced with the problem of adding such an original text to John may have felt it necessary to change the names in order to erase the Markan formula. So it makes sense that the names Peter, James and John, would be overwritten with uniquely Johannine names to accomplish this. Hence, we have a natural and coherent theory of how the unlikely but strictly Johannine trio of "Simon Peter, Thomas, and Nathanael" came to appear in the strange context of a fishing motif.

In addition the original Markan text would have named the Sea of Galilee as the place where this event occurred. However, the Gospel of John mentions the Sea of Galilee only once, and in so doing it tells us that another name for it was the Sea of Tiberias (6:1). To complete the effect then, the editors may have felt compelled to change the name to the Sea of Tiberias. The result is that Mark's well recognized formula "Peter, James, and John by the Sea of Galilee" appears to have been rewritten as the unprecedented "Simon Peter, Thomas called the Twin, and Nathanael by the Sea of Tiberias." Such an alteration of the text would obliterate the Markan signature and replace it with a strong indication of Johannine authenticity. This seems to have been the only purpose for these names, for Thomas and Nathanael are not mentioned again in the chapter. Seen in this light the apparent editing looks indelicate, but one cannot deny that it has helped assure many readers through the centuries of the authenticity of John 21.

Now the first three names are exclusively Johannine in usage, but the reference to the "sons of Zebedee" is not. These two brothers, James and John, are unknown in the Gospel of John. However, they and Peter are the three prominent disciples in Mark. Their inclusion here is a strong indicator that the text had a Markan origin. So we have a problem: if the editors were attempting to link the text intimately with the Gospel of John, why would the sons of Zebedee be included? Two answers are intuitively plausible.

First, we may note that the beloved disciple, who appears later in the chapter at 21:7 is not included in this list. Those who equate the beloved disciple with John, the son of Zebedee, will argue that at minimum the sons of Zebedee needed to be named in 21:2 since first century readers already identified John the son of Zebedee as the beloved disciple. It is possible that this is the correct interpretation.

However, we must also consider the further oddity of the final reference in 21:2 to "two others of his disciples." Now this seems like an extraneous reference. What possible meaning could this have after listing five disciples by name?

One proposal has been made by LaGrange which is speculative but certainly plausible: the list as composed in the original editing of the text read "*Simon Peter, Thomas called the Twin, Nathanael of Cana in Galilee, and two others of his disciples.*" There was no reference to the sons of Zebedee. LaGrange proposed that someone made a margin note in the original manuscript or one of the early copies identifying these two unnamed disciples as the sons of Zebedee. Eventually as the text was reproduced the marginal note began to be copied as part of the actual text. Thus the original list of five disciples became seven; the reference to "two others" is a duplicate reference to the sons of Zebedee and is an extraneous note in the text, just as it appears to be. This theory harmonizes well with the idea that the editors overwrote the original "Peter, James, and John." For just as inserting Thomas and Nathanael lends Johannine authenticity, referring to James and John as "two others of his disciples" obscures the Markan origin.

There is no way to determine the truth of the matter, nor is there a need to. What is important about the opening list of names is that (a) the first three names ensure the appendix would be perceived as integral to the Johannine tradition, and (b) the reference to the sons of Zebedee, whether it originated as part of the original editor's text or as a subsequent scribal margin note, is suggestive of Markan influence on the part of those who reproduced the gospel.

Now if the names in the opening verses of John 21 have been changed to lend the text Johannine authenticity, we may expect that other uniquely Johannine words would have been inserted for the same reason. We noted in the previous chapter two Greek words for "fish"--*ichthys* and *opsarion*. In John 1-20, *opsarion* appears twice, and *ichthys* not at all. In Mark, *ichthys* is used exclusively, and *opsarion* does not appear. In John 21, both words appear three times each, but *opsarion* (cooked fish) is misused where Jesus says, "Bring some of the fish *(opsarion)* that you have just caught" (21:10), and Peter goes to retrieve them from the net.

The present theory suggests an explanation for this error. It is possible that the limited meaning of the term *opsarion* would not have been known by someone outside the fishing trade. If the editor were looking through John in search of unique words to tie the gospel to the appendix, he may have found *opsarion* and, assuming it to be synonymous with *ichthys*, introduced it into the text of John 21:10 in error.

Thus in the text of John 21, we can find hints that it was rewritten to conform to Johannine style and tradition. Certainly the reference to the "third appearance" in 21:12 indicates the presence of an editor who was altering the text for conformance to John 20. If this were the case we have accounted for the strange blend of Johannine and synoptic influences which permeate the text. Yet it will be obvious that no amount of stylistic analysis will yield a definitive conclusion, for the editor's apparent purpose was to conceal the origin of the text. Perhaps the very inconclusiveness of the stylistic studies performed thus far is the best argument in support of the theory.

The Original Ending of Mark

The analysis of Mark and John 21 shows that the ideal literary fulfillment of the Gospel of Mark is found in the text of John 21:1-19, less the editorial changes introduced after the fact. In summary, the evidence accumulated is this:

1. The Gospel of John contains hostile anti-Petrine rhetoric which is negated by John 21. The appendix appears to have been added by pro-Petrine editors for this purpose.

2. John 21 contains a mix of Johannine and Markan traditions and styles; it appears to have been edited for appending to John.

3. John 21 was originally composed as a first resurrection appearance of Jesus in Galilee. Mark anticipates such an appearance.

4. John 21 shows that Peter is forgiven and restored after his denials. Mark anticipates this reconciliation. In particular, John 21:15-17 is a precise literary fulfillment of Mark 14:27-30.

5. The premise of the disciples' return to their fishing boats in John 21 is coherent with the indication in Mark that the women did not tell the disciples about the empty tomb.

6. When the story of John 21:1-19 is appended to Mark 16:8, the Gospel of Mark appears as a complete and unified literary work. The entire ministry of Jesus is framed between the grand theme "Follow me, and I will make you become fishers of men." Such framing is consistent with Mark's technical use of bracketing for interpretive purposes, and it is in complete harmony with the message of the gospel.

It is extremely remote that so many literary elements between the Gospel of Mark and John 21 could have fallen into place randomly and without any literary design. The cumulative weight of evidence points to the conclusion that John 21:1-19 was originally composed by the author of Mark, and that subsequent editors removed it from Mark, added Johannine elements, and appended it to the Gospel of John.

Why was Mark's Ending Used to Append John?

Since the Gospel of John contains an unsavory characterization of Peter, it is easy to discern the motive for the early church to finish the gospel on a more positive note. So the appending of John 21 makes sense. However, this theory raises another important question: Why was a pro-Petrine text not written from scratch rather than taking it from the Gospel of Mark? Why not leave the Gospel of Mark intact as it was originally written?

An answer suggests itself once John 21 is removed from the Fourth Gospel and added to Mark. Once we perform this proposed reconstruction, the two gospels stand in bold relief as opposing political documents. The result is the following:

1. John is clearly an anti-Petrine work, written with a political motive to discredit Peter as a legitimate leader of the movement. The author highlights Peter's three denials as a monumental and singular failure of this disciple. In his place, the Beloved Disciple is promoted as the rightful leader.

2. If we made no assumption about the chronological sequence of John and Mark, it would appear that Mark was composed as a political and theological response to John. The author repeats the most damaging allegation against Peter found in John, then uses it as the foundation for the meeting between Jesus and Peter in which Peter is confirmed as the authorized leader of the movement.   Mark also pointedly usurps John's shepherd metaphor to elevate Peter to a position above all other disciples. These reactionary elements make the two gospels appear to be in conflict with one another.

3. The two original gospels appear to have reported conflicting stories regarding the resurrection of Jesus. John said Jesus appeared first to Mary Magdalene at the tomb, after which she promptly brought the news to the disciples; then Jesus appeared to the disciples twice in Jerusalem. Mark said Jesus did *not* appear to the women at the tomb, and the women did not announce the resurrection to anyone. Nor did Jesus appear to the disciples in Jerusalem; instead he appeared for the first time to the disciples in Galilee. The historicity of the resurrection, which was to become a cornerstone of the movement's crystallizing orthodoxy, may have been perceived as compromised by having two irreconcilable traditions in circulation.

4.   Both gospels claimed equal authority in that they each represented the teachings of one of the twelve disciples of Jesus. Hence, one could not easily be dismissed in favor of the other.

Given these factors, the deletion of the end of Mark would have accomplished two important things. First, by eliminating the promotion of Peter as the new shepherd, it made the Second Gospel much less obvious as a rebuttal of John. Second, it removed the historical conflict in the resurrection tradition. Indeed, Mark 16:9-11 and 16:14-16 were added to bring Mark further into harmony with John. Therefore, just as John 21 appears to have been added to the Fourth Gospel to support a reconciliation between two sects of the Jesus movement, so the deletion of the original end of Mark may have been similarly motivated.

Furthermore, adding the text to John mitigated the negative portrait of Peter and made John also less obvious as a politically motivated document. Finally, John 21 causes the Fourth Gospel to harmonize with Mark's anticipation of an appearance in Galilee during which Peter is reconciled.

Implications of the Theory

The findings of this chapter have several implications for NT studies. The first is that they challenge the consensus opinion on the dating of these two gospels. If Mark was written around 70 CE, and John in the 90s, how could Mark have been a response to John? Furthermore, how could the deletion of the end of Mark soon after it was written in 70 CE be at all related to the appendix of John, which must have been added either late in the 90s or after the turn of the century? Clearly, the theory cannot be sustained if the conventional dates assigned to the gospels are correct.

There are only two possibilities here: either the theory is wrong or the dating of the gospels is wrong. Since the theory explains a great deal of textual evidence, the dating of the gospels must be called into question. A resolution may be found either by dating Mark later, or by dating John earlier, or both, such that Mark was written after John.

However, to move Mark much later into the first century begins to pose difficulties with the dating of Matthew and Luke, which are widely presumed to have been based on Mark as a source document. Redating Mark later would move the balance of the synoptic tradition into the first part of the second century. Though there is no reason why this is inconceivable, neither is there any independent data suggesting that a dating of Mark later in the century would be warranted.

Conversely, the placement of John in the 90s CE has been subject to periodic challenge in the twentieth century. We have already noted that the Fourth Gospel is missing many traditions which we might expect to find in a late first century document. Thus there are grounds to suspect that John may not be a late work. Further, since conventional theories on John have largely failed to recognize the formidable political struggle which motivated its composition, it is possible that the dating of the gospel has been misconstrued as well.

The second implication is that the Johannine community did not exist in isolation from that of Mark. Rather, the two communities were intimately aware of each other, and apparently considered one another a threat to the establishment of true doctrine. Indeed, it may be inappropriate to think of these as two distinct communities, but rather one in which there was substantial factional conflict.

A third implication is that the entire Gospel of Mark may have been composed as a rebuttal of John. Recall that many scholars argue John must have been aware of Mark due to the many striking literary connections which seem difficult to explain otherwise. On the other hand, many others believe John could not have known Mark due to the absence of several of the grandest Markan traditions. Perhaps scholars on both sides of the argument are right; perhaps there is indeed a direct literary dependence between John and Mark, and John was not aware of Mark. The discovery that Mark was the later of the two, and that it was written to correct John, would confirm that the observations made by scholars on both sides of the debate are correct.

❖   *4*   ❖

The Priority of John?

To suggest that John may have been the first of the four gospels to be written is to risk annoying many NT scholars. In the academic community, this is considered to be a field well plowed and not worthy of further attention. Yet the priority of John is a theory which will not die; it is a phoenix which continues to rise from its own ashes.

In 1985 a book entitled *The Priority of John* by Bishop John A. T. Robinson was published posthumously. This was the last great attempt to argue for a reconsideration of the Gospel of John in terms of its dating and historicity. Robinson believed the gospel was more appropriately dated to the decade of the 50s rather than the 90s as most contemporary scholars would hold. Such a dating would substantially increase its perceived historical value. A. N. Wilson, in his book *Jesus, A Life*, writes:

> I can vividly remember when John Robinson's book, *The Priority of John*, was first aired, as some posthumous letters (the 1984 Bampton Lectures), read aloud by another New Testament scholar, Charles Moule, to the congregation of St. Mary's Church in Oxford. The New Testament scholars were all shaking their heads and thinking that poor Bishop Robinson had gone off the rails before he died. No longer the firebrand who had made himself famous in the 1960s by writing a short book called *Honest to God*, which seemed to call into question Christian orthodoxy, he had devoted what turned out to be the last years of his life to establishing cranky theories about the Fourth Gospel.
>
> I believe that the scholars missed the point when they shook their heads. Robinson wrote his book, I am convinced, partly as a donnish tease. He intended to give us pause. He asked the theologians to suspend their prejudices and to look afresh at the New Testament.[1]

---

[1] Wilson, A. N., *Jesus, A Life*, W. W. Norton, 1992, p. 58-9

Wilson's comment that Robinson's book might be considered a "donnish tease" may be the most sympathetic review the book ever received. J. Louis Martyn's assessment of Robinson's earlier work *Redating the New Testament* captures the essential sentiment of most scholars toward Robinson's theories on John: "I can say only that Robinson's arguments seem to me to be designed to make water run uphill."[2] Thus *The Priority of John* has largely been ignored by NT scholars. Though a more compelling argument for this thesis will be proposed here, there is no disagreement that the significant portion of Robinson's work has been rightly passed over. Oddly enough, though it contains many interesting observations, it does not offer a sustained argument for the priority of John.

Robinson approached the problem along three lines. First, he argued that the reasons for the conventional dating of John in the 90s do not hold water. Second, he demonstrated that there is a greater ideological compatibility between John and the synoptic gospels than is generally conceded. Third, he demonstrated that there are numerous instances where John seemed to contain elements of historical data which predate the synoptic traditions.

Most scholars would say that, while all of these things may be true, they do not add up to a demonstration of the priority of John. Rather, they simply indicate that the gospel *may* have been composed earlier than has been presumed, that it may not have developed in as much isolation as has been presumed, and that the author relied on certain traditions which have an equal or better claim to historical accuracy than counterparts found in the synoptic gospels. Further, they would be correct in pointing out that none of this gives us any reason to redate the gospel.

Unfortunately, *The Priority of John* may have done more harm to the thesis than good. It appears to be an exhaustive study; hence it leaves the impression that it has rendered the best possible case in support of its controversial thesis. Yet this it has not done; the most formidable arguments in favor of the priority of John do not appear between its covers.

---

2 Martyn, J. Louis, *History and Theology in the Fourth Gospel*, Second Edition, Abingdon Press, 1979, p. 57 n.

This chapter will introduce the evidence scholars rely upon to date the gospel in the 90s. It will be shown that, in spite of the general consensus of opinion, there is no firm evidence to support this conclusion. For, as we will see, each of the arguments advanced for the late dating of John are ultimately inconclusive.

Arguments for the Late Dating of John

What is the evidence from which scholars have inferred that the Gospel of John is a product of the 90s? There are five independent arguments which support the theory that John is a late work. In brief they are as follows:

1. It is believed that professing Christians were excommunicated from the synagogues by the institution of a Benediction Against Heretics around 85-90 CE. It is argued that awareness of this excommunication is reflected in John, thereby placing its date subsequent to the enforcement of the benediction.

2. It is argued that John contains a view of Jesus which is advanced beyond that found in the synoptic gospels. Hence, it is presumed that John must be a later composition.

3. It is believed that an awareness of the destruction of the temple in 70 CE is reflected in John 2:19. Hence, this indicator would place the composition after this date.

4. Many argue that the author of John was aware of Mark. This would place the date of John after Mark, or after about 70 CE.

5. Some have suggested that John reflects thought forms consistent with proto-gnostic influence; it has been argued that this influence would not have developed before the end of the first century.

These arguments in combination are presumed to constitute good evidence for dating John near the end of the first century. Yet each of these observations is based on a set of facts which are subject to more than one interpretation. We will consider each of these issues in detail, and find that they ultimately do not contribute any meaningful information regarding the date of John.

1. *The Benediction Against Heretics.* The Gospel of John reflects a hostile relationship between Jesus' followers and the synagogues. This hostility is unique among the four gospels. Three times in the text of John the Greek word *aposynagogos*, translated in the RSV *put out of the synagogue*, is used in reference to the penalty befalling those who proclaim Jesus.[3] In addition, the term "Jews" is used with a pejorative tone in a number of passages.[4] Jesus attacks the Jews for their unfaithfulness, and some-times he even speaks as if he were not a Jew himself.[5]

Thus, it is generally agreed that the Fourth Gospel must have been composed in a situation where the Johannine community's relations with the Jewish community were hostile. What would have caused this hostility to exist, and in particular, what would have caused those professing Jesus as Messiah to be put out of the synagogue?

J. Louis Martyn has advanced the theory that the term *aposynagogue*, literally *away from the synagogue*, reflects a formal excommunication of believers resulting from the Jewish enactment of an official Benediction Against Heretics (the *birkat ha-minim*).[6] This Benediction, which amounted to a curse against heretics, was to be recited as part of formal synagogue liturgy. It is commonly thought to have been instituted sometime between 85 and 90 CE.

---

[3] John 9:22; 12:42; 16:2

[4] John 9:18; 10:31; 18:12, 36-38; 19:12

[5] "In *your* law it is written . . ." (John 8:17) See also John 7:19 and 10:34.

[6] A translation of the Benediction is as follows:
"For the apostates let there be no hope
And let the arrogant government be speedily uprooted in our days.
Let the Nazarenes [Christians] and the Minim [heretics] be destroyed in a moment
And let them be blotted out of the Book of Life and not be inscribed
    together with the righteous.
Blessed art thou, O Lord, who humblest the proud."

Martyn's theory has gained wide acceptance among contemporary scholars, and today it is the strongest single argument for dating John in the 90s. If Martyn is correct in identifying an awareness of the Benediction Against Heretics in the gospel, there is little chance that it could have been composed prior to 90 CE. Therefore an examination of his argument is an important element of this study.

Martyn infers that the Benediction Against Heretics had been instituted prior to the composition of John from one line in the gospel:

> . . . for the Jews had already agreed that if anyone should confess him to be Christ, he was to be put out of the synagogue. (John 9:22)

In this sentence Martyn sees four key points. First, a *formal decision* has been made. Second, it has been made by *an authoritative body within Judaism*. Third, it relates specifically to Jews who profess Jesus as the Christ. Fourth, the penalty is excommunication. Martyn suggests that since the excommunication of Christians appears to have been a formal decision, it must relate to some institutionalized move against Christians. Since the only official action we know of resembling a formal decision is the Benediction Against Heretics, it is most probably the Benediction which is reflected in 9:22.[7]

However, Martyn's analysis of 9:22 is subject to question. The phrase *the Jews had already agreed* does not expressly connote a formal institutionalized policy established in all rabbinic synagogues. It only indicates that an agreement had been made by authorities in control of the synagogue(s) from which the Johannine believers had been excluded. How formal the action was, and how widespread it was, cannot be determined from the references in the gospel.

In reading this passage we must bear in mind that it is written by a Johannine believer who has interpreted the conflict from his perspective. He has said a mere confession of Christ would be cause for expulsion from the synagogue. However, what may have been a dutiful confession of faith to him may have been aggressive and offensive proselytizing to the Jews. John contains some of the most

---

[7] Martyn's entire argument can be found in his work *History and Theology in the Fourth Gospel*, pp. 37-62

caustic anti-Semitic rhetoric in the NT. If Johannine believers were disrupting synagogue worship by standing and proclaiming that the leaders were liars and children of the devil (John 8:44), that they were no longer true children of Abraham (John 8:39), that those who did not believe in Jesus were condemned (John 3:18), and the wrath of God would rest upon them (John 3:36), the Jews of these congregations may understandably have decided to bar them from synagogue worship. Such an action could have been localized to the synagogue(s) from which the Johannine believers were excluded, and the reference in 9:22 would remain entirely coherent. Furthermore, synagogue authorities may have distinguished between followers of Jesus who embraced the radical Johannine dogma and those who did not, and elected to bar only those from the Johannine sect. This could account for the evidence in John that numerous followers of Jesus had not yet separated from the synagogue.

Therefore, there is no way to determine from the text whether this agreement of the Jews was a formal excommunication of all Christians from all rabbinic synagogues, or whether it was a dispute limited to Johannine experience and perhaps brought on by Johannine invective. Thus Martyn's conclusion that 9:22 most likely refers to a formal policy established for all synagogues is without foundation.

The argument is confused all the more by Martyn's translation of the key word *aposynagogos* as *an excommunication from the synagogue*. The word *excommunication* explicitly connotes a formal institutionalized legal banishment. Yet it is not clear that *aposynagogos* is meant to carry such a connotation. The word *aposynagogos* is known only by its usage in the Gospel of John. It does not appear anywhere else in the NT, nor does it appear in any other Greek literature. Its meaning can only be inferred from its literal translation *away from the synagogue*, and from the context of its use in John. Since its context does not necessarily imply that the believers have been put out by force of an institutional decree, then to define them as *excommunicates* is not warranted. They are simply those who have been *put out of the synagogue*, just as the RSV renders it.

Thus, Martyn's argument is built upon premises which cannot be proven or even demonstrated as probable. He assumes the phrase *the Jews had already agreed* refers to a formal institutionalized decision; yet the nature and scope of this agreement cannot be determined from the text. He defines *aposynagogos* as referring to excommunication, though there is no reason to apply to it such a restrictive translation. Having thus predefined 9:22 as a reference to an institutional action, he then points to the Benediction Against Heretics as the most probable explanation for it. However, the conclusion follows only if the premises are correct, and in this case, there is no reason to suppose that they are. Thus no firm connection between the Benediction and 9:22 has been established, and the hypothetical link between the two cannot be used to date the Gospel of John in the 90s.

Actually, the opposite is true: one must demonstrate independently that John was composed in the 90s in order to establish the mere *possibility* that 9:22 refers to the Benediction. Therefore, the evidence is only able to demonstrate that *if* John was written after the Benediction Against Heretics was instituted, then the Benediction *may* have been the cause of believers being put out of the synagogue.

Unfortunately, the focus on whether the Benediction Against Heretics is referred to in 9:22 has served to cloud a more substantial issue regarding John's use of the term *aposynagogos*. As noted above the term occurs three times in John. We have already seen that the betrayal theme is cast in sets of three. Peter denies Jesus three times; there are three bracketed sequences foreshadowing the triple denial; there are three references to Judas' father Simon. The fact that *aposynagogos* occurs three times is a signal to examine the context of its use. Is this unique word related in any way to the betrayal theme?

The first use of *aposynagogos* is the one we have just seen in John 9. This chapter presents the healing of the man born blind, and the entire chapter is dedicated to this one story. This is not simply a healing story designed to show Jesus' miraculous power. If it was, the episode would have ended at 9:12. The balance of the chapter is a commentary on the duty to proclaim Jesus once one has been healed, regardless of the consequences. John 9 is structured in seven distinct segments:

9:1-5	Prologue -- "I am the light of the world"
9:6-7	Jesus Heals the Blind Man
9:8-12	Blind Man's discussion with neighbors
9:13-17	Pharisees interview the Blind Man
9:18-23	Pharisees interview his parents
9:24-34	Blind Man teaches the Pharisees and is cast out
9:35-41	Epilogue-- "For judgment I came into the world"

The centerpiece of the text is the reflection on the penalty for doing so--to be put out of the synagogue. Between the first and second interviews of the blind man by the Pharisees is the key sentence of 9:22, and bracketed on either side of it a note on the responsibility of the blind man to speak for himself:

A. "Ask him, he is of age, he will speak for himself." (9:21b)

B. *If anyone should confess him to be Christ,*
he was to be put out of the synagogue (9:22b)

C. His parents said, "He is of age, ask him." (9:23b)

Having drawn attention to the duty and ability of the healed man to speak for himself, the text shows that the healed man boldly proceeds to lecture the Pharisees on their inability to recognize the hand of God. For his trouble he is then cast out of the synagogue (9:24-34). After he is cast out, Jesus finds him and assures him that he has acted correctly (9:35-39).

The entire episode is a reflection on the necessity of those who have been healed by Jesus to confront the leaders of the synagogue, to proclaim Jesus, and to suffer the consequence of being cast out. From this story we may infer that there are many Christian believers in the synagogues who have not yet separated from them. The author has addressed this story of the proclamation of the blind man to them in order to encourage them to speak out against the synagogue authorities. If they have been spiritually healed by Jesus, if they are of age, if they are able to stand and speak for themselves, they must do so as the blind man did, though it means they will be cast out. Once they have so spoken and are cast out, Jesus will find them and assure them that they have done the right thing.

The first use of the word *aposynagogos* appears in the context of a story designed to encourage believers to speak out against the authorities and separate themselves from the synagogue. The second time the word appears, it is in the same context. In John 12 we find the same sequence of themes which appear in John 9. Jesus is the light, and those that believe in the light may become sons of light (12:35-36). The world has been blinded (12:37-40). Then comes the reference to those believers who still maintain fellowship in the synagogue:

> Nevertheless many even of the authorities believed in him, but for fear of the Pharisees they did not confess it, lest they should be put out of the synagogue: for they loved the praise of men more than the praise of God. (John 12:42-43)

Here it is clear that the author is speaking of believers in the synagogue who do not confess their belief, at least in a form consistent with Johannine doctrine. Yet we may assume they have confessed it in some manner, or they would not have been known by the author. Thus we can detect in the text of John a group of believers who have not been excluded from the synagogue. The gospel is addressed in part to these believers with the objective of persuading them to separate from the synagogue.

The third occurrence of *aposynagogos* is again within the same context (16:2). For the author of John, true believers must be separated from the synagogue. Though the gospel indicates this is due to a decision on the part of the Jews, we may infer from Johannine rhetoric that they choose to separate themselves as well. The exclusion from the synagogue is to be worn like a badge of honor for proclaiming the true radical doctrine of the Johannine community. Part of the price of being a believer, according to John, is to be hated by the world:

> I have said all this to keep you from falling away. They will put you out of the synagogues; indeed, the hour is coming when whoever kills you will think he is offering service to God. (John 16:1-2)

> If the world hates you, know that it has hated me before it hated you. If you were of the world, the world would love its own; but because you are not of the world, but I chose you out of the world, therefore the world hates you. Remember the word I have said to you, 'A servant is not greater than his master.' If they persecuted me, they will persecute you; if they kept my word they will keep yours also. (John 15:18-20)

Thus the arguments in John are designed to convince believers in the synagogues that they must separate from them in order to join the true fellowship. A critical inference may be drawn from this repeated theme in John: *the presence of a large group of believers in the synagogues is incompatible with the notion that an institutional excommunication of Christians had been put in force.* If it had, one might imagine a few secretive believers on the fence may have still attempted to maintain ties with their Judaic traditions, but surely these few would not have warranted the attention directed toward them in the gospel. To the contrary, the evidence in John points to a visible and rather large group of believers with whom John is in doctrinal conflict over the issue of separation from the synagogue. It is unlikely that such a group could have continued to worship in the synagogues after the institution of a ban which formally condemned them. It is also unlikely that they would have wanted to.

Furthermore, if the Benediction Against Heretics had already been established as a formal liturgical prayer that Christians might be "destroyed in a moment and blotted out of the Book of Life," it is almost inconceivable that the author of John would not have referred to it explicitly in support of his argument. Given all the anti-Semitic language in John, surely this Benediction, had it been in force, would have created fodder for further anti-Semitic oration.

For these reasons, it appears that the Gospel of John was composed at a time prior to the institution of a formal ban of Christians from the synagogues, in a situation where there was a visible group of believers still trying to maintain ties with them. For the author of John, being put out of the synagogue is not a tragic formal action of the Jewish authorities; rather it is a doctrinal necessity. Yet there are many believers who remain in the synagogue fellowship, refusing to embrace Johannine doctrine. It is, in part, for these that the Gospel of John appears to have been composed.

In Chapter Two, we found that the Fourth Gospel had as one of its objectives the calling of Peter's followers into the Johannine fold. Here we find that John is aware of believers who have not separated from the synagogues; the gospel calls them to renounce their ties to the synagogues. Thus an obvious question is raised: Was separating from the synagogue one of the doctrinal conflicts between the Johannine and Petrine communities? Does the Fourth Gospel's insistence on being put out of the synagogue have its roots in a dispute with Peter rather than in a dispute with the Jews? Are the three reflections on the believers who have not been "put out of the synagogue" due to their failure to confess Jesus related to Peter's triple failure to confess Jesus? In essence, did the author of John think Peter and his followers were betrayers of the Jesus movement because they refused to renounce synagogue traditions?

There is evidence to suggest this may have been the case. Paul identifies Peter as the apostle to the Jews just as he was the apostle to the gentiles (Gal 2:7). Further he accuses Peter of trying to compel gentile converts to live like Jews by submitting to circumcision (Gal. 2:11-14). From such a dispute we may infer Peter's belief that gentiles, and indeed all believers, were still subject to Judaic traditions. Further, the Gospel of Matthew, which is the strongest advocate of Peter among the four gospels, also contains the most developed argument that the Jesus movement is a fulfillment of Judaism rather than a replacement of it. To the extent that Peter's teachings may be reflected in Matthew, it would be consistent with the notion that Peter would have conducted his ministry within the synagogues and with a greater respect for Judaic tradition than is apparent in the Gospel of John. We will return again to the question of conflict between the Johannine community and Peter later in this chapter.

We may summarize the response to Martyn's theory as follows:

1. The phrase *the Jews had agreed* does not necessarily imply a formal decision on the part of rabbinic leaders.

2. From this phrase nothing can be assumed about how widespread or institutionalized this agreement may have been.

3. The word *aposynagogos* does not necessarily imply excommunication in an institutional or legal sense.

4. Johannine doctrine, if proclaimed in the synagogue, could have led to a local expulsion of Johannine believers. Such an action could have left other Christians who did not subscribe to Johannine dogma welcome.

5. The gospel presupposes a large group of believers who have not yet separated from the synagogues with whom the Johannine community was in doctrinal conflict.

6. A large group of believers still involved in synagogue worship indicates a situation prior to the enforcement of the Benediction.

Therefore, there is no substantive evidence in favor of the proposal that John 9:22 reflects the Benediction Against Heretics, and nothing conclusive regarding the date of the Fourth Gospel may be derived from it.

2. *Depth of Theological Reflection.* The second popular argument in favor of a late date for John is the claim that it contains a view of the nature of Jesus which is advanced beyond that which is found in the synoptic gospels. John's characterization of Jesus as a pre-existent heavenly being who was with God before the world began, and who came down from heaven in the person of Jesus, is unique among the four gospels. In the synoptic gospels, there is no hint of Jesus as a preexistent divine being.

Furthermore, in the Fourth Gospel, "Jesus *is* the gospel, and the gospel is Jesus," as C.K. Barrett has put it.[8] The entire focus of John is

---

[8] Barrett, Ibid. p. 70

on the person of Jesus; it is the *who*ness of Jesus that is the critical issue. Conversely, in the synoptics we find that Jesus has come to introduce a new kingdom of God on earth. Jesus comes to reveal the kingdom of God and a new covenant between God and his people. This vision of Jesus' purpose is almost absent from John. The word *kingdom* itself appears only twice in John as compared to twenty times in Mark, forty-six times in Luke, and fifty-five times in Matthew.

Scholars often view the shift of focus from the kingdom of God to the person of Jesus as a profound theological development which must have taken some time to materialize. During this time the idea that Jesus was a preexistent being allegedly evolved as well; based on this it is assumed that the Gospel of John must have appeared later in the first century.

However, there is a fundamental assumption implied by this argument which does not hold. It assumes that the comparison of John's christology[9] with that of the synoptic gospels is the primary relevant comparison to be made between the two traditions for the purpose of dating them. Such is not the case. For instance, we may easily propose that the gospels' views of the apocalyptic end of the world are just as relevant. We could argue that since the synoptics have more developed visions of the end of the world than those found in John, the synoptic tradition might therefore be later than John. One might also propose that it is the moral traditions which are the most relevant. Here one could argue that the synoptics contain a higher moral vision than that found in John; hence, they must be writings from a later period in the movement's evolution.

The point is that restricting the comparison of John and the synoptics to any one particular subject such as christology is not justified. If all (or most) of the teachings on a variety of issues in John

---

[9] Christology is the study of the claims regarding the nature of Jesus as documented in the NT writings. Since each writing or group of writings has a different perspective on the nature of Jesus, each may be said to have a different Christology. Thus NT scholars speak of Pauline Christology, Johannine Christology, etc. Furthermore, Christologies are said to be high or low based on the degree to which Jesus is identified as divine. So the Johannine Christology is considered high because the Fourth Gospel proclaims Jesus to have been a preexistent eternal heavenly being. Conversely, Markan Christology may be considered low since Mark emphasizes his human nature and makes no attempt to depict Jesus as preexistent or eternal.

appeared to be more evolved than their counterparts in the synoptics, then there would be a logical basis for concluding John was a later gospel. However, since there are many synoptic traditions which appear to have greater evolved substance than their Johannine counterparts, the evidence is conflicting, and no definitive position can be taken. Therefore, to argue the lateness of John based on its high christology while ignoring the fact that it appears undeveloped in other areas of thought does not take full account of the evidence at hand.

There is a related assumption in this argument which also does not hold--that a comparison of John with the synoptic gospels is the most relevant test. This is not necessarily true either. A comparison of the ideas in John with the teachings of Paul also has a bearing on the inquiry. Thus if we find a teaching in John which appears more advanced than its counterpart in the synoptic gospels, we might assume it was a later tradition. However, if this same teaching is found in the authentic letters of Paul, which were all written in the 50s and early 60s (prior to the synoptic gospels), then the comparison with the synoptics becomes moot. For if the Pauline writings establish that an apparently "evolved" idea in John already existed before the synoptics were written, its absence from the synoptics becomes irrelevant as a factor in dating John.

Therefore, the question is straightforward: are researchers correct in assuming John is later than the synoptics because of its higher christology? We may start by agreeing that the observations them-selves are correct. John is indeed fully focused on the person of Jesus; a demonstration of his heavenly nature is a primary objective of the gospel. It is also clear that the portrait of Jesus in John is different than the Jesus we meet in the synoptic gospels. Finally, the focus on the *person of Jesus* in John versus the *kingdom of God* in the synoptics is apparent.

However, to conclude from this that John's perspective is the more profound and thus the later tradition does not follow; as it turns out this line of reasoning is purely speculative. There is no way to objectively determine whether the historical development of John's ideas about Jesus occurred prior to, concurrently with, or after the teachings of the synoptic gospels. Indeed, there is no reason why

John's unique perspective of Jesus could not have appeared very early in the century. In fact, the teachings of Paul show that sophisticated ideas about the nature of Jesus were in circulation by the middle of the century. The letters of Romans and 1 Corinthians, which date to the mid-50s, contain more developed perspectives on Jesus and the meaning of his death and resurrection than do the synoptic gospels.

Jesus as Preexistent Man from Heaven

One of the most notable themes which distinguishes John from Matthew, Mark, and Luke, is the portrayal of Jesus as a preexistent eternal being who was with the Father before the beginning of the world. However, this idea can also be found in Paul's letters. Jesus as the "man from heaven" is found in both John and 1 Corinthians:

John:

John the Baptist speaking of Jesus: "After me comes a man who ranks before me, for he was before me" (1:30) "He must increase, but I must decrease. He who comes from above is above all; he who is of the earth belongs to the earth, and of the earth he speaks; he who comes from heaven is above all." (3:30-31)

[*Jesus said,*] "For I have come down from heaven, not to do my own will, but the will of him who sent me." (John 6:38)

Paul:

Thus it is written, "The first man Adam became a living being"; the last Adam became a life-giving spirit. But it is not the spiritual which is first but the physical, and then the spiritual. The first man was from the earth, a man of dust; the second man is from heaven. As was the man of dust, so are those who are of the dust; and as is the man of heaven, so are those who are of heaven. Just as we have borne the image of the man of dust, we shall also bear the image of the man of heaven.(1Cor15:45-49)

It is not suggested that the teaching of John and Paul on the idea of the man from heaven is identical. Paul's "Second Adam" thesis is distinct from John in certain respects. However, what must be noted is the similarity of their ideas that Jesus was a man from heaven, and one who had entered creation from above. In this particular characterization of Jesus, there is no reason to suppose John's idea would have taken any more time to develop than Paul's. Indeed they could have existed contemporaneously in two different sects of the movement.

Related to the idea that Jesus is a man from heaven is the notion of his preexistence. In John, the idea that Jesus existed before the world began is explicit. In Paul, though this teaching is not as pronounced, it is evident in passages which imply that Jesus must have been in existence before his appearance on earth:

John:

> Father, glorify thou me in thine own presence with the glory which I had with thee before the world was made (17:5)

Paul:

> . . . yet for us there is one God, the Father, from whom are all things and for whom we exist, and one Lord, Jesus Christ, through whom are all things and through whom we exist. (1Cor 8:6)

> For God has done what the law, weakened by the flesh, could not do: sending his own Son in the likeness of sinful flesh and for sin, he condemned sin in the flesh . . . (Rom 8:3)

Paul's idea that God *sent his own Son* implies that he must have been in heaven prior to being sent to earth. Further, the teaching that Jesus is the one "through whom all things are" is very close to the explicit reference in the prologue of John, "He was in the beginning with God; all things were made through him, and without him was not anything made that was made" (John 1:2-3).

The Hierarchy: God, Jesus, and Creation

Another teaching which is in harmony between John and Paul is the vision of a hierarchical standing: God is the Father, and the greatest divine being; Jesus is a lesser being and clearly subordinate to the Father; finally, all creation is subordinate to Jesus:

John:

The Father loves the Son, and has given all things into his hand (3:35)

The Father judges no one, but has given all judgment to the Son, that all may honor the Son, even as they honor the Father (5:22-23)

For as the Father has life in himself, so he has granted the Son also to have life in himself, and has given him authority to execute judgment, because he is the Son of man (5:26-27)

[Jesus said,] "All that the Father has is mine" (16:15)

[Jesus said,] "The Father is greater than I." (14:28)

Paul:

"For God has put all things in subjection under [Jesus'] feet." But when it says, "All things are put in subjection under him," it is plain that he is excepted who put all things under him. When all things are subjected to him, then the Son himself will also be subjected to him who put all things under him, that God may be everything to every one. (1 Cor 15:25-28)

In these passages we can discern a number of common elements. First, God is greater than the Son. Second, all creation has been put under Jesus' dominion. Third, it is through a specific grant of the Father that Jesus is Lord over all creation. Therefore a remarkable correlation exists between several key teachings regarding the nature of Jesus in John and Paul. Both contain the vision of Jesus as a man from heaven. John explicitly indicates, and Paul strongly implies, that Jesus was a preexistent divine being prior to his appearance in human form. Both John and Paul teach that Jesus is subordinate to the Father, but has had all creation placed under him by a grant of the Father.

The Doctrine of the Holy Spirit

A third important concept which John and Paul share is that of the indwelling Holy Spirit who comes to the believer. The first thing to note is that both authors use interchangeable terminology for the

143

Holy Spirit, as if the Holy Spirit were an amorphous concept. John uses the terms Counselor, Spirit of truth, and the Holy Spirit, as if he were attempting to define this entity by giving it several names. Further, he is confused about whether it is Jesus or the Father who will send the Holy Spirit, and whether it is Jesus or the Holy Spirit, or both, who will dwell in the believer:

> And I will pray the Father, and he will give you another Counselor, to be with you for ever, even the Spirit of truth, whom the world cannot receive, because it neither sees him nor knows him; *you know him, for he dwells with you, and I will be in you.* I will not leave you desolate; I will come to you. (John 14:16-18)

> But the Counselor, the Holy Spirit, *whom the Father will send in my name,* he will teach you all things, and bring to your remembrance all that I have said to you. (John 14:26)

> But when the Counselor comes, *whom I shall send you from the Father,* even the Spirit of truth, who proceeds from the Father, he will bear witness to me. (John 15:26)

> It is to your advantage that I go away, for if I do not go away, the Counselor will not come to you; but if I go, *I will send him to you.* (John 16:7)

Similarly, Paul frequently uses terms such as the *Spirit, Christ,* the *Spirit of God,* and the *Spirit of Christ* as if they were virtually synonymous. Also the same confusion of terms exists in the attempt to describe the indwelling of the believer:

> But you are not in the flesh, you are in the Spirit, if in fact the Spirit of God dwells in you. Any one who does not have the Spirit of Christ does not belong to him. But if Christ is in you, although your bodies are dead because of sin, your spirits are alive because of righteousness. If the Spirit of him who raised Jesus from the dead dwells in you, he who raised Christ Jesus from the dead will give life to your mortal bodies also through his Spirit which dwells in you. (Rom 8:9-11)

Three distinct elements common to John and Paul may be noted. The first is the idea that the Spirit will *dwell in the believer*.[10] Though John and Paul both explicitly state that the Holy Spirit is an indwelling being, the synoptic gospels do not. In Matthew, Mark, and Luke, we find the idea that the Holy Spirit may come upon a person, may speak through a person, and may lead a person, but the notion that the Spirit *dwells continuously* with the believer is not present. Some may suggest that it is implied, although this is not the point at issue. The critical element here is that John and Paul expressly describe the indwelling of the Spirit whereas the synoptics do not. In this regard John and Paul are in greater harmony.

Second, the Johannine and Pauline teachings on the indwelling of the Holy Spirit are so similar that they both use interchangeable references to the indwelling entity. Both say that a Spirit of God or a Spirit from the Father will dwell in the believer. Yet both also say that Christ himself will dwell in the believer. There is no explicit or implied reference in the synoptic gospels that Christ himself will dwell in the believer.

Third, both John and Paul go to significant length to describe the nature and role of the "counselor" or "Holy Spirit" as if their readers are not familiar with the teaching. John says the Spirit is one who will come so the believer is not left desolate (14:18); the Spirit will teach (14:26) and guide the believer in all the truth (16:13). The author of John writes as if the indwelling of the Spirit is a new concept for his readers, for the function of the Spirit must be spelled out.

Paul also explains the role of the Holy Spirit to his readers:

> Likewise the Spirit helps us in our weakness; for we do not know how to pray as we ought, but the Spirit himself intercedes for us with sighs too deep for words. And he who searches the hearts of men knows what is the mind of the Spirit, because the Spirit intercedes for the saints according to the will of God. (Rom 8:26-27)

---

10 John and Paul use two different Greek words which are both translated "to dwell" in the RSV. The word in John 14:17, *meno*, means "to remain." Paul in Romans 8:11 uses *oikeo*, "to use or have a house." The point here is that the concept of the Holy Spirit coming to remain with or make a home with the believer is synonymous.

> To each is given the manifestation of the Spirit for the common good. To one is given through the Spirit the utterance of wisdom, and to another the utterance of knowledge according to the same Spirit, to another faith by the same Spirit, to another gifts of healing by the one Spirit . . .   All these are inspired by one and the same Spirit, who apportions to each one individually as he wills. (1 Cor. 12:7-9, 11)

Both John and Paul are writing for audiences which seem in need of some explanation of the nature and function of the Holy Spirit. Furthermore, between John and Paul, it is Paul's detailed formulations which appear to be the more developed of the two. If we were to make a comparison of the Holy Spirit teachings of John and Paul, without any preconceived notion of their dates of origin, we would conclude that Paul's was the more evolved and therefore later work.

There are numerous other similarities between John and Paul which may be noted briefly. Both focus their teachings on the *person of Jesus* as central to their message while neither shows much awareness of or interest in the parables and moral teachings of Jesus which are so prevalent in the synoptic gospels. Both writers teach that eternal life comes though a state of mind; John says he who *believes* in Jesus shall not perish but have eternal life (3:16); Paul says the believer is justified by *faith* and has peace with God through Jesus Christ "so that . . . grace might also reign through righteousness to eternal life." (Rom 5:21). Both contain the doctrine that God actively chooses who is to be saved and who is not (John 6:65; 17:6; Rom 8:28-30). Therefore a comparison of John and Paul shows that many of the ideas which are central to John are also dominant themes in the writings of Paul. There is one last doctrine which requires attention before we move to the next issue for dating John. It is the teaching that Jesus was actually God in human form.

Incarnation Theology in John

Some may suggest that John depicts Jesus as an incarnation of God, and that this idea is absent from the authentic letters of Paul. Does John not tell us Jesus was the human embodiment of God himself? After all, the gospel does say the "Word was God," and "the Word

146

became flesh and dwelt among us" (John 1:1,14). Is this not a concept which would have taken additional time to evolve?

It is true that several verses in John might imply that Jesus was God in human form. However, since the large majority of sayings in the gospel do not support such a concept, there is a serious question whether the author really meant for these infrequent references to be construed in this manner. The few verses in John which might be understood to say that Jesus was God in human form are usually subject to more than one interpretation. For example, when Jesus says, "I and the Father are one," (John 10:30), we might suppose Jesus was claiming to be God, or we might say Jesus was claiming to be of one harmonious spirit with the Father, in the sense that he is reflecting the will of the Father.

If we are to read verses such as this as a claim by Jesus that he is God in human form, we immediately run into an array of difficult verses in John which do not support the interpretation. For example:

> So Jesus said, "When you have lifted up the Son of man, then you will know that I am he, and that I do nothing on my own authority but speak thus as the Father taught me. He who sent me is with me; he has not left me alone, for I always do what is pleasing to him." (John 8:28-29)

In this saying of Jesus, we are not listening to the voice of God. Rather it is the voice of a man who believes he is sent from God, who wishes to do God's will, and who wishes to please God. Regarding this verse in particular, C.K. Barrett makes the point clear:

> It is simply intolerable that Jesus should be made to say, "I am God, the supreme God of the Old Testament, and being God, I do as I am told."[11]

Most of Jesus' sayings in John which touch upon his relation-ship with the Father are subject to the same observation, for he is most frequently shown as clearly distinct from and subservient to the Father:

> What I say, therefore, I say as the Father has bidden me. (12:50)

> The Father is greater than I. (14:28)

---

[11] Barrett, C.K., *Essays in John*, Westminster Press, 1982, p. 12f; 69-71

I have kept my Father's commandments, and abide in his love. (15:10)

I am not alone, for the Father is with me (16:32b)

The idea that Jesus was God in human form is contradicted by most of the teachings in John. John the Baptist's testimony at the beginning of the gospel confirms that Jesus is a *man* from heaven, one who is greater than John the Baptist, and one who existed before him:

> The next day [John the Baptist] saw Jesus coming toward him, and said, "Behold, the Lamb of God, who takes away the sin of the world! This is he of whom I said, 'After me comes a man who ranks before me, for he was before me.'" (John 1:29-30)

It is within this context of the gospel's predominant claim of Jesus as the preexistent *man* from heaven that the two passages often cited as equating Jesus with God must be interpreted. The first, which is found in the opening prologue, has already been noted:

> In the beginning was the Word, and the Word was with God, and the Word was God. (1:1)

> And the Word became flesh and dwelt among us, full of grace and truth; we have beheld his glory, glory as of the only Son from the Father. (1:14)

In this reference to Jesus as the Word, or self-expression of God, some have made the interpretation that God has himself become a man. However, this is not what the passage says. The *Word*, from the Greek *logos*, refers to the self-expression of God, or the speech of God.

Thus the gospel is telling us that in Jesus we find an incarnation of the *self-expression* of God; Jesus is a human manifestation of God's speech; he is in essence a reflection of the will of God. The will of God, or the self-expression of God, which manifests itself in human form is entirely different from *God himself* becoming flesh. To illustrate, we may think of an author writing a book. The book is the *word* of the author, and is clearly the self-expression of the author. However, no one would sensibly conclude from this that the author *was* the book.

When these verses are seen in this light, they are consistent with the balance of the gospel. Jesus says at one point, "the Son can do nothing of his own accord, but only what he sees the Father doing; for whatever he does, the Son does likewise." (John 5:19-20). Thus, the Word become flesh is to be understood as the incarnation of God's expression or God's will. Since this is the more coherent reading within the gospel's context, this passage cannot be cited as evidence that the author intended to teach that Jesus was God himself.

The other passage frequently cited to support the idea that Jesus was God is John 8:58, in which Jesus says, "Before Abraham was, I am." The "I AM" is the divine name as found in the Old Testament (Exodus 3:14). Has not Jesus appropriated the divine name for himself, thereby implying he is God?

If the rest of the gospel had supported this interpretation, one might read this into the text. However, since it does not, the more literal rendering is the more consistent: Jesus has made a claim only that he preexists Abraham, and by implication that he is preexistent and eternal. This reading squares with the Baptist's testimony above, in which he identifies Jesus as a man who came before him. So again within the context of the gospel, since the passage can be easily interpreted in a manner consistent with the theology of the gospel at large, it must be accorded this interpretation. Thus the Gospel of John does not teach that Jesus was God in human form. Neither do the authentic letters of Paul, or the synoptic gospels.[12]

---

[12] The closest reference in the NT to Jesus as the Deity himself is in Colossians: *for in [Christ] the whole fulness of deity dwells bodily* (Col 2:9).

Colossians is not considered by most scholars to be an authentic letter of Paul since it contains both a linguistic style and certain teachings which are foreign to the letters known to have been penned by Paul. However, the letter is in the NT, and its suspicious authorship is not a solid reason to discount it.

The more compelling reason to dismiss Col 2:9 as a reference to the Deity of Jesus is that such an interpretation is internally inconsistent with with other references in the letter itself. Col 1:15 says Jesus "is the image of the invisible God, the first-born of all creation," a sentiment which is compatible with Jesus as the self-expression of God, and as a preexistent heavenly being.

In Col 3:1, we are admonished to "seek the things that are above, where Christ is, seated at the right hand of God." In the spirit of C.K. Barrett, it is intolerable to assume the author believes that Jesus is God, and that God is seated at his own right hand. There is clearly a hierarchical ranking here as everywhere else in the NT; Jesus is a being subservient to the Father.

The idea that Jesus was God in human form is not a NT teaching. It is a Christian doctrine developed during the second, third, and fourth centuries. Over this period of time the church developed the doctrine of the Trinity, which teaches that God the Father, God the Son, and God the Holy Spirit were to be visualized as Three Persons of the Godhead. The word "trinity" does not appear anywhere in the NT. To be sure, there are isolated verses in several NT documents which, when taken out of context, can be interpreted to support the doctrine of the Trinity. However, each one of these verses becomes internally inconsistent with other teachings within the document in which it appears when such an interpretation is forced upon it.

Therefore, there is no coherent teaching in the Gospel of John that Jesus was an incarnation of God. John clearly states he was a preexistent heavenly being, that he was subordinate to the Father, and was sent by the Father to do what the Father had bidden him. Though one may believe that Jesus was an incarnation of God based on the teachings of the church, this doctrine cannot be supported by the Gospel of John unless the verses noted above are removed from their context and the author's intent is set aside.

In summary, a comparison of John and Paul shows that several key elements of Johannine "high christology," along with numerous other doctrinal concepts, have a striking similarity to ideas found in Paul's writings. Paul's letters are known to have been in circulation in the 50s, or several decades before the synoptic gospels were composed. So there is no logical ground for setting John and the synoptic gospels side by side and inferring from the comparison that John must have been a later work. Based on what had already developed in the preaching of Paul by the 50s, there is nothing in John that would have required several decades more to evolve. Thus, the argument that John shows "advanced theological reflection" as compared to the synoptic gospels provides no reliable guidance for dating John.

3. Allusion to the Destruction of the Temple. A third common argument for a late dating of John is based on Jesus' statement, "Destroy this temple and in three days I will raise it up" (John 2:19). It is presumed by many that this reference indicates the author's awareness of the destruction of the temple by the Romans in 70 CE. If so, this would place the composition of the gospel at least subsequent to that event.

There is no doubt it can be interpreted in this manner. However, in order to determine how strong the evidence is, we must look at the larger context of the passage. This is the first of three Passovers mentioned in the gospel; Jesus is in the temple, and the story unfolds as he commands the moneychangers to leave:

> "Take these things away; you shall not make my Father's house a house of trade." His disciples remembered that it was written, "Zeal for thy house will consume me." The Jews then said to him, "What sign have you to show us for doing this?" Jesus answered them, "Destroy this temple and in three days I will raise it up." The Jews then said, "It has taken forty-six years to build this temple, and will you raise it up in three days?" But he spoke of the temple of his body. (John 2:16-21)

When interpreting this passage we must bear in mind the history of the temple which would have been common knowledge among John's readers. The original temple, built by King Solomon in the 10th century BCE, was destroyed during the occupation of Jerusalem by the Babylonians which began in 587 BCE. The rebuilding effort began in 520 BCE, but the temple was not rebuilt to its prior grandeur. Then in 20 BCE, King Herod undertook a project to once again rebuild the temple, this time to restore it to its original splendor.

The spectacular new temple was largely finished by the time Jesus appeared on the scene, but work would continue on the grounds and exterior for several more decades. However, another foreign occupying force, the Romans, were in control and remained in control from the time of Jesus' ministry through the destruction of Jerusalem. The idea that the temple could again be destroyed by occupying hostile forces might reasonably have been a common concern at the time the gospel was composed.

However, we need not even suppose this to explain the passage. Note that the focus of the saying is on the fact that Jesus' body is the temple which is to be destroyed. The author may have simply designed a literary allusion to the original destruction of the temple, of which his audience would have been well informed. Indeed, if Jesus had in fact made a reference to the destruction of the temple, he would have been alluding to the temple's original destruction rather than the impending one forty years hence, and his audience would have interpreted it in that context.

Thus, the actual event of the destruction of the temple in 70 CE is not necessary to make sense of this passage. The thrust of the passage is that Jesus refers to his body as the temple; it is his body which is to be destroyed and which will be raised again. All we need to make the passage coherent is the author's belief that Jesus was raised in three days, that Jesus considered his body to be a temple, and a plausible reason for the audience to understand an allusion to the destruction of the new temple, which they clearly had from historical precedent. Since a rational context for the temple reference in John 2:19 existed in the decades prior to the actual destruction of the temple in 70 CE, it does not yield any substantive information about the date of the gospel.

4. *John's Reliance on the Synoptic Gospels.* A fourth argument sometimes offered for a late dating of John is that the author used one or more of the synoptic gospels as sources in creating his own work. For example, if it can be shown that the author of John used Mark as a source, then this would place the composition of John after the appearance of Mark, or around 70 CE. The literary affinities between John and Mark have caused a large minority of researchers to argue that the author of John must have used Mark as a source. Yet the absence of several strong Markan traditions from John cause others to assume that Mark could not have been known by John.

Of course, once we introduce the idea that John could have been composed earlier than Mark, then a third possibility presents itself: the literary interdependence between these two gospels exists because the author of Mark used John as a source, rather than the reverse.

This theory will be presented in Chapter Six, so we may forego the details here. It is sufficient to say that since the literary interdependence between John and Mark may be derived from either Mark's use of John or John's use of Mark, then such an interdependence provides no real clue to the date of John.

5. *Gnostic Influence.* There are several ideas in John which many have presumed were the result of gnostic ideological influence. Gnosticism was a heretical threat to the crystallizing orthodoxy of the movement. It focused on the notion that knowledge of the spiritual realm would lead to salvation. Gnostic ideology included the belief that the spiritual and material worlds were two opposing spheres of reality, and that the spirit must be separated from the material world. The spirit, through knowledge of the spiritual realm, could escape from material existence. This dualism is present in the text of John:

> That which is born of the flesh is flesh, and that which is born of the Spirit is spirit. (John 3:6)

> But the hour is coming, and now is, when the true worshipers will worship the Father in spirit and truth, for such the Father seeks to worship him. God is spirit, and those who worship him must worship him in spirit and truth. (John 4:23-24)

> If the world hates you, know that it has hated me before it hated you. If you were of the world, the world would love its own; but because you are not of the world, but I chose you out of the world, therefore the world hates you. (John 15:18-19)

One prominent element of gnostic thought was the dualism of light and darkness. Those who were saved were children of the light, or "sons of light." They were members of the kingdom of light. Those who were not were in darkness. The dualism of light and darkness is apparent in the Gospel of John:

> Jesus said to them, "The light is with you for a little longer. Walk while you have the light, lest the darkness overtake you; he who walks in the darkness does not know where he goes. While you have the light, believe in the light, that you may become sons of light." (John 12:35-36)

In these texts we find ideas in harmony with gnostic thought. However, gnosticism did not develop as a prominent ideological presence until the second century. It has been argued that, if what we see in John is the formative stage of gnostic thought, it must have been composed very late in the first century.

With the discovery of the Dead Sea Scrolls in 1945, it has become clear that the thought forms found in John which were identified as gnostic in origin were in circulation much earlier than had been presumed. The dualism of light and darkness is characteristic of the expression of the Qumran community which produced the Dead Sea Scrolls. The idea of "the holy spirit," which is almost absent from the Old Testament, is also common in the Scrolls. Pierre Benoit wrote:

> Since the discoveries at Qumran, we can see that it is no longer necessary to invoke Greek gnosticism as the original milieu of the Fourth Gospel, since now we have one, which is more ancient and closer, in Palestine itself. [13]

Hence, contemporary researchers no longer suggest that gnostic influence is a factor by which the Gospel of John can be reliably dated.

Summary of Evidence for the Late Dating of John

To recap the arguments in favor of dating John in the 90s, we have reviewed the following: (1) Though it is assumed that John 9:22 reflects the effect of the Benediction Against Heretics, no definitive link between the two has been established. (2) Though it is supposed that John's thinking on the nature of Jesus is advanced over that which is found in the synoptics, we find many of John's ideas already in circulation in the early writings of Paul. (3) The anticipation of the temple's destruction in 2:19 could have been written prior to the event. (4) The literary interdependence between John and Mark may be the result of Mark's use of John rather than John's use of Mark. (5) There is no longer any need to assume gnostic influence upon the author of John, since the ideas commonly identified as gnostic in origin have been found in the Dead Sea Scrolls, indicating they were in circulation much earlier than had been previously supposed.

In short, the evidence commonly offered for a late dating of John is sparse and inconclusive. There is no firm evidence that John was

---

[13] Benoit, Pierre, excerpt from *Paul and the Dead Sea Scrolls*, edited by J. Murphy O'Connor and James H. Charlesworth, Crossroad Publishing, 1990, p. 17

composed in the 90s. There has been a tendency to assume it is a late work based on its uniqueness as compared to the synoptics. This impression has been supported by tentative speculations regarding the temple reference in 2:19 and *aposynagogos* in 9:22. However, in the final analysis, A.N. Wilson summarized correctly:

> The Fourth Gospel stands apart from the first three in matters of style, and provenance and theology. Because it had a 'high' christology, a belief that Jesus was the pre-existent Logos, who had taken flesh and dwelt among us, concealing his true nature from all but those who saw him with the eyes of faith, it has been assumed that this was the last Gospel to be written, perhaps as late as 100 CE. But even this judgment is question-able, and the truth about the matter will probably never be known. There is no logical necessity which compels us to place a late date on the Fourth Gospel, though it is obviously different in character from the first three.[14]

So there is a widely held perception that the Gospel of John is a late work, but there is no proof of it. If there were no evidence to the contrary, a dating of John in the 90s might be as good a guess as any. However, if we are willing to place conventional ideas in temporary abeyance and look for clues which might tell another story, a fascinating new possibility emerges: John is the earliest of the Christian gospels, written during the formative years of the primitive Jesus movement. Furthermore, the clash between Peter and the Beloved Disciple which is reflected in John is an important key to the historical origins of Christianity.

---

[14] Wilson, Ibid., p. 48

5

The Original Gospel

Having determined that there is no firm evidence for the conventional dating of John in the 90s, we may now begin to look for clues which would suggest an earlier date. Our examination of John will be structured around three basic questions. First, what is missing from John that we might expect to find in a late first century gospel? Second, are the primary issues of concern to the author of John coherent as late first century issues? Finally, does John contain reports of Jesus' ministry which are more historically credible than synoptic versions of the same stories?

The answers to these questions will collectively point to the answer that John is a very primitive work. Of course no single clue will offer conclusive evidence for the theory; if it did the entire issue would not be in debate today. Rather, as each additional observation is made, the cumulative weight of evidence will ultimately tip the scale in favor of an early date for John. However, the final demonstration of the priority of John will not come from an examination of the text of John itself, but from the Gospel of Mark. After we have seen that John could have been the first gospel, we can turn to Mark for further evidence that it was written as an ideological response to John.

What is Missing from the Gospel of John?

Our first question considers those traditions and literary elements which are not in John, but which might be expected to appear in a late first century document. As has been noted previously, the amount of material absent from John is considerable. Here we will look at five categories of missing elements: (1) vocabulary, (2) parables, (3) mythical traditions, (4) moral vision, and (5) an awareness of the church as an institutionalized entity.

1. *Limited Technical Vocabulary.* The first hint that the Gospel of John was an early document is its limited vocabulary. There is quite a list of words which the Jesus movement adopted over the course of the first century to effectively communicate its new beliefs and doctrines. As the movement expanded and diversified, its language grew with it.

However, a startling number of words which quickly became integral to Christian expression never appear in the Gospel of John. Yet most of these words appear frequently in the synoptics and/or the letters of Paul, showing that they were in common use in various sects of the movement much earlier than John is alleged to have been composed. The following is a partial list of words which are absent from John, along with the Greek word from which they are translated:[1]

apostle *(apostolos)*	heal *(therapeuo)*
church *(ekklesia)*	hell *(geena, gehenna)*
faith *(pistis)*	parable *(parabole)*
fellowship *(koinonia)*	pray *(proseuchomai)*
gentile *(ethnos)*	repent *(metanoeo)*
gospel *(euaggelion)*	

What can we infer from the fact that John contains none of these words? Researchers have noted this phenomenon, and a common explanation is that the Johannine community evolved as a separate and isolated group which was out of touch with developments in the mainstream church. For example, it is apparent that Paul was

---

[1] In each case it is the Greek word which is missing from the text of John. In several instances, two or more different Greek words may be translated by the same English word. For example *therapeuo* and *iaomai* are both usually translated "heal" in the RSV. In this case, *therapeuo* appears 28 times in the Synoptic Gospels, yet is absent from John; *iaomai* appears 15 times in the Synoptics, and three times in John (4:47; 5:13; 12:40))

responsible for developing the technical use of the term "gospel," and that the term was already in use by the time his earliest surviving letter, 1st Thessalonians, was written (around 52 CE). Yet the term *gospel* does not appear in John. Helmut Koester writes:

> The absence of [the term gospel] in the Johannine writings is only one among other pieces of evidence which prove that the beginnings of the Johannine community lay outside the scope of the Pauline mission area.[2]

Following this logic we might then also infer that, since many of the words in the list above appear frequently in the synoptic texts, the Johannine community also must have lain outside the scope of influence of those that developed Matthew, Mark, and Luke.

This isolation theory, which is advanced to explain much of the uniqueness of John, is troublesome for several reasons. First, it is not easily explained how a community of believers which produced such a formidable gospel could have remained isolated from the development of the mainstream church for half a century, from the community's inception in the 30s or 40s until the gospel was presumably composed in the 90s. During this period of time the church spread throughout the Roman Empire and North Africa. So to allege that the Johannine community was out of touch to the degree required to create such a language barrier poses more questions than it answers.

Second, the gospel's anti-Petrine rhetoric implies an acute awareness of Peter and his teachings. The author writes with the intent of persuading the followers of Peter to leave him and join the Johannine community. He writes with a vehemence which implies Peter is a threat to his community and its leadership. Thus, to suggest that the Johannine community was isolated from other sects of the Jesus movement is inconsistent with the evidence in the gospel itself. No language barrier would have existed if the Petrine and Johannine communities were in competitive dialogue with one another.

Third, in spite of its presumed isolation, the Johannine community had access to a number of stories about the life of Jesus which also appear in the synoptic gospels, some with a host of details intact. In

---

[2] Koester, Helmut, *Ancient Christian Gospels*, Trinity Press International, 1990, p. 9

particular, as noted previously, the similarities between John and Mark in terms of storyline, sequence, and detail have convinced many scholars that John must have used Mark as a source document. This is also contrary to the notion of an isolated Johannine community.

An alternative explanation for the missing vocabulary could be that the Gospel of John was written very early in the life of the church, before the words in the list above evolved as part of the Jesus movement's self-expression. Thus, we might suspect that "apostle" is missing because John was written before this title was applied to the original twelve disciples; "church" is missing because John was written before this term was applied to the community of believers; "gospel" is missing because John was written before the word came to be equated with the message of the movement, etc.

2. *The Absence of Parables.* As noted above, the Greek word for parable, *parabole*, does not appear in John. In fact, the entire tradition that Jesus' taught in parables is missing from John.[3]

By the time Matthew, Mark, and Luke were written, the sects of the Jesus movement represented by these gospels had developed the idea that the primary teaching form of Jesus was the parable; the parables of Jesus were studied, memorized, passed on to others, and used for instruction in church gatherings. However, it was not just the parables themselves that constituted the parable tradition. A key element of the tradition was the *reason* Jesus taught in parables, a reason which is explained in this statement of Jesus to his disciples:

> To you has been given the secret of the kingdom of God, but for those outside everything is in parables; so that they may indeed see but not perceive, and may indeed hear but not understand; lest they should turn again, and be forgiven. (Mark 4:11-12)

---

[3] The *parable* is a simile, metaphor, or short story told in simple terms that symbolically embodies a larger meaning; generally the parables of Jesus in the synoptic gospels are intended to reveal some particular truth or wisdom related to the kingdom of God. The Parable of the Mustard Seed is a good example of the simile form (Mark 4:30-32). For examples of the short story form of parable, see the Parable of the Prodigal Son (Luke 15:11-32), the Parable of the Unjust Steward (Luke 16:1-9), and the Parable of the Laborers in the Vineyard (Matt. 20:1-16).

The author of Mark, after recounting a number of parables tells us:

> With many such parables [Jesus] spoke the word to them, as they were able to hear it; he did not speak to them without a parable, but privately to his own disciples he explained everything. (Mark 4:33-34).

So the parable was understood, at least in the synoptic tradition, as the method by which Jesus revealed the kingdom of God. Only those to whom it had been given to understand the parables could partake of Jesus' message. How is it, then, that John could have written a gospel at the end of the first century which virtually ignored the entire parable tradition of the Jesus movement? It is difficult to imagine why he would have done so; it also seems odd that the movement would have accepted such a gospel as authoritative.

It is on this issue that John A. T. Robinson missed an opportunity to press for the priority of John. He argued that the parable tradition is not missing from John, and listed numerous sayings which were alleged to qualify as parables of Jesus, including the following:

> Truly, truly, I say to you, unless a grain of wheat falls into the earth and dies, it remains alone; but if it dies, it bears much fruit. (John 12:24)

> When a woman is in travail she has sorrow, because her hour has come; but when she is delivered of the child, she no longer remembers the anguish, for joy that a child is born into the world. (John 16:21)

> Truly, truly, I say to you, he who does not enter the sheepfold by the door but climbs in by another way, that man is a thief and a robber; but he who enters by the door is the shepherd of the sheep. To him the gatekeeper opens; the sheep hear his voice, and he calls his own sheep by name and leads them out. When he has brought out all his own, he goes before them, and the sheep follow him, for they know his voice. A stranger they will not follow, but they will flee from him, for they do not know the voice of strangers. (John 10:1-4)

Robinson argues at length that many of Jesus' sayings in John are compatible in form with the parables in the synoptic gospels. Yet the point seems to be overlooked that the *parable tradition* as Jesus' preferred method of teaching is itself what is missing from John. So the fact that there are numerous sayings which might be identified as parable-like in their form and structure only means that the traditions out of which John and the synoptic gospels emerged are more harmonious than is often acknowledged. This is true as far as it goes. Yet it is the difference rather than the similarity between John and the synoptics which may yield a clue to their temporal sequence.

Very little of the text of John might be said to consist of parable-like sayings. The large majority of the text is made up of long monologues (John 14-16; 17), shorter monologues woven into a dialogue format (John 6:25-65; John 10), and actual conversational dialogues. Though such dialogues are present in the synoptic gospels, they are relatively infrequent and notably less caustic and confrontational than they are in John.

Thus, we find that instead of the structured parables which make up a large portion of the synoptic texts, John gives us lengthy and detailed dialogues of Jesus either with his disciples or with his adversaries. Most of the conversations are foreign in both structure and content compared to what we find in the synoptic gospels. Not only does this create a puzzle for us today, but it seems that it would have been suspicious to the church as well if this gospel had appeared at the end of the first century. Why would a church steeped in the traditions of the synoptic gospels have accepted such a divergent work as authoritative?

The Evolution of the Parable Tradition

One possible answer may be found in the development history of the parable itself. Scholars believe that the parable was a teaching form, perhaps initiated by Jesus, but certainly developed by the church over time. In the absence of written documents or standard liturgical forms of worship, the parable was an efficient form of oral teaching developed and to propagate the message of the church effectively.

Some of the parables may have originated with Jesus, but the degree to which the parable was used by Jesus as a teaching form is not known. Conversely, some of them were clearly developed by the church to address issues of concern later in the first century. For example, the Parable of the Ten Virgins, found only in Matthew, was developed to address the apparent delay of Jesus' second coming, and the need to stand firm in the faith in spite of the delay:

> Then the kingdom of heaven shall be compared to ten maidens who took their lamps and went to meet the bridegroom. Five of them were foolish, and five were wise. For when the foolish took their lamps, they took no oil with them; but the wise took flasks of oil with their lamps. As the bridegroom was delayed, they all slumbered and slept. But at midnight there was a cry, "Behold the bridegroom, come out to meet him!" Then all those maidens rose and trimmed their lamps. And the foolish said to the wise, "Give us some of your oil, for our lamps are going out." But the wise replied, "Perhaps there will not be enough for us and for you; go rather to the dealers and buy for yourselves." And while they went to buy, the bridegroom came, and those who were ready went in with him to the marriage feast; and the door was shut. Afterward the other maidens came also, saying, "Lord, lord, open to us." But he replied, "Truly I say to you, I do not know you." Watch, therefore, for you know neither the day nor the hour. (Matt. 25:1-13)

In this parable, the reference to the "delay of the bridegroom" is an implicit reference to the delay of Jesus' return. We may assume that this parable was developed to respond to a growing frustration that Jesus had not yet appeared again. The parable warns that only those who are steadfast and wise in their preparations for Jesus' return shall be saved. In similar manner, the Parable of the Good Servant and the Wicked Servant (Matt. 24:45-51; Luke 12:41-46) was developed to address the same issues. It also was designed to encourage faithfulness in spite of the tardiness of Jesus' return. It declares that those who fall away shall be punished with the unfaithful.

The Parable of the Talents (Matt. 25:14-30; Luke 19:11-27) is another interesting example of parable development to meet evolving concerns. Here the issue is not the delay of the second coming, but the need for believers to remain active participants in the movement rather than sit by in idle anticipation of Jesus' return. It appears that it may have been developed earlier than the parables noted above, for it does not address the issue of the delayed return. Rather, it addresses a problem posed by those who "supposed the kingdom of God was to appear immediately" (Luke 19:11), and who therefore were not leading active and productive lives in the meantime. It encourages believers to anticipate that the kingdom will not appear immediately, and that they should remain productive while anticipating it. Those who do not will have their reward taken away.

Parables such as these would have made no sense to an audience that did not anticipate the resurrection. The Gospel of John indicates that the disciples did not expect him to rise from the dead:

> Then the other disciple, who reached the tomb first, also went in, and he saw and believed; for as yet they did not know the scripture, that he must rise from the dead. (John 20:9)

Without any notion of a resurrection, the idea of a second coming could not have been part of the historical dialogue either. So the parables noted above could not have originated with Jesus. They are clear evidence that the Jesus movement added to the parable tradition over time as an means to address evolving concerns of believers. In these examples, the parables were created and attributed to Jesus to encourage steadfastness of faith in the light of Jesus' anticipated return. However, if parables were developed to address eschatological concerns, it is likely that the parable format was used to assimilate a variety of doctrinal ideas as they became part of the church's expression.

If this is true, an early composition date for John may explain the absence of parables from its text. We may surmise that many of the parables did not originate with Jesus and had not yet been developed at the time John was composed. Since the author did not have either the synoptic gospels or the tradition of the parables as a reference, they do not appear in his document. Further, the absence of them would not have looked strange to the very early Jesus movement if the teaching form of the parable had not yet become a major part of its traditions.

Furthermore, the long conversational style found in John is not the type of teaching which would have been successfully passed from generation to generation in oral form. Nor would many of the long dialogues make theological sense if extracted from the gospel and circulated separately as smaller written works. Since they are not the product of oral epitomizing and refinement, the format of Jesus' teachings in John is precisely the opposite of what we might expect from a collection of traditions handed down over half a century.

So the absence of a developed parable tradition, and the presence of a teaching style not conducive to oral transmission, both tend to support the proposal that John may have been an early work. It would not be surprising to find that the parable-like sayings in John that Robinson pointed to actually reflect a primitive stage of parable development out of which the full parable tradition eventually grew.

3. *The Absence of Major Mythical Traditions.* In addition to the missing vocabulary and the absence of the parable tradition, many of the significant mythical traditions of Jesus' life are missing from John also. There is no virginal conception of Mary by the Holy Spirit, no angels at his birth, no temptation by Satan, no casting out of demons, no transfiguration on the mountain, and no ascension into heaven.

The omission of all of these stories is remarkable given that John presents the most mythical characterization of the nature of Jesus. How is it that John's account of the earthly visit of the preexistent man from heaven is not attended by any of the supernatural events so well documented in the synoptic gospels? Certainly John could have used some of this synoptic imagery effectively. For example, would not his concept of Jesus as the man from heaven have been wonderfully illustrated by the story of the virginal conception? Would not Jesus' return to heaven have been enhanced by the story of the ascension?

The question raised here is whether these stories were part of the beliefs of the primitive movement, or whether they were stories developed by the church over time. As evidence of the latter, it is worth noting that the authentic letters of Paul do not mention any of these mythical events either. Further, as we consider the synoptic gospels we find that Mark, which is presumed to be the earliest of the three, does not contain the virginal conception or the ascension, and it only briefly mentions the temptation of Jesus by Satan. It is only the later synoptic gospels which offer all of these stories in their most evolved form.

It would be consistent with the evidence at hand to suggest that many of the great mythical stories of Jesus' life were developed by the church over a period of time. They are reflected only in the later writings of the NT due to the fact that they had not yet become part of the expression of the church when the earlier writings were composed. If this is the correct scenario, then their absence from the Gospel of John is compatible with the theory of its early composition.

John: The Natural Gospel

Not only does John avoid the great mythical traditions, but with the one exception of its idea of Jesus as a preexistent being, it is clearly the least mythologized of the four gospels. Not only are supernatural events like the virginal conception or the temptation by Satan missing from John, but the earthly stage upon which Jesus conducts his ministry is rarely subject to disturbance by supernatural forces. There are no angels descending from on high; there are no earthquakes or eclipses of the sun or tearing of the temple curtain at the time of Jesus' death; there is no resurrection of the saints to walk the streets of Jerusalem. Other than the miracles performed by Jesus himself, John depicts a natural world which remains largely undisturbed by heavenly forces.

In fact, there are only three "supernatural" events in John which are not miracles performed by Jesus. They are the spirit descending upon Jesus as witnessed by John the Baptist (1:32-34), a voice from heaven (12:28-30), and the angels at the tomb (20:11-13). Yet even these are very odd as supernatural events, for they are portrayed by John in a comparatively natural manner. For example, this is John's account of the spirit descending from heaven:

> And John bore witness, "I saw the Spirit descend as a dove from heaven, and it remained on him. I myself did not know him; but he who sent me to baptize with water said to me, 'He on whom you see the Spirit descend and remain, this is he who baptizes with the Holy Spirit.' And I have seen and borne witness that this is the Son of God." (John 1:32-34)

In contrast, this is the same story in Matthew:

> And when Jesus was baptized, he went up immediately from the water, and behold, the heavens were opened and he saw the Spirit of God descending like a dove and alighting on him; and lo, a voice from heaven, saying "This is my beloved Son, with whom I am well pleased." (Matt 3:16-17; see also Mark 1:10-11; Luke 3:21-22))

Matthew's version indicates that the "heavens were opened" and that there was a "voice from heaven." Mark and Luke contain both of these elements as well. However, the heavens do not open in John, nor is there a voice from heaven; the voice which identifies Jesus as the Son of God is that of John the Baptist himself. Furthermore, the experience of the "Spirit descending as a dove" is a private experience of the Baptist, albeit one to which he testifies. In the synoptic versions, there is a greater implication that this was a supernatural event witnessed by those at hand.

John's tendency to render supernatural events in a natural manner is also evident in another story unique to John which reports a voice from heaven:

> [Jesus said,] "Father, glorify thy name." Then a voice came from heaven, "I have glorified it and I will glorify it again." The crowd standing by heard it and said that it had thundered. Others said, "An angel has spoken to him." Jesus answered, "This voice has come for your sake, not for mine." (John 12:28-30)

Note that the author draws attention to the fact that the crowd perceived the "voice" as thunder. He further tells us that others said, "an angel has spoken to him," indicating that they did not recognize this as the voice of God, nor did they understand the words, for they interpreted the voice as angelic words which were spoken only to Jesus. If the author is attempting to convince readers that God had spoken from heaven, why would he indicate that the eyewitnesses did not interpret it as such? If this story was a mythical creation for theological purposes, why did he introduce eyewitnesses to contradict the claim of the miraculous?

It is this inherent conflict in the account which makes it appear as though the story may be based on an eyewitness account; a legitimate explanation of the passage is that the voice from heaven was indeed thunder, and the eyewitnesses interpreted it as a message from God due to the ironic timing of the thunder clap. Note that the voice's response to Jesus does not contain any message other than an affirmation of Jesus' request. In essence, the words reported in the text are the verbal equivalent of what a properly timed thunder clap would have communicated to the observers. This account is written as though it could be a literal recording of an actual historical event, with the eyewitness interpreting the well-timed thunder as a response from God. Such a reading of the passage is allowed by what the author himself has told us. We do not find any similar discord on the part of witnesses to mythical events in the synoptic gospels. They are reported as straightforward supernatural events which are not subject to interpretive confusion.

John's third supernatural event, the story of the angels at the tomb, contains precisely this same natural patina:

> But Mary stood weeping outside the tomb, and as she wept she stooped to look into the tomb; and she saw two angels in white, sitting where the body of Jesus had lain, one at the head and one at the feet. They said to her, "Woman, why are you weeping?" She said to them, "Because they have taken away my Lord, and I do not know where they have laid him." Saying this, she turned round and saw Jesus standing, but she did not know that it was Jesus. (John 20:11-13)

This account is astonishing in comparison to angelic appearances accounts in the synoptic gospels. Here the angels bring no message, they do not frighten anyone by their presence, and indeed, Mary responds to them as if they were human beings. The 'angels' appear to have virtually no role in the story. In contrast once again we may refer to Matthew's version of the same event:

> Now after the Sabbath, toward the dawn of the first day, Mary Magdalene and the other Mary went to see the sepulchre. And behold, there was a great earthquake; for an angel of the Lord descended from heaven and came and rolled back the stone, and sat upon it. His appearance was like lightening, and his raiment white as snow. And for fear of him, the guards trembled and became like dead men. But the angel said to the women, "Do not be afraid; for I know that you seek Jesus who was crucified. He is not here; for he has risen, as he said."(Matt. 28:1-6a)

Here Matthew portrays the classic angelic appearance. The angel descends in glory, its presence frightens the humans who see it, and it comes with a specific message from heaven. So when we return to

John's account, we must ask how is it that such an inconsequential angelic appearance came to be written into the text? Why would the author suggest the beings were angels if they were to act like and be responded to as if they were human?

Again we may suspect that the story originated from the report of an eyewitness to an actual historical event. For it is easy to imagine that Mary actually did see two human beings in the tomb. She reported what she saw to the disciples. After interpreting the entire event as a resurrection, the author supposed these two unidentified persons must have been angels attending the resurrection. So he identifies them as such in his gospel. Yet the account remains unembellished, as it was originally reported to the author.

Such an explanation is of course speculative. The point is that the author of John does not embellish his story with details that appear to us to be mythical in substance as Matthew clearly does. He tells us they were angels because he apparently believed they were angels. However, he gives us no reason to make the same assumption.

So when we take a close look at the three "supernatural" events in John (excluding again the miracles performed by Jesus), they each lend themselves to a natural interpretation. When we consider that these are the only three supernatural events recorded by the author of John other than the miracles of Jesus, the enigma of the gospel becomes pronounced: how is it that the author came to tell the story of the mythical man from heaven while virtually eliminating the tradition of supernatural activity which the synoptic gospels say attended his coming? A possibility is that John was composed much earlier than the synoptic gospels--the absence of supernatural embellishment is due to its composition prior to the development of many of the mythological traditions.

4. *Limited Moral Vision.* Another major component of the Jesus tradition which is missing from John is the portrayal of Jesus as a moral visionary. The Fourth Gospel records few teachings which bear upon moral conduct and attitude, whereas this type of teaching is prevalent in the synoptics. Further, the character of Jesus as portrayed in John lacks the moral vitality and compassion which is so evident in the synoptic gospels. These are notable omissions. To illustrate the problem, the following are sayings which do not appear in John:

> You shall love the Lord your God with all your heart, and with all your soul, and with all your mind. This is the greatest and first command-ment. And the second is like it, You shall love your neighbor as yourself. (Matt 22:37-39)

> Love your enemies, do good to those who hate you, bless those who curse you, pray for those who abuse you. (Luke 6:27-28)

> If anyone strikes you on the right cheek, turn to him the other also. (Matt 5:39)

> Judge not, that you not be judged. For with the judgment you pronounce you will be judged. (Matt. 7:1-2)

> Do not lay up for yourselves treasure on earth, where moth and rust consume, and where thieves break in and steal, but lay up for yourselves treasure in heaven . . . for where your treasure is, there will your heart be also. (Matt 6:19-21)

> Beware of practicing your piety before men in order to be seen by them; for then you will have no reward from your Father who is in heaven. (Matt 6:1)

> "Blessed are the meek, for they shall inherit the earth . . . blessed are the merciful for they shall obtain mercy . . . blessed are the peacemakers, for they shall be called sons of God." (Matt. 5:5, 7, 9)

These sayings indicate that, for the authors of the synoptic gospels (Luke and Matthew in particular), the content of Jesus' teaching had important substance in its own right. What Jesus taught regarding proper thought and conduct was integral to his ministry and message. Conversely, for the author of John, the only significant element of Jesus' message was that he proclaimed himself to be the Son of God; whatever he may have taught regarding moral conduct and thought was almost irrelevant to this greater theme.

Yet it is not just the teachings themselves which are missing from John. The Fourth Gospel lacks the characterization of Jesus as a compassionate teacher which is prominent in the synoptic tradition.

Compare for example the story of the Anointing at Bethany as rendered by John and Mark (Figure 4.1). In this story the compassion of Jesus is more pronounced in Mark's version of the story. Jesus remains centered on the sacrificial act of the woman which is worthy of his praise and attention. Jesus graciously affirms her act in spite of the complaints from the other disciples. Conversely in John, Jesus does not affirm the woman, and turns attention to himself.

Figure 4.1: The Anointing at Bethany

John 12: 1-8	Mark 14:3-9
1 Six days before the Passover, Jesus came to Bethany, where Lazarus was, whom Jesus had raised from the dead. 2 There they made him a supper; Martha served, and Lazarus was one of those at table with him. 3 Mary took a pound of costly ointment of pure nard and anointed the feet of Jesus and wiped his feet with her hair; and the house was filled with the fragrance of the ointment. 4 But Judas Iscariot, one of his disciples (he who was to betray him), said, 5 "Why was this ointment not sold for three hundred denarii and given to the poor?" 6 This he said, not that he cared for the poor but because he was a thief, and as he had the money box he used to take what was put into it. 7 Jesus said, "Let her alone, let her keep it for the day of my burial. 8 The poor you always have with you, but you do not always have me."	3 And while he was at Bethany, in the house of Simon the leper, as he sat at table, a woman came with an alabaster flask of ointment of pure nard, very costly, and she broke the flask and poured it over his head. 4 But there were some who said to themselves indignantly, "Why was the ointment thus wasted? 5 For this ointment might have been sold for more than three hundred denarii, and given to the poor." And they reproached her. 6 But Jesus said, "Let her alone, why do you trouble her? She has done a beautiful thing to me. 7 For you will always have the poor with you, and whenever you will, you can do good to them; but you will not always have me. 8 She has done what she could; she has anointed my body beforehand for burying. 9 And truly, I say to you, wherever the gospel is preached in the whole world, what she has done will be told in memory of her.

As we shall see in Chapter Six, the Anointing at Bethany is not a unique or isolated example. In many stories common to John and Mark, we may observe a compassion and refinement of character in the Markan Jesus which is missing from John's portrayal.

However, this is not to say that the moral content of Jesus' sayings or the compassion of his character are missing entirely from John. Rather, it is that these elements are muted and diminished in John as compared to the synoptics. For instance, we may compare the "love" commandments in the gospels. In John, Jesus tells his disciples to love one another (15:12). The instruction is limited to those who are fellow believers, and thus is restricted compared to the more generalized Markan formula, "love your neighbor as yourself," or the admonition in Matthew and Luke to "love your enemies," which is widest in scope of all.

The only story told in John expressly for the purpose of instructing on proper conduct is the Woman Caught in Adultery (7:53-8:11). However, the earliest manuscripts of John do not contain this passage, and it is not considered authentic to the original gospel. It is not unreasonable to suspect this story was added specifically to lend the gospel a much needed infusion of moral vision.

So once again we have the problem of explaining missing traditions. How is it that teachings as formidable as the Great Commandments do not appear in John? Further, if John is a "deep theological reflection" on the person of Jesus, why does it disregard the tradition of Jesus as a moral luminary? Why does it show a Jesus of limited compassion? Such a portrait does not fit comfortably with the idea that John is an evolved theological meditation on the nature of Jesus.

By the decade of the 90s, we may infer from the circulation of the gospels of Mark, Matthew, and Luke, and the letter of 1 Clement,[4] that the characterization of Jesus as a moral visionary was widespread. So if John had simply enhanced the synoptic portrait of Jesus with a pre-existent heavenly dimension, it would not have been surprising. Such

---

[4] Clement was the fourth Bishop of Rome, following after Peter, Linus, and Anencletus. The First Epistle to the Corinthians (1 Clement), dated c. 96 CE, is one of the earliest writings of the church to have survived outside the NT. Its characterization of Jesus as a teacher of moral wisdom will be reviewed below.

a vision would be easier to imagine as a product of evolved thought. However, this is not what we find in John. The Fourth Gospel tells of Jesus' heavenly origin while simultaneously diminishing the moral component of Jesus' character. Thus it is more difficult to envision John as a product of mature thought. Further, it is a wonder that the established church would have accepted such a work as an authoritative record of the life of Jesus.

When might we expect the proclamation of Jesus' heavenly nature to have overshadowed the importance of his moral character? Is it necessary to conceive of this as a late phenomenon? To answer this question a comparison with Paul is once again illuminating. For Paul does not characterize Jesus as a teacher of wisdom and ethics. Whatever Jesus may have taught was incidental to Paul's theology, just as it was for the author of John.

In the letters of Paul, the critical message is that the death and resurrection of Jesus as the Son of God provided a substitutionary death for all believers. Paul taught that Jesus is Lord, that he is the Second Adam who has redeemed the race of man, and that nothing can separate the believer from the love of God because the risen Lord intercedes for him. Thus, for Paul the great cross-centered themes of resurrection, faith, and salvation constituted the meaning of Jesus' life. Conversely, the moral and wisdom teachings of Jesus are almost inconsequential. It is rare for Paul to quote a saying of Jesus. This implies that Paul did not consider the essential message of the gospel to be derived from the teachings of Jesus.

So just as John and Paul are in harmony on many explicit aspects of their teachings regarding Jesus, God the Father, and the Holy Spirit, so are they similar in their dismissal of the teachings of Jesus as being relevant to the gospel message. For both writers, it is belief in the resurrected Jesus which is the essence of the gospel. This for them outweighed any need to portray Jesus as a moral luminary.

With documents such as Mark, Matthew, and Luke, and (allegedly) Q in circulation, it is apparent that the tradition of Jesus as a moral sage and compassionate teacher had gained prominence by the end of the first century. Clement, a bishop of Rome, wrote the following in his first Epistle to the Corinthians in 96 CE:

More particularly, let us remember what the Lord Jesus Christ said in one of His lessons on mildness and forebearance. "Be merciful," He told us, "that you may obtain mercy; forgive, that you may be forgiven. What you do yourself, will be done to you; what you give, will be given to you; as you judge, so you will be judged; as you show kindness, so it will be shown to you. Your portion will be weighed out for you in your own scales." May this precept, and these commands, strengthen our resolve to live in obedience to His sacred words, and in humility of mind . . .[5]

The churches at Rome and Corinth were founded by Paul, and in the letters of Paul there is little reference to the moral teachings of Jesus. Yet in the letter of 1 Clement we find evidence that Jesus' moral teachings were quoted and revered as sacred in these same two churches just forty years after Paul. So 1 Clement lends further support to the idea that by the end of the first century the teachings of Jesus were widely understood to have a meaningful and significant moral content. Accordingly, as this tradition of Jesus grew more prominent it would have been less likely for a gospel which simply ignored the moral tradition to have been produced or accepted.

In short, the limited moral substance of the Fourth Gospel is contrary to the notion that it is an advanced meditation on the nature of Jesus which evolved over many decades. The evidence from Paul indicates that advanced christological ideas were extant in the 50s, and that these ideas were not accompanied by any prominent vision of Jesus as moral sage. For these two reasons, the lack of moral substance in John would be compatible with a finding that John is a much earlier work than normally presumed.

5. *Absence of Institutional Development in the Church.* The last component of thought which is mysteriously absent from John is an awareness of the church as an institution. We have already noted that several words which came to form part of institutional expression are missing from John, including *apostle, church, gospel,* and so forth. Further, there are no liturgical formulas in John. The Lord's Prayer is missing, as is the sacrament of the Eucharist. The Great Commission

---

[5] 1 Clement 13, excerpt from *Early Christian Writings*, Penguin Books, 1968, p. 28

by which Jesus sent the disciples into the world has no clear institutional form in John. There is no concept of apostolic succession, by which church leadership is handed down in pre-ordained order.

It is interesting to draw an ideological comparison between John as an alleged document of the 90s, and 1 Clement. Since 1 Clement is usually dated 96 CE, it is presumed by most to be contemporary with the writing of John. The relevance of 1 Clement is the degree to which it demonstrates the advance of institutional organization in the church by the end of the first century.

In 1 Clement, the writer speaks of bishops and deacons as authorized leaders of the church.[6] The word laity is used for the first time in Christian literature,[7] indicating that the church had already begun to distinguish between professional clergy and a congregation of lay persons. One of the problems addressed by Clement in this letter is the dissension in the congregation as to who was qualified to hold the title of bishop. The concept of apostolic succession is present in a highly developed form:

> Now, the gospel was given to the Apostles for us by the Lord Jesus Christ; and Jesus the Christ was sent from God. That is to say, Christ received his commission from God, and the Apostles theirs from Christ. The order of these two events was in accordance with the will of God. So thereafter, when the Apostles had been given their instructions, and all their doubts had been set at rest by the resurrection of our Lord Jesus Christ from the dead, they set out in the full assurance of the Holy Spirit to proclaim the coming of God's kingdom. And as they went through the territories and townships preaching, they appointed their first converts--after testing them by the Spirit--to be bishops and deacons for the believers of the future (1 Clement 42).

Not only had a hierarchy of church leadership taken form by the end of the first century, at least for the churches in Rome and Corinth, but Clement also reveals that a well established ritual and liturgy had appeared as well. Rules of conduct, worship, and order had been established:

---

[6] 1 Clement 42, Ibid., p. 40

[7] 1 Clement 40, Ibid., p. 39

. . . there ought to be strict order and method in our performance of such acts as the Master has prescribed for certain times and seasons. Now, it was His command that the offering of gifts and the conduct of public services should not be haphazard or irregular, but should take place at fixed times and hours. Moreover, in the exercise of His supreme will He has Himself declared in what place and by what persons He desires this to be done, if it is all to be devoutly performed in accordance with His wishes and acceptably to His will.[8]

In the same way, my brothers, when we offer our own Eucharist to God, each one of us should keep to his own degree. His conscience must be clear, he must not infringe the rules prescribed for his ministering, and he is to bear himself with reverence.[9]

Clement also uses institutionalized language which is not free prose, but rather a formal liturgical declaration of faith:

In conclusion, may the all-seeing God, the Ruler of spirits and Lord of all flesh, who has chosen the Lord Jesus Christ, and through Him ourselves to be a people for his possession, grant to every soul that is called by His glorious and holy Name such faith and fear, such peace and patience, such forebearance, self-restraint, purity and sobriety, that they may be pleasing to His Name; through our High Priest and Protector Jesus Christ, by whom be glory, majesty, might and honor to Him both now and forever, world without end. Amen.[10]

Thus, the letter of 1 Clement indicates that the churches at Rome and Corinth manifested a high degree of institutional organization by the end of the first century. It is not suggested that all sects of the Jesus movement would be expected to have taken on the same organizational structure, or indeed have been ritualized to the degree that the church of Rome appears to have been. However, what is puzzling in John is the virtual absence of any sign of organizational structure or liturgical expression. The gospel does not recognize any hierarchy between the original twelve disciples of Jesus and the rest of the believers. It does not contain any awareness of the Eucharist as a ritual established by Jesus during the Last Supper. The author rarely uses language which would appear to have a developed liturgical form.

---

[8] 1 Clement 40a, Ibid., p. 39
[9] 1 Clement 41a, Ibid., p. 39
[10] 1 Clement 64, Ibid., p. 49

The most obvious inference is that the gospel was composed much earlier in the century, before the Jesus movement had developed its institutional structures. It represented the expressions and beliefs of the Johannine community at the time it was written; since the community was in a rudimentary stage of development, the gospel reflects primitive, non-institutionalized expression.

The Issue of the Eucharist in John

Before leaving the discussion of missing traditions, we must return to one point made above. It is that the tradition of the Eucharist does not exist in the Fourth Gospel. While there is no debate that it is not explicitly described, many scholars find an awareness of the Eucharist in John 6:

> "I am the living bread which came down from heaven; if any one eats of this bread, he will live forever; and the bread which I shall give for the life of the world is my flesh."
> The Jews then disputed among themselves, saying, "How can this man give us his flesh to eat?" So Jesus said to them, "Truly, truly, I say to you, unless you eat the flesh of the Son of man and drink his blood, you have no life in you; he who eats my flesh and drinks my blood has eternal life and I will raise him up at the last day. He who eats my flesh and drinks my blood abides in me and I in him." (John 6: 51-56)

The key question here is whether the author wrote this as an allusion to a tradition of the Eucharist he was already aware of, or conversely, whether the passage itself is an extremely primitive tradition of a saying of Jesus which led to the development of the Eucharist. Since most scholars are predisposed to think of John as a late gospel, most believe it was the former. As C.K. Barrett says, "few dispute that the Eucharist is alluded to in this part of the discourse."[11]

This is the primary example of a technique alleged by many scholars to have been used by the author of John. It is supposed that the author was aware of the synoptic stories, but rewrote them in order to render them historically non-specific. C.K. Barrett explains:

[11] Barrett, Ibid., p. 297

What is perhaps most striking in a comparison of John and the synoptic gospels is that several of the most important synoptic incidents are omitted by John, though he seems to show indirectly knowledge of some of them . . . It is unthinkable that he dismissed such incidents as unimportant; in fact, it seems that he regarded them as far more important than mere 'incidents'. The narratives as they stand in the synoptic gospels are in general readily detachable from their contexts; this followed inevitably from the mode in which the traditional material out of which the gospels were made was handed down. For this reason even the most significant events could easily become incidental, and could even, if removed from their proper setting, be dangerously misunderstood. John safeguards their meaning by stripping them of their historical individuality and building them into the theological framework of his Gospel.[12]

In other words, Barrett argues that John deconstructed several synoptic stories, eliminated references to concrete times and places, and wove the essential meaning of the events into his text without reference to their historical origin; further, he did this so that essential meanings could not be misconstrued. Barrett's foremost illustration of this is the allusion to the Eucharist in John 6 above. His argument is plausible if the gospel was composed late in the decade, for we would have good reason to believe the author was aware of the tradition of the Eucharist. If the author had such awareness, then John 6 cannot be interpreted except as an allusion to it.

The difficulty with this explanation is that it would not seem to address the objectives Barrett suggests are the motive for John to have created such an allusion. Does John really "safeguard" the essential meaning of the Eucharist by casting it in such literal terms? Does he protect the tradition from being "dangerously misunderstood?" One might allege this was John's intent, but it is a long reach to demonstrate he actually met his objective. When the conversation in John 6 which alludes to the Eucharist creates confusion among Jesus' listeners, in what way is the meaning of the Eucharist kept from being misunderstood?

Note that it is the presumption of John's late composition which compels most scholars to see John 6 as an allusion to the Eucharist. For

---

[12] Barrett, Ibid., pp. 51-2

if we were to presume that John was composed much earlier, when we are not sure what traditions the author may have been aware of, then the passage above might as easily be interpreted as a primitive saying from which the Eucharist was subsequently developed.

Fortunately, additional light is shed on the subject by Paul. Scholars universally agree that the earliest reference to the Eucharist as a sacramental tradition in the NT is found in 1 Corinthians:

> For I received from the Lord what I also delivered to you, that the Lord Jesus on the night when he was betrayed took bread, and when he had given thanks, he broke it, and said, "This is my body which is for you. Do this in remembrance of me." In the same way also the cup, after supper, saying, "This cup is the new covenant in my blood. Do this, as often as you drink it, in remembrance of me." For as often as you eat this bread and drink the cup, you proclaim the Lord's death until he comes. Whoever, therefore, eats the bread or drinks the cup of the Lord in an unworthy manner will be guilty of profaning the body and blood of the Lord. (1 Cor. 11:23-27)

There is one striking comment in this passage--Paul says he has received this tradition from the Lord himself. In other words, it was given to him through a direct revelation. This comment would make no sense if the tradition had been established by Jesus at the Last Supper and passed down through Peter and the other disciples who were present. So it would appear that it was Paul who introduced the concept of the Eucharist, and invested it with the meaning that would subsequently be adopted by the movement. His letter to the Corinthians is dated in the mid-50s. Each of the synoptic gospels is dated long afterward, and the tradition of the Eucharist which we find in them is evidently based on this passage in 1 Corinthians (See Mark 14:22-25; Matthew 26:26-29; Luke 22:15-20).

Since John is the only gospel in which the Eucharist does not appear, one possible explanation is that it was composed before Paul's revelation gained prominence in the movement. In fact, since the author of John reports that those who listened to Jesus' teaching were offended by it to the extent that even many of Jesus' followers "drew back and no longer went about with him" (John 6:66), we may wonder whether Paul's revelation was motivated by a desire to transform John's offensive teaching into a tradition more palatable and functional for the evolving movement. Of course, such a suggestion would assume that the tradition in John predates 1 Corinthians. However, from the evidence so far, the scenario may be allowed.

The Virginal Conception

The Eucharist is only one of several traditions alleged to have been deconstructed by John. As another example, Barrett sees a possible allusion to the virginal conception in this passage:

> But to all who received him, who believed in his name, he gave power to become children of God; who were born, not of blood nor of the will of the flesh nor of the will of man, but of God. (John 1:12-13)

The statement here indicates believers become children of God through their belief and through a corresponding act of God. The story of the virginal conception teaches that Jesus was the Son of God from birth, also through an act of God. Hence, the two have some degree of broad conceptual similarity. Yet there is nothing in the words above which would cause us to assume a prior knowledge of the virginal conception on the part of the author. It is not a tangible allusion to the virginal conception in the same way the earlier passage could be seen as an allusion to the Eucharist. So it is difficult to infer that the essential meaning of the virginal conception is captured here.

However, the source of the problem is clear. The tenuous reasoning arises from the attempt to bridge the gap between a fact and a working presupposition in conflict. The fact is that John contains none of the major synoptic legends. The presupposition is that John was written in the 90s and must have known these legends. Barrett does not question the presupposition; so he assumes the author of John knew these stories and "safeguards their meaning by stripping them of their historical individuality." However, if John was written early, and the author did not know the synoptic legends, it is surely evident that the facts can be interpreted in the reverse: the essential meanings existed in prototypical form in the primitive church; to safeguard the primitive message, they were mythologized into simple stories designed to propagate these beliefs accurately and efficiently.

So the question is whether these clues of indirect knowledge derive from a later deconstruction of the synoptic legends, or whether are they early precursors to them? Did John strip the story of the virginal conception of its historicity in order to safeguard its meaning, or was the story subsequently created to illustrate the idea of Jesus as a heavenly being? From the evidence so far, a plausible answer is that John does not show awareness of developed traditions; rather it reflects an embryonic stage of belief out of which the legends eventually grew.

Historical Credibility in the Fourth Gospel

In the previous chapter we found that the conventional arguments for dating the Gospel of John in the 90s are not strong enough to warrant such a conclusion. So far in this chapter we have found that a host of traditions which we might expect to find in a late first century document do not exist in John. In Chapter Two we discovered that the Gospel of John was composed by someone who was intent upon maligning the character of Peter. Such an attack would make more sense if Peter was alive at the time the gospel was written. These three factors combined suggest that John may be a much earlier work than typically assumed.

This is not the end of the discussion, however. There is more evidence in John which also points to early authorship. When we compare John with the synoptic gospels, we find that in many instances there are conflicts between the way the two traditions have reported the same events. This is fortunate for two reasons. First, the existence of obvious contradictions indicates that the gospels were not extensively rewritten by the early church to bring them into harmony after the fact. Though we have seen that Mark and John show obvious signs of editing to achieve a semblance of political harmony, their inherent inconsistencies attest that they were treated by the church with a certain respect for their integrity as originally composed.

Second, when the contradictions between John and the synoptics are compared, it often appears as though John's version has greater historical credibility. It is as if the author of John relied upon a more accurate source of information than did the synoptic writers. To the extent that John has greater historical credibility, it implies that the author may have been closer to historical events, or that the Johannine accounts were subjected to less revisionist interpretation over time. Either of these lends tacit support to an early dating of John.

We will look at four notable discrepancies between John and the synoptics. First, John reports that Jesus and John the Baptist conducted concurrent ministries in competition with one another, while the synoptics indicate that Jesus did not begin his ministry until after the Baptist was imprisoned. Second, John maintains that the disciples first gathered around Jesus within the milieu of John the Baptist's ministry, whereas the synoptics say the first disciples were called while fishing by the Sea of Galilee. Third, John places the Last Supper on the evening before the Passover, while the synoptics say that the Last Supper was the Passover meal. Finally, we will look at several inconsistencies in the accounts of the interrogation of Jesus by Pontius Pilate.

1. *The Concurrent Ministry of John the Baptist.* The first major point of historical conflict between John and the synoptic gospels is their depiction of the ministry of John the Baptist as a background for Jesus' ministry. All four gospels present John the Baptist as a prophet figure whose role was to herald the coming of Jesus. He is reported to have proclaimed in reference to Jesus, "After me comes he who is mightier than I, the thong of whose sandals I am not worthy to stoop down and untie" (Mark 1:7; see also Matt 3:11; Luke 3:16; John 1:26-27). The early Jesus movement identified the Baptist's role as one of a subservient forerunner preparing the way for Jesus and identifying him as the chosen one of God.

A discrepancy exists because the synoptics report Jesus began his ministry and called his first disciples *after* the arrest of John the Baptist. This scenario is explicit in Mark and Matthew, and implied in Luke:

> Now after John was arrested, Jesus came into Galilee, preaching the
> Gospel of God, and saying, "The time is fulfilled, and the kingdom of
> God is at hand; repent, and believe in the Gospel." And passing along
> by the Sea of Galilee, he saw Simon and Andrew the brother of Simon
> casting a net by the sea; for they were fishermen. And Jesus said to
> them, "Follow me, and I will make you become fishers of men." And
> immediately they left and followed him. (Mark 1:14-18; see also Matt
> 4:12,17; Luke 3:20)

According to Mark and Matthew, since Jesus waited until after
John the Baptist was imprisoned before beginning his own work, he
did not establish a ministry in competition with the Baptist. Rather,
the Baptist performed his brief role as the forerunner to Jesus, then
disappeared from the scene before Jesus commenced his activities.

The Gospel of John tells a different story. In this account Jesus
begins to attract disciples within the context of the Baptist's ministry.
In fact the first disciples follow Jesus because the Baptist identifies him
as the "Lamb of God":

> The next day again John [the Baptist] was standing with two of his
> disciples; and he looked at Jesus as he walked and said, "Behold, the
> Lamb of God!" The two disciples heard him say this, and they
> followed Jesus. Jesus turned, and saw them following, and said to
> them, "What do you seek?" And they said to him, "Rabbi, (which
> means Teacher), where are you staying?" He said to them, "come and
> see." They came and saw where he was staying; and they stayed with
> him that day, for it was about the tenth hour. One of two who heard
> John speak, and followed him, was Andrew, Simon Peter's brother.
> He first found his brother Simon, and said to him, "We have found
> the Messiah." (John 1:35-41)

So the Fourth Gospel says that the disciples come to Jesus at the
direction of John the Baptist. Jesus' first disciples are followers of the
Baptist, and Jesus' ministry begins as a splinter group from the Baptist's
activities. Jesus' ability to attract followers of the Baptist implies that he
was most likely an active leader in John's ministry prior to the split.
However, it is crucial to note that though John the Baptist has
supposedly identified Jesus as the Christ, he does not follow Jesus
himself. Rather, he continues his own ministry independent of Jesus'
activities:

> After this Jesus and his disciples went into the land of Judea; there he remained with them and baptized. John was also baptizing at Aenon near Salim, because there was much water there; and people came and were baptized. For John had not yet been put in prison. (John 3:22-24)

Further, the gospel does not hide the fact that Jesus and John the Baptist were conducting competing ministries:

> Now when the Lord knew that the Pharisees had heard that Jesus was making and baptizing more disciples than John . . . he left Judea and departed again to Galilee. (John 4:1-3)

Thus, the Fourth Gospel poses a difficult scenario from a theological perspective. If John the Baptist's mission was to act as a forerunner to Jesus, and if he had recognized Jesus as the Christ, why did he not become a disciple of Jesus himself? Why did he continue to conduct his own ministry of baptism independent of Jesus' activities? With respect to Christian dogma, this is a serious inconsistency. However, the problem is eliminated in the synoptic accounts by the assertion that Jesus did not begin his ministry until after John was arrested.

Which of these accounts is historically more plausible? All four gospels are unanimous on the fact that John the Baptist was a prophet-like figure who was imprisoned by Herod. Further, it is clear from the writings of the first century historian Flavius Josephus that the Baptist had a substantial following. Josephus' account of John the Baptist, presumed to have been written around 90 CE, shows a remarkable awareness of the teaching of the Baptist for an historian writing sixty years after the fact. Note that Josephus does not associate John the Baptist with Jesus, but rather treats him as a formidable religious leader in his own right:

> Herod had put [John the Baptist] to death, though he was a good man and had exhorted the Jews to lead righteous lives, to practice justice toward their fellows and piety towards God, and so doing join in baptism. In his view this was a necessary preliminary if baptism was to be acceptable to God. They must not employ it to gain pardon for whatever sins they committed, but as a consecration of the body implying that the soul was already thoroughly cleansed by right

behavior. When others too joined the crowds about [John the Baptist], because they were aroused to the highest degree by his sermons, Herod became alarmed. Eloquence that had so great an effect on mankind might lead to some form of sedition, for it looked as if they would be guided by John in everything that they did. Herod decided therefore that it would be much better to strike first and be rid of him before his work led to an uprising, than to wait for an upheaval, get involved in a difficult situation and see his mistake. (Antiquities 18.5.2)

That an historian writing in the late first century would have been so aware of John the Baptist implies that he was not an insignificant figure. Indeed, Josephus appears to be more aware of the ministry and message of John the Baptist than he is of Jesus'. It is possible that, for a number of years after their deaths, the movement of John the Baptist may have been as large as or perhaps even larger than, the Jesus movement. So the synoptic reduction of John the Baptist to a relatively insignificant character who existed merely to announce Jesus is not an historically plausible portrayal of him.

In comparison, the Fourth Gospel's indication that the Jesus movement was a group which split off from the ministry of John the Baptist is credible, as is the report that they conducted parallel ministries for some period of time. The statement in John 4:1 that "Jesus was making and baptizing more disciples than John" implies that they were competing with one another.

Such an inference brings several other comments in the Fourth Gospel into perspective. One of the significant recurring themes in John is that *John the Baptist was not the Messiah:*

There was a man sent from God, whose name was John. He came for testimony, to bear witness to the light, that all might believe through him. *He was not the light,* but came to bear witness to the light. (John 1:6-8, emphasis added)

. . . we have beheld [Jesus'] glory, glory as of the only Son from the Father. (John bore witness to him, and cried, "This was he of whom I said, 'He who comes after me ranks before me, for he was before me.'") (John 1:14b-15)

> And this is the testimony of John, when the Jews sent priests and Levites from Jerusalem to ask him "Who are you?" *He confessed, he did not deny, but confessed, "I am not the Christ."* (John 1:19-20, emphasis added)

The insistent rhetoric on this subject implies that some of the author's intended readers recognized John the Baptist as the Messiah. Furthermore, it appears to have been a critical issue, for in case the readers missed it the first three times, the claim that Jesus was greater than the Baptist is repeated several more times throughout the gospel:

> And they came to John and said to him, "Rabbi, he who was with you beyond the Jordan, to whom you bore witness, here he is, baptizing, and all are going to him." John answered, "No one can receive anything except what is given him from heaven. You yourselves bear me witness, that I said, *I am not the Christ*, but I have been sent before him." (John 3:26-28, emphasis added)

> [Jesus said,] "You sent to John, and he has borne witness to the truth. Not that the testimony I receive is from man; but I say this that you may be saved. He was a burning and shining lamp, and you were willing to rejoice for a while in his light. But the testimony which I have is greater than that of John; for the works which the Father has granted me to accomplish, these very works which I am doing, bear me witness that the Father has sent me. (John 5:33-36)

> [Jesus] went away again across the Jordan to the place where John at first baptized, and there he remained. And many came to him; and they said, "John did no sign, but everything that John said about this man was true." (John 10:40-41)

This prominent theme in the Gospel of John which insists that John the Baptist was not the Christ is unique among the four gospels, and indeed among the NT writings. It indicates that the author was writing for at least one audience which was steeped in controversy over the roles of John and Jesus. In the eyes of the author, John the Baptist was formidable enough to represent a competitive threat for the messianic title.

The prominence of John the Baptist is at odds with the synoptic reduction of him as a brief forerunner to Jesus. However, even within

186

the synoptic gospels there are oblique references which imply the legend and movement of John the Baptist lived long after him. Mark refers to the disciples of the Baptist as holding to the tradition of fasting, while Jesus' disciples did not (Mark 2:18). Mark also says that as Jesus' name became known, "some said he was John the Baptist raised from the dead." (Mark 6:14). In Luke, the disciples asked of Jesus, "Lord, teach us to pray, as John taught his disciples" (Luke 11:1). The implication is that the Baptist's movement was perceived as a model which the Jesus movement could emulate.

Further, in all three synoptic gospels, Jesus is confronted by Jewish leaders who demand to know from whence Jesus derives his authority. Jesus responds, "Was the baptism of John from heaven or from men?" By this question, Jesus presumably placed his adversaries in a difficult spot. They had not supported John the Baptist, so they could not admit his ministry was from heaven. Yet if they were to say he was not a prophet, they risked a negative reaction of the crowds-- "they were afraid of the people, for all held that John was a real prophet." (Mark 11:27-33 and pars.) This story would not have made sense to the readers of the synoptic gospels unless they recognized the Baptist as a prophet in his own right. From the combined evidence in all historical sources, it is apparent that John the Baptist was more prominent as a competitor to Jesus than as a forerunner as Christian tradition has maintained.

The Debate over Messiahship: Jesus vs. John the Baptist

It is only the Gospel of John which contains the insistent rhetoric that the Baptist was not the Christ and should not be mistaken as such. How did this come to be such a vital issue for the author of the Fourth Gospel when it was apparently irrelevant for every other NT writer? This question has implications for the dating of the gospel; the first problem it poses is when a debate over the roles of Jesus and the Baptist would most likely have been extant?

Since it is presumed that John the Baptist died in 29 CE and Jesus in 30 CE, and since both left in their wake followers who proclaimed each respectively as the Messiah, a natural assumption is that this debate would have been a prominent issue in the years immediately following their deaths. Such a debate could have continued for many decades, and perhaps beyond the end of the first century. However, what is less probable is the notion that a visible conflict between followers of the Baptist and Jesus materialized late in the first century after having been a non-issue in the intervening decades.

On this point the silence of the rest of the NT is resounding. None of the NT documents other than John, which all date from the 50s on, show any awareness of John the Baptist as a rival of Jesus for the messianic title. Though the silence on this issue in all of these writings cannot prove that the Johannine community did not face the Baptist conflict in the 90s, it renders the suggestion suspicious.

Furthermore, it does not make intuitive sense that, after many decades of synoptic tradition which placed the start of Jesus' ministry after the imprisonment of the Baptist, a gospel writer would suddenly introduce the serious difficulty that the Baptist, after identifying Jesus as the Messiah, proceeded to conduct his own ministry in competition with Jesus.

In short, the Johannine treatment of John the Baptist is improbable as a product of the 90s. However, it appears credible once we assume that it is the earliest and most historically accurate version of the story. Through the window of the Fourth Gospel we see a clearer view of the historical relationship between Jesus and John the Baptist. Within the Johannine stories of the Baptist we can discern a layer of historical fact which is absent from the synoptic gospels; the indications of competition between Jesus and John the Baptist are most probably rooted in actual historical events.

2. *The Call of the Disciples.* Another discrepancy between the Fourth Gospel and the synoptics exists in their divergent reports of the calling of the disciples. This is related to the John the Baptist issue, but is distinct and warrants further attention. In the Gospel of Mark, Jesus' first act is to call the first four disciples. They are called while fishing by the Sea of Galilee:

And passing along by the Sea of Galilee, he saw Simon and Andrew the brother of Simon casting a net in the sea; for they were fishermen. And Jesus said to them, "Follow me and I will make you become fishers of men." And immediately they left their nets and followed him. And going on a little farther, he saw James the son of Zebedee and John his brother, who were in their boats mending their nets. And immediately he called them; and they left their father Zebedee in the boat with the hired servants, and followed him (Mark 1:16-20).

The Johannine account of Jesus meeting the first disciples is quite different. As we have seen, this occurs within the setting of John the Baptist's ministry, at a place outside Jerusalem which the author calls "Bethany beyond the Jordan." Here the first disciples, one of whom is Andrew, take the initiative to seek Jesus, it is not Jesus who calls them (John 1:38, 42). Second, Andrew seeks out his brother, Simon Peter, and introduces him to Jesus. Third, Jesus calls Philip (1:43). Finally, Philip finds Nathanael and brings him to Jesus (1:45-46). After a dialogue with Jesus, Nathanael decides to follow him.

In the Fourth Gospel the disciples begin to collect around Jesus because they are attracted to his message and his person. John's story grants them a degree of personal autonomy and integrity; they see Jesus, they listen to him, and they decide to follow him. The first disciples are predisposed to hearing Jesus' message, as they have already sought out John the Baptist and become his disciples. The story's premise that Jesus appears among those following the Baptist and is able to attract some of those on the scene is plausible.

Conversely, in Mark the first four disciples are not engaged in any religious pursuit and are not associated with the Baptist at all. They are busy making a living as fishermen. When Jesus walks by and calls them, they appear to be struck as under a trance, and without apparent reason they drop what they are doing and follow Jesus without question or dialogue. Their unconditional and immediate response is puzzling since people would not usually react this way. At the very least, one gets the feeling something crucial has been left out of the story. Thus, once again John's account has historical texture whereas Mark's appears theologically motivated.

189

3. *The Days of the Last Supper and Crucifixion.* All four gospels show that the evening before Jesus' crucifixion he was together with his disciples for an event traditionally referred to as the Last Supper. The synoptic gospels represent this as the Passover meal (Mark 14:12-15; Matt. 26:17-19, Luke 22:7-13). However, the Gospel of John is clear that this meal occurred the night before the feast of the Passover, that is, twenty-four hours earlier than the report in the synoptic gospels.

This discrepancy is crucial, for if the Last Supper was the Passover meal, it would mean that Jesus would have been condemned and crucified on the high Sabbath. It is improbable that the Jewish authorities ostensibly involved in the interrogation, and condemnation of Jesus would have been engaged in such an activity on a high Sabbath.

In point of fact, the synoptic gospels are confused internally on the sequence of events. First, they describe the Last Supper as the Passover meal:

> And on the first day of Unleavened Bread, when they sacrificed the Passover lamb, his disciples said to him, "Where will you have us to go and prepare for you to eat the Passover?" (Mark 14:12; Matt. 26:17; see also Luke 22:7-9)

After partaking of the Passover meal, the synoptics then say that Jesus was crucified on the day of Preparation, that is the day before the Passover (Mark 15:42; Matt. 27:62; Luke 23:54). In other words, the synoptics literally indicate the Last Supper occurred *after* the crucifixion.

It is unlikely that this was a mistake all three authors made out of carelessness. A more likely explanation is that the date of the Last Supper was intentionally altered in the movement's tradition to coincide with the Passover meal and thus generate a greater symbolism of Jesus as the Passover lamb. Recall that in these same three gospels, Jesus introduces the sacrament of the Eucharist--the consumption of the bread and wine as symbols of his body and blood--at this Last Supper. The symbolism of Jesus as the lamb consumed at the Passover is completed by having the Last Supper and the Passover coincide.

In essence, the confusion in the synoptic gospels is not accidental, but rather once again influenced by theological concerns. However, the fact remains that John is the only gospel of the four which records an historically plausible sequence of events--the Last Supper must have occurred on the evening before the Passover meal. Here we find another instance in which John appears to record a story which has not been altered by the synoptic writers or other early church tradition for theological or evangelical purposes.

4. The Interrogation of Jesus by Pontius Pilate. One final example of apparent historical credibility in the Gospel of John is to be found in the encounter between Jesus and the Roman governor, Pontius Pilate (John 18:28 - 19:16). The story begins after Jesus' interrogation by the high priest, when he is taken to the praetorium (the residence of the Roman governor):

> Then they led Jesus from the house of Caiaphas to the praetorium. It was early. They themselves did not enter the praetorium, so that they might not be defiled, but might eat the Passover. So Pilate went out to them and said, "What accusation do you bring against this man?" (John 18:28-29)

Here the author indicates that the Jewish authorities who had brought Jesus to the governor refused to enter the building so that they might not be defiled. It is not clear what risk of impurity the author had in mind, but the idea that they stood outside to avoid defilement is a striking detail. It leads to a cumbersome situation in which Pilate goes back and forth between Jesus inside the building and the Jews outside as he conducts an ongoing dialogue with both.[13]

After discovering the charges which have been brought against Jesus by the Jews, Pilate goes into the praetorium to interrogate Jesus personally while the Jews remain outside (18:33). After Pilate's first discussion with Jesus, Pilate then "went out to the Jews again, and told them, 'I find no crime in him'" (18:38). They object, and Pilate has Jesus scourged, then brought out to the Jews (19:1-4). They demand that he be crucified. Pilate, and by implication, Jesus as well, reenter the praetorium and have a further discussion (19:8). After the second discussion, Jesus is led outside again and "sat down on the judgment seat at a place called The Pavement, and in Hebrew, Gabbatha" (19:13).

---

[13] The uniqueness of John's account in this regard has been noted by scholars. See Raymond Brown, Ibid., pp. 843-872.

The synoptic gospels do not record any of this detail of Pilate and Jesus going in and out of the praetorium, nor do they mention that the Jewish leaders stayed outside to avoid defilement. In the synoptics, the entire encounter appears to occur outside. Compared with the lengthy account in John, Mark tells the same story in a condensed form which is about one-third the length of John's:

> . . . and they bound Jesus and led him away and delivered him to Pilate. And Pilate asked him, "Are you the king of the Jews?" And he answered him, "You have said so." And the chief priests accused him of many things. And Pilate again asked him, "Have you no answer to make? See how many charges they bring against you." But Jesus made no further answer, so that Pilate wondered.
>
> Now at the feast he used to release for them one prisoner for whom they asked. And among the rebels in prison, who had committed murder and insurrection, there was a man called Barabbas. And the crowd came up and began to ask Pilate to do as he was wont to do for them. And he answered them, "Do you want for me to release for you the Kings of the Jews?" For he perceived that it was out of envy that the chief priests had delivered him up. But the chief priests stirred up the crowd to have him release for them Barabbas instead. And Pilate again said to them, "Then what shall I do with the man whom you call the King of the Jews?" And they cried out again, "Crucify him." And Pilate said to them, "Why, what evil has he done?" But they shouted all the more, "Crucify him." So Pilate, wishing to satisfy the crowd, released for them Barabbas; and having scourged Jesus, he delivered him to be crucified. (Mark 15:1b-15)

In Mark, there is a large crowd assembled to press for the execution of Jesus. The chief priests are said to have "stirred up the crowd" in order to pressure Pilate to condemn Jesus, and Pilate succumbs to the clamor of the crowd. This version of the story is implausible for two reasons. First, the position of high priest was politically aligned with the Roman administration. It was the Romans who installed the high priest, and it was the function of the high priest to promote the stability of the administration and to act on behalf of Roman interests. The high priest was chosen from a number of prominent citizens who were chief priests, and who were sympathetic to the Roman administration. During the Passover and the concurrent week-long Feast of Unleavened Bread, for which thousands of pilgrims had arrived in

Jerusalem, the administration's primary interest would have been to ensure that peace and calm were maintained. So Mark's account of the chief priests stirring up an emotional crowd in order to force the Roman governor to act on their behalf makes little historical sense.[14]

Second, the Roman governor Pontius Pilate was accustomed to suppressing social unrest with brutal force. It is dubious that he would have meekly submitted to a crowd of riotous Jews clamoring for the crucifixion of Jesus. If such a crowd had assembled he would most likely have called upon his military to dispel it. The notion that he would throw up his hands and give the mob what they demanded is incomprehensible. Hence, Mark's story requires that we accept unlikely behavior on the part of the chief priests as well as Pilate.

In both John and Mark, it is clear that Pilate finds no crime in Jesus, but delivers him to be crucified based on the demands of those who have made the accusations against him. However, in John there is no crowd which is stirred up by the chief priests. The confrontation occurs between Pilate and the chief priests and officers who had brought Jesus before him. It is they who have the discussion with Pilate, and it is upon their insistence that Jesus be executed. Also, John's account says the "Jews" (in context referring specifically to the chief priests and officers, 19:6), argued that Pilate may be guilty of disloyalty to Caesar if Jesus is released.

In John, the final argument which causes Pilate to consent to the execution is the charge from the Jewish authorities that Pilate himself may be seen as disloyal to the emperor if he allows Jesus to go free. This detail appears nowhere in the synoptic gospels. However, since both Pilate and the chief priests were instruments of the Roman administration, such a dialogue is historically plausible. Furthermore, if we may presume Jesus had challenged the authority of the chief priests and the politicized temple cult which they controlled, their interest in seeing Jesus executed makes sense as well.

---

[14] In Mark's version, the chief priests explicitly inflame the crowd (Mark 15:11); Matthew's version softens the tradition by saying the chief priests "persuaded" the people (Matt 27:20); In Luke there is no statement that the chief priests stirred up the multitude, but it may be inferred from the context (Luke 23).

Therefore, John's account of the interrogation before Pilate contains several details which do not appear in the synoptic gospels, and which have a sense of historical credibility. Also, the unlikely synoptic scenario of the chief priests inciting a large crowd to pressure Pilate into condemning Jesus does not exist in John. Once again there is a sense of historical trustworthiness in the Fourth Gospel which is absent from the other three.

Historical Tradition in John

Though scholars usually consider John to be a theological reflection of little historical consequence, they have recognized that the gospel has an array of details which makes it appear to be rooted in historical tradition. C. H. Dodd, in his classic work *Historical Tradition in the Fourth Gospel*, summarizes these observations:

> Particulars of time and place [in the gospel of John] are frequent; a dialogue takes place at Jerusalem, in the temple, in the treasury, in Solomon's cloister; or in the synagogue at Capernaum; or at a city of Samaria called Sychar, near the property which Jacob gave to his son Joseph, where Jacob's well was. One dialogue takes place in the middle of the Feast of Tabernacles, another on the last day of the same festival, another at the Encaenia in winter. Individual characterization, again, which is slight in the synoptics, sometimes emerges strikingly in John: the Samaritan Woman at the well, and Pontius Pilate, are full-length character studies like nothing that the synoptics offer, and even characters more lightly sketched, such as those of Caiaphas the High Priest (11:49-50), the blind beggar badgered by the court (9:24-34), the apostle Thomas, with his odd but entirely convincing combination of pessimism and impulsiveness (11:16; 20:24-5, 28), and others, go beyond almost anything in the synoptic dialogues . . .[15]

Though the richness of apparent historical detail in John is recognized by scholars, it is rarely interpreted as an indication of the gospel's early composition or historical integrity. The spiritual and theological elements of the gospel, which are assumed to be late developments, dominate its interpretation. Thus, any inference that

---

[15] Dodd, C. H., *Historical Tradition in the Fourth Gospel*, Cambridge University Press, 1963, p. 317

the historical detail in John may be the result of its early composition is precluded. If "apparent historical detail" were the only indicator, such a conclusion might be justified. However, the literary analysis we have seen thus far has contributed independent evidence that the gospel is indeed an early composition. John's apparent historical detail, which is so well recognized, may be now be brought into service as further supporting evidence that the gospel is a primitive work.

Summary

We found in Chapter Four that the evidence which is typically advanced in support of a late dating of John is inconclusive, and that no certain determination of date can be made from it. Our study of the Gospel of John in Chapters Two and Three, as well as the present chapter, has produced a number of observations which collectively point to one conclusion--that John was the first of the surviving gospel narratives to appear in the life of the primitive church. The evidence may be summarized as follows:

1. The Beloved Disciple vs. Peter. The Fourth Gospel was composed with a primary objective to show that Peter was a betrayer of the Jesus movement, and that he could not be trusted as a leader. The gospel upholds the Beloved Disciple as the authorized leader, and calls the followers of Peter to join the Johannine community. This dispute does not make sense as an issue of the 90s. Rather, there must have been an active conflict between Peter and the Beloved Disciple at the time the gospel was composed. Church tradition holds that Peter was crucified in the mid-60s. Whether this actually occurred or not cannot be independently verified, but the natural life span of Peter would not be expected to have extended much beyond this time frame. Thus, this evidence suggests a composition date prior to the mid-60s.

2. The Conflict with John the Baptist. The Gospel of John reflects a dispute between followers of Jesus and followers of John the Baptist as to which was the authentic Messiah. This dispute, while not inconceivable as a late first century issue, is more comprehensible as an issue faced by the primitive movement in the years immediately following the deaths of these two leaders. The fact that the balance of the NT documents show no awareness of the dispute is tacit evidence that it was an early conflict which was resolved as the Jesus movement matured during the course of the century. The presence of this conflict in the gospel points to an early composition date.

3. The Issue of Separating from the Synagogues. John displays an acute awareness of a doctrinal struggle regarding separation of Christians from traditional synagogue worship. Since this was an issue the Pauline churches were facing as early as 50 CE, and since many Christian churches had developed a substantial institutional form of worship independent of the synagogues by the 90s, the dispute reflected in John points to a composition date much earlier in the century, when such a conflict would be more coherent with the historical milieu.

4. The Missing Traditions. The Gospel of John shows no awareness of the tradition that Jesus taught in parables, or that his teaching had a significant moral content. It shows no awareness of a host of mythical stories which were attributed to the life of Jesus over time, and which would have been compatible with John's vision of Jesus as a man from heaven. The gospel shows no awareness of the church as an institutionalized entity. Finally, there is a remarkable list of vocabulary which rapidly became integral to the movement's expression, but which does not appear in John. Collectively, these missing traditions suggest a composition date for John prior to time they evolved as part of the church's expression.

5. Historical Credibility. The Gospel of John frequently contains accounts of events which differ from the synoptic gospels, and which manifest a higher degree of historical credibility than do the synoptic versions. These accounts collectively suggest that the author of John had access to traditions which had not been altered by the movement for theological purposes. The evidence suggests that John was an earlier composition.

6. John 21 as the Ending of Mark. The finding that John 21:1-19 was in its original form the missing ending of Mark suggests that the two gospels may be restored to approximate their original scope. Once the substance of John 21:1-19 is removed from John and appended to Mark 16:8, the two gospels stand as completely resolved and integrated literary works. A comparison of the two indicates that Mark was most probably composed as a response to John. This evidence suggests that John was written prior to Mark, or prior to about 70 CE.

Thus, a variety of independent clues all lead to the same conclusion: John's Gospel was a product of the primitive Jesus movement. It gives us a unique view of the early years of the movement, prior to the time when the synoptic legends began to dominate its expression.

Those who would resist this conclusion face a difficult problem: Why would the church of the 90s accept as authoritative a document, written several generations after the fact, which (a) contained numerous historical and doctrinal conflicts with the established synoptic tradition, (b) portrayed Jesus as one with little moral vision, (c) ignored the tradition that Jesus taught in parables, (d) highlighted an unattractive squabble between two prominent apostles of Jesus, and (e) introduced the notion that John the Baptist was a competitor of Jesus who some thought was the authentic Messiah after all?

The answer is self-evident: it is highly improbable that the church at the end of the first century would have accepted such a document. Therefore, we must default to a solution which brings all of the evidence into harmony. The reason the Gospel of John survived, and was included in the New Testament, is that it was recognized in the first century church as the original gospel of Jesus.

❖   *6*   ❖

The Second Gospel

The recognition of the Gospel of John as the first narrative gospel has important consequences for the quest for the historical Jesus. This gospel, which is so frequently dismissed as historically irrelevant, becomes a vital source of information about the beliefs of the primitive Jesus movement in the early part of the century. Furthermore, the priority of John has momentous implications for our interpretation of the synoptic gospels. In the belief that Mark and Q are the earliest traditions, scholars have relied heavily upon the synoptics for reconstruction of Jesus' life and message. We may now consider the possibility that they were later works, written with the awareness of, and in reaction to, the Gospel of John. The "tyranny of the synoptic Jesus" as it has often been called, comes to an end.

The next important link in the chain is to determine whether the author of Mark was aware of John, and whether the Gospel of Mark was written in response to John. We know that the author of John was motivated to discredit the apostle Peter. His gospel was produced in the midst of an ideological struggle with Peter to define the meaning of Jesus' ministry. It is also clear that the synoptic tradition holds Peter in a positive light, affirming him as the leading apostle. The data suggest, then, that the Johannine and synoptic traditions may be seen in broad terms as two opposing voices in a common dialogue.

Furthermore, church tradition holds that the author of Mark was a follower of Peter, and that the Gospel of Mark was written to document the teachings of Peter. Bishop Eusebius, a fourth century church historian and theologian, had this to say regarding Mark and his relationship with Peter:

So brightly shone the light of true religion on the minds of Peter's hearers that, not satisfied with a single hearing or with the oral teaching of the divine message, they resorted to appeals of every kind to induce Mark (whose Gospel we have), as he was a follower of Peter, to leave them in writing a summary of the instruction they had received by word of mouth, nor did they let him go till they had persuaded him, and thus became responsible for the writing of what is known as the Gospel according to Mark.[1]

If there were no further evidence, we could not reasonably determine whether the reference in Eusebius is accurate. However, the finding in Chapter Three that John 21 was constructed from the missing ending of Mark adds independent corroborating evidence. Once the Gospel of Mark is restored with this ending, it becomes apparent that the author's intent was to show Jesus and Peter reconciled after the denials, and to thereby affirm Peter's leadership status in the movement. This lends credence to the assessment of Eusebius.

Therefore, the evidence suggests an obvious scenario. The Gospel of John's attack on Peter would most likely have been perceived as scandalous and shameful by the Petrine community, and we may expect that they would have responded to it in some manner. If Mark was the writer commissioned to document the teachings of Peter, it is reasonable to suspect that part of his commission would have been to answer the charges in the Gospel of John.

With this as background, we may now turn to the Gospel of Mark to seek textual evidence that the gospel was indeed written as an ideological response to John. This chapter will show that the evidence is substantial. It will show that the Gospel of Mark was written as a firm corrective, if not a full rebuttal of the teachings of John.

The Triple Failure of the Disciples

We found in Chapter Two that the Gospel of John casts the betrayal theme in sets of three. There are three denials of Peter, three bracketed sequences which foreshadow this event, three references to Judas' father Simon, and three references to believers who fail to

---

[1] Eusebius, *History of the Church*, Book II, 2.15, Penguin Books, 1965, p. 49

separate themselves from the synagogues. The author developed this literary device as a method for framing the condemnation of Peter within the context of a betrayal of the movement.

The first significant sign that Mark is a deliberate response to John is that the author of Mark uses precisely this same literary technique to answer the Johannine charges. He has constructed his response in sets of three as well. There are three separate predictions by Jesus that he will suffer at the hands of the authorities, be killed, and rise after the third day. These form the backbone of Mark's response to John. The first passage which begins with the passion prediction follows. Note that the text is actually continuous, but it has been spaced into three segments to highlight three distinct elements which have been carefully placed in sequence:

> And he began to teach them that the Son of man must suffer many things, and be rejected by the elders and chief priest and the scribes, and be killed, and after three days rise again. And this he said plainly.
>
> And Peter took him, and began to rebuke him. But turning and seeing his disciples, he rebuked Peter, and said, "Get behind me, Satan! For you are not on the side of God, but of men."
>
> And he called to him the multitude with his disciples, and said to them, "If any man would come after me, let him deny himself, take up his cross, and follow me." (Mark 8:31-34)

The passage opens with Jesus' reflection upon his impending death. Following this, Peter fails to comprehend his meaning, and Jesus rebukes him sharply. This passage has contributed to the notion held by some scholars that the Gospel of Mark may have had an anti-Petrine orientation. Yet as we will see, this interpretation cannot stand within the larger context of the gospel. Clearly the author is not afraid to show that Peter did not understand the larger issue at hand. However, it is not just Peter who fails in Mark, but James and John as well. Note in this passage that Peter's failure to understand is followed immediately by a teaching that self-denial is the essence of Jesus' message. The passage opens with Jesus' personal self-denial, and closes with a teaching that self-denial is also required of the disciples.

The Second Bracketed Sequence

The second passage in Mark which begins with the prediction of the passion is this:

> For he was teaching his disciples, saying to them, "The Son of man will be delivered into the hands of men, and they will kill him; and when he is killed, after three days he will rise."

> But they did not understand the saying, and they were afraid to ask him. And they came to Caper'na-um; and when he was in the house he asked them, "What were you discussing on the way?" But they were silent; for on the way they had discussed with one another who was the greatest.

> And he sat down and called the twelve; and he said to them, "If anyone would be first, he must be last of all and servant of all." (Mark 9:31-35)

In this second passage, we find the identical sequence of events as in the first. First, Jesus predicts his passion; second, the disciples fail to understand; third, Jesus teaches that self-denial is the essence of the message. Though there are no disciples mentioned here, the passage has great meaning as a response to the Gospel of John. For John is preoccupied with demonstrating that the Beloved Disciple is the greatest of the disciples, and that Peter is not to be accepted as a worthy leader of the movement. First century readers who were aware of this debate would likely have seen in this passage an indictment of John by the author of Mark.

The Third Bracketed Sequence

The third and final passage, as one might assume, reflects the same structural form as the first two. However, it is more extensive and more candid in its indictment of James and John, the sons of Zebedee, for seeking their own great reward:

> "Behold, we are going up to Jerusalem; and the Son of man will be delivered to the chief priests and the scribes, and they will condemn him to death, and deliver him to the Gentiles; and they will mock him, and spit upon him, and scourge him, and kill him; and after three days he will rise."

And James and John, the sons of Zeb'edee, came forward and said to him, "Teacher, we want you to do for us whatever we ask of you." And he said to them, "What do you want me to do for you?" And they said to him, "Grant that we may sit, one at your right hand, and one at your left, in your glory." But Jesus said to them, "You do not know what you are asking. Are you able to drink the cup that I drink, or to be baptized with the baptism with which I am baptized?" And they said to him, "We are able." And Jesus said to them, "The cup that I drink you will drink, and with the baptism with which I am baptized, you will be baptized; but to sit at my right hand or my left is not mine to grant, but it is for those for whom it has been prepared." And when the ten heard it, they became indignant at James and John.

And Jesus called them to him and said to them, "You know that those who are supposed to rule over the Gentiles lord it over them, and their great men exercise authority over them. But it shall not be so among you; but whoever would be great among you must be your servant, and whoever would be first among you must be slave of all. For the Son of man also came not to be served but to serve, and to give his life as a ransom for many." (Mark 10:33-45)

In this passage, all three segments have been expanded. The prediction of the passion contains more detail than the previous two; the treatment of James and John is extensive; and finally, the reflection upon self-denial is more fully developed. However, the sequential construction of this passage as a third episode in the series is unmistakable. Each passage opens with Jesus' personal sacrifice, and closes with the required sacrifice of the disciples. Between these brackets in each is a specific judgment of the disciples for not comprehending that self-denial is the essence of the gospel message.

It now becomes more apparent why the author was willing to show Peter as uncomprehending. Though he was severely rebuked, his failure was one of understanding. In the second two episodes, not only do the disciples fail to comprehend, but they seek their own glory and status as well. Within the context of the Johannine community's implicit affirmation of "the disciple whom Jesus loved" as the greatest of the disciples, the implied indictment of Johannine doctrine would have been clear.

Three Bracketed Sequences as Foreshadowing

Just as there are three bracketed sequences in John which are used to foreshadow Peter's three denials, Mark uses the three episodes we have just seen to foreshadow a triple failure of all three disciples-- Peter, James, and John:

> And they went to a place which was called Gethsem'ane; and he said to his disciples, "Sit here, while I pray." And he took with him Peter and James and John, and began to be greatly distressed and troubled. And he said to them, "My soul is very sorrowful, even unto death; remain here, and watch." And going a little farther, he fell on the ground and prayed that, if it were possible, the hour might pass from him. And he said, "Abba, Father, all things are possible to thee; remove this cup from me; yet not what I will, but what thou wilt." And he came and found them sleeping, and he said to Peter, "Simon, are you asleep? Could you not watch one hour? Watch and pray that you may not enter into temptation; the spirit indeed is willing, but the flesh is weak." And again he went away and prayed, saying the same words. And again he came and found them sleeping, for their eyes were very heavy; and they did not know what to answer him. And he came the third time, and said to them, "Are you still sleeping and taking your rest? It is enough; the hour has come; the Son of man is betrayed into the hands of sinners. Rise, let us be going; see, my betrayer is at hand." (Mark 14:32-42)

In this passage, all three disciples fail to stand by Jesus in his time of need. They sleep while he prays. The fact that they are caught sleeping three times is a key to the passage. Three times they are unable to remain awake with Jesus, and he must face his destiny alone. It is also important to note that Jesus specifically took Peter, James, and John aside for support during this time, and it is all three of them who could not stay awake. Yet the author is careful to construct the failure as stemming from human frailty rather than willful abandonment. *The spirit is willing but the flesh is weak.* For the author of Mark, all three disciples failed Jesus out of their human limitations.

Therefore, the author of Mark has appropriated John's technique of bracketing as well as his repetition of sets of three to construct his response to the denial/betrayal issue. Within Mark's response, Peter indeed fails to comprehend, but the other two disciples, in addition to misunderstanding, are shown to seek their own glory, which by most standards would constitute the greater sin.

Peter's Denials in Mark

It is against this background in Mark that the triple denial of Peter must be interpreted. Mark was careful to note that *all* the disciples committed to stand by Jesus (14:31), and *all* disciples fled and scattered (14:50). Mark also indicated that Peter was grieved when he recognized what he had done in denying Jesus (14:72). Finally, Mark foreshadowed the reconciliation between Jesus and Peter (16:7).

Peter's three denials are, therefore, to be interpreted as related to forgivable human limitations, just as the disciples unintentionally fell asleep three times. Just as Jesus is compassionate in his understanding the spirit is willing but the flesh is weak, so Jesus will be compassionate in his forgiveness of Peter. Therefore, according to Mark, Peter's denials do not reveal a unique character flaw for which he should be condemned, as the Gospel of John charges.

The Shepherd Metaphor in Mark

The literary affinity between Mark 14:27-30 and John 21:15-17 has been reviewed in Chapter Three, however with the foregoing as background, it is worth another look:

> And Jesus said to them, "You will all fall away; for it is written, 'I will strike the shepherd, and the sheep will be scattered.' But after I am raised up, I will go before you to Galilee." Peter said to him, "Even though they all fall away, I will not." And Jesus said to him, "Truly, I say to you, this very night, before the cock crows twice, you will deny me three times." But he said vehemently, "If I must die with you, I will not deny you." And they all said the same. (Mark 14:27-31)

The shepherd metaphor is a dominant Johannine literary device which is developed in John 10, where Jesus is identified as the good shepherd, and where it is shown that the hireling (most likely Peter) cannot be trusted to take care of the flock in the manner of the shepherd. Conversely, the shepherd motif is not Markan, though it appears this one time in the passage above.

The author's use of it within the context of the failure of the disciples and the triple denial of Peter is not accidental. Mark has intentionally inserted this Johannine motif to foreshadow the reconciliation scene in which Jesus instructs Peter to feed the sheep. Though this scene now exists in John 21:15-17, with the evidence that Mark responded to John's betrayal theme by appropriating its literary devices of bracketing and formatting the theme in three's, the fact that he also used John's shepherd metaphor strengthens the conclusion that Mark was the original architect of John 21.

It is now clear that Mark intended to fulfill the anticipated reconciliation between Jesus and Peter not only by using John's literary device of threes, but through the use of his shepherd metaphor as well. Thus the very literary devices used by John to undermine the credibility of Peter were used by Mark to turn the tables on John, and to construct a formidable rebuttal of Johannine rhetoric.

Mark's Negative Portrait of James and John

Mark presents Peter, James, and John as constituting an inner circle of those closest to Jesus. These three are the only disciples allowed to witness the raising of Jairus' daughter (5:37) and the transfiguration on the mountain (9:2). They are the ones Jesus separates from the larger group and confides in on the night of his arrest (14:33). They, with Andrew, are the first disciples to be called by Jesus (1:16-20), and they appear as the first three on the list of the twelve disciples (3:14-19). So the author of Mark has isolated Peter, James, and John as the key figures in the story.

However, as prominent as they are, John only speaks twice in the gospel, and his brother James only once. In the previous instance where James and John appear together, they are castigated by the author, not for their lack of comprehension of Jesus' purpose, but for their preoccupation with advancing their own interests. In the following passage, it is John alone who speaks. Once again the text is continuous, but has been spaced to highlight the bracketing:

> And he took a child, and put him in the midst of them; and taking him in his arms, he said to them, "Whoever receives one such child in my name receives me; and whoever receives me, receives not me but him who sent me."
>
> John said to him, "Teacher, we saw a man casting out demons in your name, and we forbade him, because he was not following us." But Jesus said, "Do not forbid him; for no one who does a mighty work in my name will be able soon to speak evil of me. For he that is not against us is for us. For truly, I say to you, whoever gives you a cup of water to drink because you bear the name of Christ, will be no means lose his reward.
>
> "Whoever causes one of these little ones who believe in me to sin, it would be better for him if a great millstone were hung around his neck and he were thrown into the sea." (Mark 9:36-42)

Several elements are important in this passage. First, John is portrayed as one who would exclude and denounce persons who believe differently from himself. In this instance the issue is exorcism. This is of greater consequence that it might appear. Exorcism is a practice which is notably absent from the Gospel of John, and presumably not part of the beliefs of the Johannine community. That John, the son of Zebedee, is represented as one who would forbid the exorcist lends support to the church's tradition that the Gospel of John is, in fact, the gospel of this disciple.

Second, Jesus' response indicates that there are others included in the movement who do not believe precisely as John does. There is a need to be open-minded regarding how people express their faith, "for he that is not against us is for us." This recalls the criticism that the Gospel of John levied against those believers who have chosen to retain their association with the synagogues. Given this conflict as background, it is apparent that the author of Mark constructed this passage to condemn the divisiveness and exclusiveness which are characteristic of Johannine doctrine.

A third key element in this passage is that the author has bracketed the dialogue between Jesus and John with reflections on the need to receive new believers as children, and to nurture them at their own level. Exclusive and rigorous doctrine is not appropriate for the movement, according to Mark. The bracketing serves to underscore this theme which is already present in the dialogue itself.

A final element in this passage is that the phrase "whoever receives me, *receives not me but him who sent me*" appears to be a correction of a statement in John:

> Truly, truly, I say to you, he who receives any one whom I send receives me; and he who receives me receives him who sent me. (John 13:20)

The corrected statement in Mark pointedly underscores the Markan position that Jesus is not to be confused with the one who sent him. This reflects the doctrinal argument of the nature of Jesus which existed between the Johannine and Markan communities. It is noteworthy that it appears within the context of this critique of the disciple John.

Who was the Beloved Disciple?

Church tradition holds that the disciple whom Jesus loved was John, the son of Zebedee. However, there is no direct indication of this in the Fourth Gospel, nor is there any independent confirmation of the tradition. Thus scholars have usually set aside the tradition as indeterminate, and held that the identity of the Beloved Disciple cannot be known. Scholars such as Rudolf Bultmann have even suggested that the Beloved Disciple was not an historical figure, but rather a literary symbol of the entire fellowship of believers.

The conflict in church politics between Peter and this disciple precludes such an interpretation. However, the question is whether we have uncovered enough new evidence in the course of this analysis to identify the Beloved Disciple. The facts and observations which bear upon this are these:

1. Peter and the Beloved Disciple were two prominent leaders of the primitive church in competition with one another.

2. The Gospel of John indicates that the Beloved Disciple was one of the twelve by showing him present at the Last Supper.

3. The Beloved Disciple had enough latent authority to challenge the leadership of Peter. This independently suggests that he must have been one of the twelve, since it would seem unlikely that anyone further removed from Jesus would have been able to contest Peter's authority.

4. The Gospel of John indicates that Peter and the Beloved Disciple were the two prominent disciples among the twelve; it never mentions James and John, the sons of Zebedee.

5. The Gospel of Mark indicates that Peter, James, and John were the three prominent disciples among the twelve; it never mentions the Beloved Disciple.

6. The Gospel of John was composed, in part, to attack Peter.

7. The Gospel of Mark was composed to answer the attack on Peter; in so doing, it castigates James and John on issues which appear related to the dispute with the Johannine community.

8. The gospels of John and Mark were both edited to remove some of their adversarial tone. This indicates that the communities of Peter and the Beloved Disciple reconciled, and that the Petrine community had gained ascendancy.

9. In the Acts of the Apostles, Peter and John appear together numerous times; Peter is always named first, and is generally the spokesperson for the two of them. Thus, Acts provides independent evidence that these two disciples joined forces and were both prominent as leadership figures in the early church.

These observations collectively point to the conclusion that the Beloved Disciple was indeed John, the son of Zebedee. Even if there were no church tradition to this effect, there is adequate textual evidence to make this historical inference. So the findings in this study serve to confirm the credibility of the church's tradition.

Summary

The author of Mark constructed a response to the Gospel of John using the same literary devices that appear in the Gospel of John. John uses three bracketed sequences to foreshadow the failure of Peter. Mark uses three bracketed sequences to foreshadow the failure of Peter, James, and John collectively. The shepherd metaphor appears in Mark only within the context of the prediction of the disciples scattering and Peter denying Jesus. This is independent evidence that the author of Mark methodically lifted literary elements from John in order to turn the tables on John. The Gospel of John condemns Peter as a betrayer of the movement. The Gospel of Mark, in response, condemns James and John for seeking their own glory, and John alone for promoting divisive doctrine.

These findings are in harmony with church tradition that the Gospel of John contains the teachings of the disciple John, the son of Zebedee, and that the Gospel of Mark was composed by a follower of Peter. The evidence, then, is compelling that the author of Mark composed his gospel as an ideological response to the Gospel of John.

The Doctrinal Conflict

In some ways it is remarkable that the Gospels of John and Mark exist side by side in the same New Testament, for as religious documents they are opposed to one another on a wide range of topics. Each gospel individually would be sufficient as the foundation of a new religion, but Johannine "Christianity" and Markan "Christianity," had they evolved separately, would have had little to do with one another. Indeed the only significant element they would have had in common is an origin in a person known as Jesus of Nazareth. Yet even their perceptions of who Jesus was and what he taught are so divergent that it is hard to imagine the Johannine Jesus and the Markan Jesus as having been the same person.

John and Mark are in direct contradiction with each other on a number of issues, including the nature of Jesus, the personal demeanor of Jesus, and the key teachings of Jesus. Foremost among the doctrinal conflicts is their characterization of the nature of Jesus. John presents him as a preexistent eternal being who came down from heaven on a mission from the Father, and who fulfilled his mission and returned to his place in heaven. While he was here he suffered no temptation, and was in control of his destiny. He approached the trial and crucifixion in a serene manner, rhetorically asking Peter, "Shall I not drink the cup which the Father has given me?" (John 18:11). There is no indication that Jesus had any sense of mental or physical anguish even during this ordeal.

Mark, on the other hand, reveals a human dimension of Jesus. The Markan Jesus was subject to all the pain, doubt, fear, and temptation than any human being struggles with in life. He is baptized at the beginning of his ministry, and he is tempted by Satan and ministered to by angels. He approaches the trial and crucifixion with fear and trepidation, praying if it be possible that the "cup" be removed from him (Mark 14:35-36). On the cross, Jesus dies in pain and a sense of abandonment, crying, "My God, my God, why hast thou forsaken me?" (Mark 15:34).

Thus the understanding of Jesus' nature is radically different between John and Mark. In John, he appears to be the embodiment of a heavenly being. In Mark, he is a human being who, in spite of having been granted mysterious heavenly power, does not lose his essential human nature.

The Johannine "I Am's" and Signs vs. the Markan Messianic Secret

As John and Mark are opposed on the nature of Jesus, they also conflict on the issue of Jesus' self-proclamation. One of the most prominent features in John is Jesus' repeated assertions that he is the one who came from heaven, who is sent by God, and through whom eternal life is to be gained. The Johannine Jesus makes this clear through numerous proclamations about himself:

> The woman said to him, "I know that Messiah is coming (he who is called Christ); when he comes, he will show us all things." Jesus said to her, "I who speak to you am he." (John 4:25-26)

"Truly, truly, I say to you, he who hears my word and believes in him who sent me, has eternal life; he does not come into judgment, but has passed from death to life." (John 5:24)

If you believed Moses, you would believe me, for he wrote of me. (John 5:46)

"I am the bread of life; he who comes to me shall not hunger, and he who believes in me shall never thirst." (John 6:35)

"I am the living bread which came down from heaven" (John 6:51)

"I am the light of the world; he who follows me will not walk in darkness." (John 8:12b)

"I am the good shepherd; I know my own, and my own know me, as the Father knows me and I know the father." (John 10:14-15a)

"I am the resurrection and the life; he who believes in me, though he die, yet shall he live." (John 11:25b)

"I am the true vine, and my Father is the vinedresser." (John 15:1)

Jesus as Miracle Worker

In the Gospel of John there is a companion theme to Jesus' proclamation as the one sent from God. Jesus is portrayed as a miracle worker who produced his miracles as "signs" of his messianic status. When Jesus turned the water into wine, the author says it was the "first of his signs . . . and manifested his glory" (John 2:11). When Jesus was in Jerusalem for the first of three Passovers, the author indicates "many believed in his name when they saw the signs which he did" (John 2:23). One argument which the author used to discredit the notion that John the Baptist was the Messiah was that he "did no sign" (John 10:41). The Johannine Jesus is said to have been glad that he was not present when Lazarus died (John 11:15), for he now had an opportunity to produce a miracle so that they might believe (John 11:40-42).

In John, those who saw Jesus' miracles, and believed in him accordingly, were destined for eternal life. For the author, the bold proclamations of Jesus about who he was, and the signs or miracles which he did to demonstrate his power, went hand-in-hand with the key elements of the gospel message. Indeed, the final sentence of the gospel says "Jesus did many other signs in the presence of the disciples which are not written in this book; but these are written that you may believe that Jesus is the Christ . . " (20:30-31)

Mark objects strenuously to this characterization of Jesus. In Chapter Three the prominent Markan theme known as the "Messianic Secret" was introduced. Though there are many elements in the gospel which are said to contribute to the theme of the Messianic Secret, the most notable are those which show that Jesus would not allow himself to be announced as the Messiah or the Son of God, nor would he allow many of his miracles to be publicized. The demons are commanded to be silent when they indicate they know who Jesus is (Mark 1:23-26). The disciples are told to keep the raising of Jairus' daughter a secret (5:41-43a). They are also told to remain quiet about Peter's recognition of him as the Christ (8:27b-30), and to keep secret the transfiguration as well (Mark 9:9-10a).

The *Messianic Secret* in Mark has puzzled researchers for centuries. What could account for the author's repeated insistence that Jesus did not proclaim his Messiahship? Why did the author depict Jesus as one who did not want his miracles publicized? From the context of Mark itself, there is no clue as to why the author would have been so sensitive to these issues.

However, once we consider that Mark was written as a response to John, it becomes apparent that the Messianic Secret has the effect of negating the characterization of Jesus in John as one who performed miracles to demonstrate his power and divine nature. In so doing, Mark portrays an entirely different Jesus from the one we find in John. The Markan Jesus does not draw attention to his Messianic status, but instead to the new kingdom of God. He does not manifest the self-focused personality traits which are characteristic of the Johannine Jesus. He wants people to follow him because of the content of his message, not because they have become mesmerized with his power or his celebrity.

The two gospels are in direct conflict on Jesus' use of signs to reveal his status. In response to the Johannine claims, Mark writes this story:

> The Pharisees came and began to argue with him, seeking from him a sign from heaven, to test him. And he sighed deeply in his spirit, and said, "Why does this generation seek a sign? Truly, I say to you, no sign shall be given to this generation." (Mark 8:11-12)

Thus Mark openly opposes John's portrayal of Jesus as one who used miracles to amaze the public in order to win a following. There are numerous miracles recorded in Mark, but they are usually performed to meet the legitimate needs of the people involved. The Feeding of the Five Thousand occurs because the people are hungry, and it is done in a manner which prevents the crowd from realizing what Jesus has done (Mark 6:35-44). Jairus' daughter is raised in the privacy of her home, with onlookers banned from the scene (Mark 5:35-43). A blind man is healed, and Jesus instructs him to go home, and not to enter the village where he might create a stir (Mark 8:22-26).

So the Gospel of Mark portrays Jesus as one who responds to the needs of the people around him, but who does not take personal advantage of his healings by highlighting his ability to do them. Therefore, since the Messianic Secret in Mark directly negates the portrait of Jesus found in John, it is not difficult to conclude that this was the author's intent.

Servanthood

Another issue over which John and Mark lock horns is Jesus' teaching on servanthood. The difference between the self-focused Jesus of the Fourth Gospel and the outwardly-focused Jesus of Mark is captured in their respective sayings of Jesus on the topic of servanthood:

> If any one serves me, he must follow me; and where I am, there shall my servant be also; if any one serves me, the Father will honor him. (John 12:26)

> Whoever would be great among you must be your servant, and whoever would be first among you must be slave of all. For the Son of man also came not to be served, but to serve, and to give his life as a ransom for many. (Mark 10:43b-45)

In this quote from John, the focal point is the need for the believer to serve Jesus; Jesus expects to be served by his followers, and the reward will be that the Father will honor such servanthood. However, in Mark we find Jesus' orientation to be one of a role model who intends to serve, and thereby encourage like behavior on the part of those who follow him.

Markan Negations of Johannine Doctrine

We have seen several instances in which a theme in John is negated by Mark. John says Jesus boldly proclaimed his Messiahship; Mark says he did not. John says he performed signs to show his power; Mark says he did not. John quotes Jesus as saying, "If anyone serves me, the Father will honor him." Mark responds with the quotation, "I came *not to be served* but to serve." Again, John quotes Jesus, "He who receives me receives him who sent me." The Markan Jesus responds, "He who receives me, receives *not me but* him who sent me."

There is, then, a pattern of rhetorical rebuttal in Mark. To John's thesis, we find Mark's antithesis. Logically antithesis always follows thesis. Therefore, the direction of argument between John and Mark is independent evidence that Mark was the second gospel, and was written as a rebuttal of John.

The Key to Eternal Life

Another significant ideological conflict between John and Mark is their teachings on what must be done to gain eternal life. The differences can be summarized in one word each; for John the key is *belief,* and for Mark it is *action*. Prominent throughout John's gospel is the message that belief in Jesus as the Christ is all that is necessary to gain eternal life:

For God so loved the world that he gave his only Son, that whoever believes in him should not perish but have eternal life (John 3:16)

He who believes in him is not condemned; he who does not believe is condemned already, because he has not believed . . . (3:18)

He who believes in the Son has eternal life; he who does not obey the Son shall not see life, but the wrath of God rests upon him (3:36)

Then they said to him, "What must we be do, to be doing the works of God?" Jesus answered them, "This is the work of God, that you believe in him whom he has sent." (6:28-29)

. . . whoever lives and believes in me shall never die. (11:26a)

. . . for the Father himself loves you, because you have loved me and believed that I came from the Father. (16:27)

. . . but these things are written that you may believe that Jesus is the Christ, the Son of God, and that believing you may have life in his name. (20:31)

Thus the Johannine doctrine is clear: a simple belief that "Jesus is the Christ, the Son of God," is both necessary and sufficient to win eternal life. Those who do not believe are condemned.

The Gospel of Mark opposes this simple formula. An unidentified man asks Jesus "what must I do to inherit eternal life?" Jesus responds, "go, sell what you have, and give to the poor, and you will have treasure in heaven; and come, follow me" (Mark 10:17-21). The need for costly self-denial and sacrifice appears again as a prerequisite for eternal life. The message of Mark is clear: "If any man would come after me, let him deny himself and take up his cross and follow me." (Mark 8:34)

In Chapter Three it was pointed out that the original grand frame of Mark was the opening and closing command to Peter, "follow me!" The theme that the disciples were to be made "fishers of men" implies that discipleship would mandate active participation in the furtherance of the kingdom of God. So Mark teaches that action and commitment are essential to a life of discipleship. Belief is a mere prerequisite, and certainly not sufficient to gain eternal life, for even the demons believe that Jesus is the Son of God (Mark 3:11; James 2:19). So for the author of Mark, many can recognize the greatness of Jesus; however, eternal life will be gained only by those who turn their belief into commitment and action. The original grand bracket of Mark, *Follow Me!*, indicated that the entire gospel of Jesus must be interpreted in terms of a call to action.

In short, the issues which form the ideological conflict between John and Mark are the core issues of Christianity. Who was Jesus? What did he teach? What must the follower do to inherit eternal life? John and Mark contain divergent answers to these questions. Independently, these two gospels could have formed the basis of two different religions. To be sure, there is enough disparity of doctrine between them to make the struggle for leadership between Peter and the Beloved Disciple of momentous import. These were not simply two egocentric individuals fighting for the top seat. Rather, they each had strong convictions and radically different visions by which they intended to define the legacy of Jesus.

A Comparison of Common Stories

The finding that Mark was written as a corrective response to John prompts the question whether particular stories common to both gospels appear to have been edited or altered by the author of Mark. In essence, does Mark's version appear to be the more evolved tradition when the two are compared? Indeed, this seems to be the case.

We have already seen a parallel comparison of the Anointing at Bethany (page 171). In this account, the Johannine Jesus appears aloof and abrupt; Mary appears to be someone of low status whose worshipful act is accepted without further comment by Jesus. The story bears an unsettling tenor that he expects to be honored in this manner, and thus it is not worthy of a gracious response. Further, in the midst of John's account, the author elects to add a parenthetic note about the unsavory character of Judas Iscariot. The author apparently thinks it is more important to point out Judas' propensity to steal the money than to retain the story's focus on the woman's act.

John's account of the Anointing at Bethany is one of the least appealing characterizations of Jesus in the gospels. Though commentators often attempt to interpret this episode in a theological light rather than a moral one, the passage in its literal form is dehumanizing to the woman who has made this sacrificial gesture of worship and subservience. In Mark's version of the same story, Jesus defends, reaffirms, and praises the woman, and grants her the honor of being remembered throughout the world for her act of generosity and kindness. The story retains the focus upon the woman's sacrificial act from beginning to end; it drops the reference to Judas all together. Jesus appears to be concerned with the needs of the woman, and graciously acknowledges the value of her gift.

The portrait of Jesus in Mark's version is compatible with the overall Markan depiction of Jesus as magnanimous and sensitive to the needs of the people around him. Note that the story as it appears in John could not have been duplicated in Mark without seriously disturbing Mark's general portrait of Jesus. In reading John's version, the author of Mark would have faced the decision either to delete the story altogether, or rewrite it to accommodate the Markan view of Jesus.

Within the story of the Anointing at Bethany are two details which are common to both, but which do not appear in Matthew and Luke. The details that the ointment was worth *300 denarii* and that it was an extract of *pure nard* are unique to John and Mark. So even though their versions of the story are different in their characterization of Jesus, the common details imply a direct literary dependence. The most straightforward inference is that the author of Mark used the text of John as a source, and rewrote the tradition to fit his portrait of Jesus. So the apparent rewrite of the Anointing at Bethany supports the theory that Mark was written to correct ideological deficiencies in John.

The Feeding of the Five Thousand

Another example of apparent Markan rewriting appears in the Feeding of the Five Thousand (Fig. 6.1) Here, as in the previous story, it appears as though Mark has revised John's account to produce a portrait of Jesus more compatible with Markan doctrine. In John's

Figure 6.1: The Feeding of the Five Thousand

John 6:1-15	Mark 6:32-44

1 After this Jesus went to the other side of the Sea of Galilee, which is the Sea of Tiberias.
2 And a multitude followed him, because they saw the signs which he did on those who were diseased.
3 Jesus went up on the mountain, and there sat down with his disciples. 4 Now the Passover, the feast of the Jews, was at hand. 5 Lifting up his eyes, then, and seeing that a multitude was coming to him, Jesus said to Philip, "How are we to buy bread, so that these people may eat?" 6 This he said to test him, for he himself knew what he would do.

7 Philip answered him, "Two hundred denarii would not buy enough for each of them to get a little." 8 One of his disciples, Andrew, Simon Peter's brother, said to him, 9 "There is a lad here who has five barley loaves and two fish; but what are they among so many?" 10 Jesus said, "Make the people sit down." Now there was much grass in the place; so the men sat down, in number about five thousand.
11 Jesus then took the loaves, and when he had given thanks, he distributed them to those who were seated; so also the fish, as much as they wanted. 12 And when they had eaten their fill, he told his disciples "Gather up the fragments left over, that nothing may be lost." 13 So they gathered them up and filled twelve baskets with fragments from the five barley loaves, left by those who had eaten. 14 When the people saw the sign which he had done, they said, "This is indeed the prophet who is to come into the world!" 15 Perceiving they were about to come and take him by force to make him king, Jesus withdrew again to the mountain by himself.

32 And they went away in the boat to a lonely place by themselves.

33 Now many saw them going and knew them, and they ran there on foot from all the towns, and got there ahead of them. 34 As he went ashore he saw a great throng, and he had compassion on them, because they were like sheep without a shepherd; and he began to teach them many things. 35 And when it grew late, his disciples came to him and said, "This is a lonely place and the hour is now late; 36 send them away, to go into the country and villages round about and buy themselves something to eat." 37 But he answered them, "You give them something to eat." And they said to him, "Shall we go and buy two hundred denarii worth of bread, and give it to them to eat?" 38 And he said to them, "How many loaves have you? Go and see." And when they found out, they said, "Five, and two fish."

39 Then he commanded them all to sit down by companies upon the green grass. 40 So they sat down in groups, by hundreds and by fifties. 41 And taking the five loaves and the two fish, he looked up to heaven, and blessed, and broke the loaves, and gave them to the disciples to set before the people; and he divided the two fish among them all. 42 And they all ate and were satisfied. 43 And they took up twelve baskets full of broken pieces and of the fish. 44 And those who ate the loaves were five thousand men.

report, Jesus has planned the event to produce a sign of his Messiahship. This is clear from the fact that he has allowed the multitude to follow him, he sits down and waits for them to come, he "tests" Philip, knowing what he is going to do, and finally, he produces the miracle to the amazement and praise of the people (v.14). So as John records it, Jesus has produced this miracle for the purpose of revealing his divine nature. Such a story could not be included in Mark's gospel without revision, as it violates the Markan view of how Jesus conducted himself.

Mark's version shows the throng outrunning Jesus to the place he is to arrive by boat. Jesus has compassion for them and sees this as an opportunity to teach them many things (v. 34). As a natural course of events, the hour grows late and the people need to be fed. Jesus empowers his disciples to feed the multitude (v. 37, 41), rather than doing it directly himself as in John. Finally, the crowd is fed and satisfied, but there is no indication that the crowd realizes that a miracle has occurred; they do not try to take him by force to make him king, as in John. Jesus, within the context of Mark's version, has taught the people many things, and has empowered his disciples to meet their needs, while keeping his power to produce a miracle of this type invisible to the crowd.

At first, it may seem strange to suggest that this miracle was not noticed by the crowd, as the interpretation of the event is informed by John's version that the multitude reacted with amazement. Should there be any doubt that Mark's Jesus intended this miracle to be invisible to the people, we may refer to a similar but separate event also recorded in Mark where 4,000 are fed, with the same non-existent reaction (8:1-10). Immediately following this miracle, the Pharisees approach Jesus "seeking from him a sign from heaven, to test him." Jesus responds by saying, "Truly, I say to you, no sign shall be given this generation." (8:11-12). In John, the miracle is calculated to bring glory to Jesus. Mark has rewritten the story to show that Jesus quietly meets the needs of the multitude so that he can continue to teach.

The Cleansing of the Temple

The episode in which Jesus drives the moneychangers from the temple (Figure 6.2) contains similar evidence that Mark revised John. Both gospels tell the story of Jesus' attack on those who engaged in the trade of selling sacrificial animals in the temple and providing money changing services for visitors from foreign jurisdictions. However, in John's account, Jesus uses a whip to beat these persons as he drives them from the temple. In Mark, this detail has been omitted.

Furthermore, for the author of John, this episode is another vehicle for proclaiming the identity of Jesus. His authority to drive the moneychangers out of the temple derives from the fact that since this is *his* Father's house, he is able to forbid it on his own authority (v. 16). The disciples understand his zeal as a sign that he is the expected Messiah (v. 17). The use of the temple as a house of trade is wrong, and this Jesus objects to. However, the point of the story is to make a statement about the nature of Jesus, not about the morality of trade in the temple. The question posed by the Jews[2] serves to underscore that Jesus cleansed the temple in order to make a statement about himself.

In Mark, the Cleansing of the Temple is ostensibly motivated by Jesus' righteous indignation at the profaning of the sacred temple by business practices conducted to support it; it is to be a house of prayer rather than a place of business. There is no reflection on the nature of Jesus in Mark's version. Jesus has not cleansed the temple to draw attention to his status as the Son of God. His purpose is to teach that the profaning of the temple is morally wrong. His adversaries react to him in fear, as they are concerned with the apparent moral authority of his teaching.

---

[2] The author uses the term "Jews" to refer to the Jewish authorities. Here, as in other references within this gospel, the term is used with a pejorative tone. Clearly Jesus, the disciples, and the author himself were Jewish, and the negative connotation was intended to apply only to the Jewish authorities with whom Jesus was in conflict. Unfortunately, these subtleties are too often lost on the average reader, and the negative references in John have served to fuel Christian anti-Semitism ever since. Alan Culpepper observed in his November, 1993 address to the Society for Biblical Literature, that in this regard, the Fourth Gospel has not served the church well as scripture.

Figure 6.2: The Cleansing of the Temple

John 2:14-17   Mark 11:15b-17

John 2:14-17	Mark 11:15b-17
14 In the temple he found those who were selling oxen and sheep and pigeons, and the moneychangers at their business. 15 And making a whip of cords, he drove them all, with the sheep and oxen, out of the temple; and he poured out the coins of the money-changers and overturned their tables. 16 And he told those who sold the pigeons, "Take these things away; you shall not make my Father's house a house of trade. 17 His disciples remembered that it was written, "Zeal for thy house will consume me." 18 The Jews then said to him, "What sign have you to show us for doing this?" 19 Jesus answered them, "Destroy this temple, and in three days I will raise it up."	15b And he entered the temple and began to drive out those who sold and those who bought in the temple, and he overturned the tables of the moneychangers and the seats of those who sold pigeons; 16 and he would not allow any one to carry anything through the temple. 17 And he taught them, and said to them, "Is it not written, 'My house shall be called a house of prayer for all the nations'? But you have made it a den of robbers. 18 And the chief priests and the scribes heard it and sought a way to destroy him; for they feared him, because all the multitude was astonished at his teaching.

In short, these three stories in John and Mark illustrate opposing perspectives on Jesus. In each case, the Johannine Jesus creates situations for the purpose of drawing attention to himself and his status as the Messiah or Son of God. Conversely, Mark's Jesus is oriented toward the needs of his audience. His purpose is to reveal the kingdom of God in his deeds and his words. He shows no desire to make an issue of his own Messiahship.

In each of these examples, the stories have been composed to support the larger ideological agenda of the gospel in which they appear. In each case, Mark's edited version retains the general struc-ture of John's story along with a host of common details, while at the same time substantially altering the portrait of Jesus.

This is a critical observation. For most researchers on the quest for the historical Jesus assume that Mark is the earliest and most historically viable narrative gospel. Yet the data here have shown that Mark's gospel did not derive from an early and independent tradition. Many of its doctrines have been introduced in response to Johannine teachings. Its treatment of the disciples is guided and informed by the political struggle between the Johannine and Petrine communities.

The Messianic Secret, and a host of other traditions, are designed to negate Johannine interpretations of the nature and teachings of Jesus. Even several of John's texts have been directly rewritten to operate in service of Markan doctrine.

Thus it cannot be sustained that Mark is an early and independent source of data on the historical Jesus. Though it may contain a variety of traditions which trace back to the historical Jesus, it is apparent that in no small measure, Mark must be interpreted as a political and ideological response to the Gospel of John.

❖   *7*   ❖

Gospel Patterns

We have seen evidence thus far that John was the first gospel, and Mark the second. If Luke and Matthew are the later gospels, is it possible to detect an evolution of Christian thought through the four gospels in this sequence? This is a key question, for if such an evolution of traditions may be discovered, it would help to isolate the earliest ideas about Jesus from those which were developed by the church as it matured.

In the prologue of this book, it was suggested that there are patterns in the gospels which fit together like pieces of a puzzle. We have begun to see a few of these patterns emerge between the gospels of John and Mark. These two gospels cannot have been developed in isolation from one another. Rather, they are two halves of the same conversation--opposing positions in a common debate.

When we date John earlier in the first century, another significant question arises which challenges established ideas. For we now appear to have three independent and early interpretations of the life of Jesus--one from John, one from Paul, and one from Mark. These three distinct historical sources have two things in common. First, they each say that the crucifixion and resurrection were the most vital events in the story of the historical Jesus. Second, none of these three sources is aware of any tradition represented by the Q gospel.

The quest for the historical Jesus has been dominated by Q research in recent years. Many are convinced that the greatest historical traditions are embedded in the sayings of Q. The discovery of Q as a "lost gospel" has led some to suppose that the historical Jesus was a formidable teacher of ethics. Yet this vision of Jesus is missing entirely from Paul and John. It only begins to emerge in Mark, which appears to be the latest of the three early traditions. Further, even Mark, with its refined moral portrait of Jesus as compared to John, shows little awareness of the great ethical and wisdom sayings which make up the Q tradition.

Therefore, the evidence from John, Paul, and Mark suggests that the primitive Jesus movement focused primarily, if not exclusively, on his crucifixion and resurrection as the defining events of his life; only later did the church begin to weave a tradition of substantial moral vision into the gospel story. Such a scenario would indicate that the Q tradition may not be as early as is often presumed. Has the heralded discovery of the Q gospel led away from, rather than toward, a discovery of the historical Jesus?

Emerging Patterns

In recognizing the Gospel of Mark as a response to John, a host of questions are raised concerning the evolution of Christian ideas during the first century. Mark contains an array of supernatural myths which do not appear in John. It also offers a notably different perspective on the character of Jesus. Since the Markan Jesus is portrayed as the humble servant of all mankind, one who was focused upon the needs of others, and who avoided drawing attention to himself, he appears to be morally advanced as compared to the Johannine Jesus, at least by twentieth century standards. Are Mark's revisions and enhancements to the gospel story part of a larger evolution of thought? May we detect the same process of development continuing in Matthew and Luke?

The answer is *yes*. There are indeed patterns of ideological growth which are pronounced in the four gospels, and which can be quantified and rendered in graphic form. This chapter will present a statistical analysis of these trends in the gospels. The results will indicate that the actual chronological sequence of the gospels was John-Mark-Luke-Matthew. Further, the results imply that each of the gospels represents a snapshot of ideological development at four distinct stages in the movement's evolution. Once they are seen in this light, a direct path of development can be charted from the most primitive expressions of the movement to the final array of beliefs which formed the foundation of institutionalized Christianity.

It must be noted at the outset that this progression is not radically divergent from generally recognized ideas of gospel chronology. Mark is widely accepted as the earliest of the three synoptic gospels. Luke and Matthew are usually thought to have been produced sometime during the decade of the 80s, but the dates cannot be pinpointed. The suggestion that Luke may have been written closer to 80 CE and Matthew closer to 90 CE fits well within the parameters of the general timeframe normally assigned to these gospels. The proposed priority of John is the only significant element of the theory which is not part of contemporary thought, yet even this has been proposed by several scholars during the twentieth century.

There are several discrete categories of thought and belief which grow incrementally in the gospel sequence John-Mark-Luke-Matthew. They are (a) the supernatural mythologies, (b) the visions of the end of the world, and (c) the moral/wisdom sayings. In this chapter, we will consider each of these categories in turn.

Growth of the Supernatural Traditions

We have already noted that John, even though it is often characterized as the most mythologized gospel, is actually the gospel which portrays the most natural earthly stage for Jesus' ministry. This phenomenon can be quantified by isolating the supernatural events in the gospels which are not miracles performed by Jesus himself. "Supernatural events" are defined here as those in which divine beings or divine powers other than Jesus have either appeared or in some other way caused a disturbance in the natural space-time continuum. They are evidence that, in the minds of the authors, supernatural beings are at work influencing the course of life on earth.

Figure 7.1 lists each of these events, and the gospel(s) in which they appear. From this chart it is clear that a great deal of synoptic supernatural mythology is missing from John. Though the Fourth

Gospel technically records three supernatural events, we noted previously that even these three are oddly natural; the voice from heaven is interpreted by the crowd as thunder, the angels do not behave like angels, and the vision of the Spirit descending as a dove is a private vision of the Baptist rather than a public event as it appears to be in Matthew and Luke. Thus there is a qualitative difference between John's natural vision of the world and the mythologized world of the synoptics.

Figure 7.1: Supernatural Events of the Gospels
(excluding miracles performed by Jesus)

Event	John	Mark	Luke	Matt
Virginal Conception			1	1
Star of Bethlehem				1
Warnings in Dreams				2
Angelic appearances	1		4	4
Heavens open upon Jesus' baptism		1	1	1
Spirit descends upon Jesus like a dove	1	1	1	1
Voice from heaven	1	1	1	1
Temptation by Satan		1	1	1
Conversations with Satan			1	1
Angels minister to Jesus in wilderness		1		1
Conversations with demons		3	3	1
Transfiguration/ Moses & Elijah appear		1	1	1
Voice from cloud during Transfiguration		1	1	1
Sky darkens on afternoon of Jesus' death		1	1	1
Tearing of the temple curtain		1	1	1
Earthquake upon Jesus' death				1
Earthquake at the tomb				1
Saints resurrected/appear in Jerusalem				1
Total Supernatural Events	**3**	**12**	**17**	**22**

John's mythological characterization of Jesus as the preexistent man from heaven has long caused scholars to think of the gospel as theologized to the point where it has little historical value. However, this has only served to mask the more vital observation that, though the character of Jesus is mythologized, the events of his life are not nearly as mythologized as they are in the synoptic tradition. We might then with equal force argue that it is the synoptic tradition, with its demons, angels, temptations by Satan, transfiguration, etc., that is to be considered the least historical in the John vs. synoptic debate. At the very least, one cannot dismiss John as non-historical due to its mythical content without applying the same logic to the synoptics.

The data in Figure 7.1 are visually represented by the bar graph in Figure 7.2:

**Figure 7.2: Distribution of Supernatural Events
in the Four Gospels**
(excluding the miracles performed by Jesus)

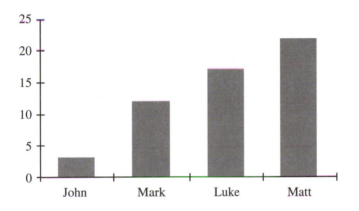

The difference in the number of supernatural events in the gospels is apparent. If we were to find that John-Mark-Luke-Matthew is the correct chronological sequence of gospel composition, then this graph would indicate that supernatural mythologies associated with the gospel story grew with time. Of course, this information by itself does not prove anything about whether the suggested sequence is correct. There is nothing unusual about the fact that the four gospels have different amounts of mythology, and the fact that they can be displayed in ascending order of mythical content says nothing about their temporal sequence. Nor does it yet prove that the number of mythological stories increased over time.

Some may suggest other explanations for the data. For instance, we might assume the distribution may be related to the absolute length of the gospels; Luke and Matthew are longer than John and Mark, and the sheer volume of text could be a determining factor in the distribution. Thus without further data there is no reason to believe the pattern in the above graph suggests anything about gospel sequence.

However, the reason this graph has been presented is that there are more data to be considered which will help to interpret it. Surprisingly, other categories of tradition manifest the same statistical patterns of evolution throughout the four gospels. This common pattern will recur as we proceed through this chapter, and its repetition will require a more substantive explanation.

The Pattern of Eschatological Teachings

Eschatology is the study of teachings related to the end of the world, the second coming of Jesus, and the day of judgment. As compared to the supernatural mythologies, it is a distinct category of thought and tradition in the early church. Yet as we will see, the degree of concern about the end of the world in each gospel is linked closely to the amount of supernatural mythology in each. However, there is no obvious reason why teachings about the anticipated end of the world should be statistically related to the supernatural tradition. Rather, if the gospels were produced by independent communities with varying concerns and beliefs, we would expect to find no correlation between what a community anticipated regarding the end of the world and what it believed about the supernatural events of Jesus' life.

However, a precise statistical correlation exists throughout the four gospels between these two seemingly unrelated categories of belief. The pattern can be illustrated in two ways. The first is a statistical measurement of the amount of text each author allocated to eschatological issues. The second is a closer evaluation of the actual content of the eschatological teachings themselves.

First, let us consider the statistical analysis of the texts. When we add up the number of verses of each gospel which refer to the last day, the second coming, or the day of judgment, and calculate these figures as a percentage of the entire gospel, we get an interesting result. The gospel with the least concern for such issues is John; only 1.5% of the text of John addresses a future "last day." By comparison, 7.2% of the text of Mark is focused on eschatological issues. Luke is third with 10.3%. Matthew shows the greatest concern for the end of the world, with a significant 14.5% of its text allocated to the subject. The following graph shows the actual percentage of each gospel's text allocated to eschatological issues:

Figure 7.3: Percentage of Gospel Text
Allocated to Eschatological Issues[1]

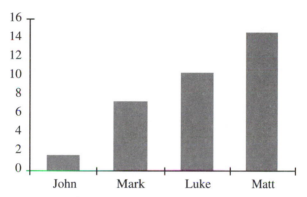

Several observations may be made about Figure 7.3. Clearly these statistics produce a curve similar to the distribution of supernatural events; indeed the graphs appear to be almost duplicates of one another. Since there is no obvious connection between teachings on the end of the world and stories of supernatural events of Jesus' life, the findings suggest that a common factor may have influenced the development of both. For it is suspicious that such a close repetition of the same statistical pattern would have occurred coincidentally.

---

[1] Based on defining the following texts as eschatological: **John** 5:26-29; 6:37-40, 44, 53, 54; 12:47,48; **Mark** 12:1-11; 13:1-37; **Luke** 10:10-15; 12:35-50; 17:20-37; 18:1-8; 19:11-27, 41-44; 20:9-18; 21:5-36; 22:28-30; 23:28-31; **Matt** 10:14-23; 11:20-24; 12:36-42; 13:24-30,36-43,47-50; 16:27-28; 21:33-41;23:32-36;24:1-51; 25:1-46; 26:64

Recall that in the previous chart we anticipated a possible objection that the greater length of Luke and Matthew might explain the fact that they have more supernatural events than John and Mark. Such an explanation does not work as well here. Note that in this graph, the statistics are rendered as percentages of the total text of each individual gospel. This should neutralize any influence on the distribution pattern which would derive from the relative length of the four gospels. For there is no reason why the percentage of text allocated to eschatology within each gospel should not be random and without any clear pattern. The fact that this distribution pattern closely echoes the previous one suggests an organizational factor other than the length of the gospels.

The Length of the Gospel Texts

Since it may be suspected that the patterns could be related to the length of the gospels, it is worthwhile to examine their length to see if this could be an explanatory factor. In point of fact, the John-Mark-Luke-Matthew sequence does not correspond to their relative length in ascending order. The absolute text length of John 1-20 is greater than Mark 1:1-16:8 by about 24%, and Luke is longer than Matthew by 9%.

A graphic representation of the comparative length of the four gospels is shown in Figure 7.4. This chart indicates that the similar distribution of supernatural events and eschatological teachings is not directly related to the length of the texts. If they were, we would expect to find a similar progression in textual length from John to Matthew. Therefore, the parallel patterns in these two traditions must be explained by alternative means, or be dismissed as coincidental. Though it is possible that these apparent growth curves reflect an evolution of thought during the first century, we have not yet seen enough supporting data to establish the theory with certainty.

Figure 7.4: Relative Length of the Gospel Texts [2]

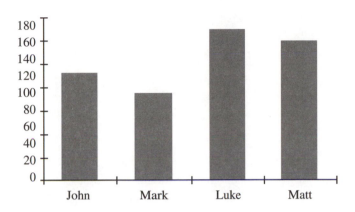

The Content of Eschatological Teachings

There is another intriguing aspect to the eschatological teachings in the gospels. Not only does the percentage of text allocated to this subject increase in the John-Mark-Luke-Matthew sequence, but the vision of the end of the world as a cataclysmic imminent judgment becomes more explicit and violent in the same sequence.

In the Gospel of John we find very little concern regarding the end of the world as a consequential future event. The "last day" is mentioned several times, but there is no association of a return of Jesus to earth with this event, nor is there any concept of a dramatic judgment of the world on that day. To the contrary, the Johannine community believed salvation and judgment were already complete with the death and resurrection of Jesus. Those who believed had already passed from death to life, and those who did not were already condemned (John 3:18).

---

[2] Measurement includes the full texts of Matthew and Luke; John 1-20; and Mark 1:1-16:8. Since the average length of a verse differs between the four gospels, we cannot use the number of total verses to measure the length of each gospel. In this case, the total words of text of each gospel have been calculated. The results were converted to a scale which indicates the relative length of the gospels as a percentage of Mark. Thus Mark has been set to 100. John has a value of 124, or 24% greater length than Mark. Luke is 75% longer than Mark, and has a value of 175. Matthew, at 161, is 61% longer than Mark.

As there is an awareness of the "last day" in John, there is also the idea that Jesus will come again. However, just as the reference to the last day is mentioned only in passing, so the event of the second coming is likewise briefly passed over. There is only one passage which might be interpreted as a prediction of the second coming:

> In my Father's house there are many rooms; if it were not so, would I have told you that I go to prepare a place for you? And when I go and prepare a place for you, I will come again and will take you to myself, that where I am you may be also. (John 14:2-3)

Though Jesus says in this passage that he will come again, there is nothing to indicate that the author means anything as momentous as a physical second coming. Rather, the larger context of John 14 indicates the second coming is not a future event, but is to be equated with the resurrection and subsequent appearance of the Holy Spirit:

> And I will pray the Father, and he will give you another Counselor, to be with you for ever, even the Spirit of truth, whom the world cannot receive, because it neither sees him or knows him; you know him for he dwells with you and will be in you. I will not leave you desolate; I will come to you. Yet a little while, and the world will see me no more, but you will see me; because I live in you, you will live also. (John 14:16-19)

> These things I have spoken to you, while I am still with you. But the Counselor, the Holy Spirit, whom the Father will send in my name, he will teach you all things . . . (John 14:25-26)

These verses indicate that Jesus will come again in the form of the Holy Spirit, who is to dwell in the hearts of the believers. There is no mention of another physical return of Jesus to earth after the resurrection.

The Future Return of Jesus in Mark

In the synoptic gospels we find a different story. Mark introduces the idea that there will be an end of time, heralded by tribulation and violence, the culmination of which will be the physical return of Jesus:

And Jesus began to teach them, saying, "Take heed that no one leads you astray. Many will come in my name, saying, 'I am he!' and they will lead many astray. And when you hear of wars and rumors of wars, do not be alarmed; this must take place, for the end is not yet. (Mark 13:5-7)

For in those days there will be such tribulation as has not been from the beginning of the creation which God created until now, and never will be. (Mark 13:19)

But in those days, after that tribulation, the sun will be darkened, and the moon will not give its light, and the stars will be falling from heaven, and the powers in the heavens will be shaken. And then they will see the Son of man coming in clouds with great power and glory. And then he will send out the angels, and gather his elect from the four winds, from the ends of the earth to the ends of heaven. (Mark 13:24-27)

Further, this event is to take place within the lifetime of those who heard Jesus' speak, and they are admonished to be alert and to watch for the signs of the end:

Truly, I say to you, this generation will not pass away before all these things take place. Heaven and earth will pass away, but my words will not pass away. But of that day or that hour no one knows, not even the angels in heaven, nor the Son, but only the Father. Take heed, watch; for you do not know when the time will come. (Mark 13:30-33)

In Mark, we find there will be an "end" of some sort which will be heralded by violence and persecutions, and which will culminate in Jesus' return. However, Mark does not call it a "day of judgment" as Matthew does. Though this might be inferred from the text, the idea that the world will be destroyed and unbelievers cast into eternal damnation is not as fully developed as it is in Luke and Matthew.[3]

---

[3] All Markan teachings regarding the end times and the second coming of Jesus are found in Mark 13; if this chapter were deleted, no other reference to eschatological issues is to be found in the remaining text. Further, Mark 13 appears to have originated as a separate literary unit, a tract or pamphlet whose purpose was to instruct specifically on the second coming. Some have suggested that the author of Mark used this older pamphlet as a source and worked it into his text virtually intact. However, one might as easily suggest that Mark 13 was a *later* addition to the original gospel, representing teachings which developed after the gospel was produced in its original form. Note there is a remarkable continuity between chapters 11, 12, and 14 which appears disrupted by chapter 13.

The End of the World in Luke and Matthew

In Luke, there is an increased focus on eschatology as compared to Mark. Luke's texts on the end of the world are more than twice the length of Mark's. Most of the text of Mark 13 can be found (in similar language) in Luke 21:5-37. However, in addition to the material derived from Mark, Luke adds language which has a heightened sense of ominous foreboding. For example, in Mark 13, the elect are cautioned to watch and to be careful they are not lead astray by false prophets and teachers. In contrast, Luke ends this portion of the discourse with the following:

> But take heed to yourselves lest your hearts be weighed down with dissipation and drunkenness and cares of this life, and that day come upon you suddenly like a snare; for it will upon all who dwell upon the face of the whole earth. But watch at all times, praying that you may have strength to escape all these things that will take place, and to stand before the Son of man. (Luke 21:34-36)

Luke also takes Mark's vision of the end one significant step further by introducing the idea that the second coming will be accompanied by the violent destruction of the world:

> As it was in the days of Noah, so will it be in the days of the Son of man. They ate, they drank, they married, they were given in marriage, until the day when Noah entered the ark, and the flood came and destroyed them all. Likewise as it was in the days of Lot -- they ate, they drank, they bought, they sold, they planted, they built, but on the day when Lot went out from Sodom fire and sulphur rained from heaven and destroyed them all -- so will it be on the day when the Son of man is revealed. (Luke 17:26-30)

Clearly Luke contains a greater sense of urgency regarding the end of the world as compared to Mark.[4] Yet it is Matthew which

---

[4] Most scholars believe that the Gospel of Luke and the Acts of the Apostles are two parts of the same literary work, which is often referred to as Luke-Acts. The claim has been made that Luke-Acts is perhaps the least eschatological work in the NT. This impression comes from the fact that there is virtually no end time teaching in Acts. However, Luke and Acts differ on this issue, and the non-eschatological orientation of Acts cannot be allowed to unduly influence the interpretation of the texts in Luke.

develops the concept to the greatest extreme. The phrase "day of judgment" occurs for the first time in Matthew (10:15; 11:22, 24; 12:36), as does the phrase "close of the age" (13:39, 40, 49; 24:3; 28:20). The explicit damnation of unbelievers to an "eternal fire" is also unique to Matthew (25:41). In particular the vision of Jesus sitting on his throne with all the nations before his divine judgment appears only in Matthew:

> When the Son of man comes in his glory, and all the angels with him, then he will sit on his glorious throne. Before him will be gathered all the nations, and he will separate them one from another as a shepherd separates the sheep from the goats, and he will place the sheep at his right hand, but the goats at the left. Then the King will say to those at his right hand, "Come, O blessed of my Father, inherit the kingdom prepared for you from the foundation of the world . . . " Then he will say to those at his left hand, "Depart from me, you cursed, into the eternal fire prepared for the devil and his angels . . ." And they will go away into eternal punishment, but the righteous into eternal life. (excerpts from Matt. 25:31-46)

The Delay of the Second Coming

Yet another element unique to Luke and Matthew is the concern regarding the delay of Jesus' return. Apparently the audiences for whom these gospels were written had lived with the expectation of Jesus' return for so long that many were becoming impatient or confused. Both Matthew and Luke include the following parable:

> Who then is the faithful and wise servant, who his master has set over his household, to give them their food at the proper time? Blessed is that servant whom his master when he comes will find so doing. Truly, I say to you, he will set him over all his possessions. But if that wicked servant says to himself, "My master is delayed," and begins to beat his fellow servants, and eats and drinks with the drunken, the master of that servant will come on a day when he does not expect him and at an hour he does not know, and will punish him, and put him with the hypocrites; there men will weep and gnash their teeth.(Matt 24:45-51; Luke 12:41-48)

In addition to this common story, the Parable of the Unjust Judge (Luke 18:1-8) and the Parable of the Ten Virgins (Matt 25:1-13) are stories unique to Luke and Matthew respectively which warn readers of the need to stand faithful in the face of the apparent delay of Jesus' return.   From a chronological perspective, it is consistent that this theme should appear in the later gospels.

In short then, the distribution of eschatological teachings in the gospels is summarized in Figure 7.5.   In this table, the pattern of evolving thought regarding the end of the world corresponds precisely with the increasing percentage of the gospels' texts allocated to these issues.   The expanding focus from John to Matthew seems to represent a growing anticipation of the second coming of Jesus as a violent cataclysmic event.   The gospels reflect an increasing need to encourage the believers to stand firm.

During the second half of the first century, the church suffered several waves of violent persecution by Roman authorities.   Many believe that Jews who had joined the Jesus movement were cursed and formally excommunicated from the synagogues under the dictates of the Benediction Against Heretics around 85 CE.   The movement's ideology would also have been influenced by the brutal destruction of Jerusalem.   Thus it is not surprising that the eschatological tradition as it evolved during this period would predict an increasingly violent retribution against the ungodly.   From an historical perspective, the evidence is compatible with the theory that the gospels reflect four distinct chronological stages of belief.

Figure 7.5: Summary of Eschatological Themes in the Gospels

	John	Mark	Luke	Matt
Damnation of unbelievers to eternal fire on day of judgment				X
Concern over delay of Jesus' return			X	X
Destruction of the world upon Jesus' return			X	X
Violence/persecution as end of age nears		X	X	X
Second coming of Jesus to earth		X	X	X
Last day/termination of present age	X	X	X	X

Moral Vision in the Gospels

In addition to the development of supernatural mythologies and ideas regarding the end of the world, a third independent tradition which appears to have evolved in the gospels is the moral content of the teachings of Jesus. Earlier we saw that Mark's versions of several stories in John show Jesus as more focused on the needs of the persons around him than the texts of John indicated. Clearly the Markan Jesus is considerably more attractive as a moral visionary than is the Johannine Jesus. This raises a question: Do these two gospels simply represent different perspectives on Jesus which coexisted in two opposing sects of the movement, or does Mark's version reflect an evolved perspective on the character of Jesus? Indeed, the trend of moral enhancement of the character and message of Jesus is continued through Luke and Matthew.

In order to quantify this we may identify and isolate the moral sayings of Jesus--those which bear upon proper conduct and right thinking as it relates to one's fellow man. These sayings may be categorically distinguished from those which instruct on the kingdom of God, salvation, and other religious or philosophical themes. For example, the commandment to love God with all one's heart may be considered a religious theme as it bears upon man's relation to God, whereas the commandment to love one's neighbor may be classified as a moral teaching since its focus is on one's relationship to society.

In anticipation of an objection, it is not suggested that the authors of the gospels would necessarily have made these distinctions. On the contrary, these are analytical categories of which they probably would not have been aware. However, there is a quantifiable difference in moral content among the four gospels. Consequently, categorizing Jesus' sayings as religious vs. moral does shed light on the authors' latent concern with the behavioral conduct of believers among themselves and within society at large.

Figure 7.6 lists the sayings of Jesus which bear upon right thinking and proper conduct in society and among fellow believers. On occasion, sayings of very similar intent or meaning have been grouped into a category rather than listed separately. For example,

Figure 7.6: Distribution of Moral Teachings in the Gospels

Moral Teaching:	John	Mark	Luke	Matt
New Commandment (Love the brethren)	x			
Healing on the Sabbath	x	x	x	x
Admonitions to forgive	x	x	x	x
Blaspheming against the Holy Spirit		x	x	x
On Fasting		x	x	x
On Divorce		x	x	x
When you pray, forgive		x	x	x
Measure you give/measure you get		x	x	x
He who would be first must serve all		x	x	x
Great Commandment (love God/neighbor)		x	x	x
Render to Caesar things that are Caesar's		x	x	x
If your hand causes you to sin, cut it off . .		x		x
What comes out of one's heart defiles him		x	x	x
Do not lay up treasures on earth		x	x	x
Make friends quickly with your accuser			x	x
Love your enemies			x	x
Turn the other cheek			x	x
Give to those who beg of you			x	x
You cannot serve God and mammon			x	x
Take the speck out of your own eye			x	x
Judge not, that you be not judged			x	x
As you wish men would do to you, do so			x	x
He who exalts himself will be humbled			x	x
Parable of the Good Samaritan			x	
Blessed are the meek . . .				x
Blessed are the merciful . . .				x
Blessed are the peacemakers . . .				x
Blessed are the pure in heart . . .				x
Do not look lustfully upon a woman				x
Do not be angry with your brother				x
Do not swear, either by heaven or earth				x
He who takes sword, dies by sword				x
Admonitions to practice faith in secret		x		x
TOTAL	**3**	**14**	**22**	**31**

Matthew contains teachings to fast in secret, to pray in secret, and to give alms without others knowing. These three sayings have been summarized in the table as "admonitions to practice faith in secret." Since Luke and Matthew are the two gospels with the greatest propensity to restate similar themes, such groupings do not alter the general distribution pattern of moral content in the gospels. The categorization of certain sayings is sometimes subjective and open to debate. Therefore, the reader is encouraged to perform an independent review of the sayings to verify to his or her own satisfaction that the statistical distribution of moral teachings is closely represented by this table.

The data from Figure 7.6 are presented in bar graph form in Figure 7.7. Note that the pattern we have already seen appears once again. There is a statistical expansion in the number and variety of moral teachings in the John-Mark-Luke-Matthew sequence. This graph reflects the same progression of thought from John to Matthew that exists in the distribution of supernatural events and eschatological teachings. To visually demonstrate the remarkable similarity of these statistical curves, Figure 7.8 presents a summary of each of the three elements discussed above. Since the vertical axis is not measured in the same units for each category, the values for the Gospel of Mark have been set to 100, and each of the values for the other three gospels have been rendered in statistical proportion to Mark.

Figure 7.7: Distribution of Moral Teachings in the Four Gospels

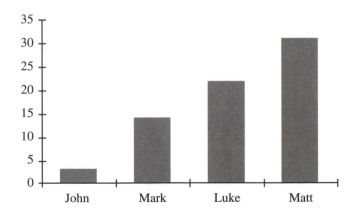

Figure 7.8: Summary of Ideological Patterns in the Four Gospels

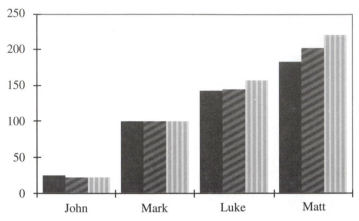

The shaded columns, which are the first in each group of three, depict the relative number of supernatural events in each gospel. The columns in position two (diagonal stripes) represent the relative percentage of text each gospel allocates to eschatological concerns. The third columns (vertical stripes) show the relative scope of moral teachings. All statistics are relative to Mark. Thus in all three categories, Mark = 100.

Explaining the Gospel Patterns

Modern scholarship has not recognized the patterns of evolving thought in the John-Mark-Luke-Matthew sequence, so there has been no attempt to explain them to date. Since they are unrecognized, they have not influenced contemporary theories of gospel chronology. However, these patterns require an explanation, for it is remote that such pronounced statistical profiles could exist by coincidence.

The most logical solution to the problem is that the John-Mark-Luke-Matthew sequence is the actual historical order of their composition. John is the most primitive of the four gospels, and each of the synoptics reflects an evolved ideological perspective over the earlier gospels. Such an inference from these statistics is in harmony with findings earlier in the book which suggested the priority of John. It is also compatible with the widely held belief that Luke and Matthew were written subsequent to Mark and their authors used Mark as a source document.

Further Evidence of Textual Evolution

As compelling as the previous data may be, there is still more evidence which supports the proposed theory. It is possible to identify the evolution of specific traditions through each of the gospels in the John-Mark-Luke-Matthew sequence. The evolution of specific texts is independent of the statistical measurements presented above, and they offer confirming evidence which is unrelated to them.

For example, the development of the Lord's Prayer (Figure 7.9) is striking. The Lord's Prayer does not exist in John. However, a root tradition behind the Prayer can be found in Mark. Then the first development of the tradition as a specific prayer taught by Jesus appears in Luke. Finally, Matthew contains the most evolved rendition. Therefore, the apparent evolutionary sequence of the Lord's Prayer is compatible with the John-Mark-Luke-Matthew hypothesis.

Figure 7.9: The Lord's Prayer

Mark 11:25	Luke 11:2-4	Matt. 6:9-13
Whenever you stand praying,	When you pray, say: Father,	Pray then like this: Our Father who art in heaven,
	Hallowed be thy name. Thy kingdom come.	Hallowed be thy name. Thy kingdom come, thy will be done, on earth as it is in heaven. Give us
	Give us	
forgive, if you have any-thing against any one; so that your Father also who is in heaven may forgive you your trespasses.	each day our daily bread; and forgive us our sins, for we ourselves forgive every one who is indebted to us; and lead us not into temptation.	this day our daily bread and forgive us our debts as we also have forgiven our debtors; And lead us not into temptation, but deliver us from evil.

The Great Commission

Another example of evolving tradition is the Great Commission (Figure 7.10). John, Luke, and Matthew each report a saying of the resurrected Jesus which sends his disciples into the world to spread the message. Since the resurrection scenes have been deleted from Mark, it is not known whether the author included a similar commissioning of the disciples in his original work. (Note: though Mark 16:15 is clearly part of the Great Commission tradition, this is part of the appendix which was added to Mark at a later time. Since we do not know when this text was added, it is disregarded here.)

However, the commission passages in John, Luke, and Matthew are interesting. These three versions of the Great Commission have two elements in common. First, Jesus is sending his disciples into the world. Second, the disciples will not be left alone, but will be empowered from heaven to do the work they are sent to do. In John, it is the Holy Spirit who is given to accompany the disciples. In Luke, the indirect reference is also to the Holy Spirit, which the author subsequently says is given to the disciples on the day of Pentecost (Acts 2). Matthew does not indicate that the Holy Spirit is the empowerment, but in this passage Jesus affirms that he will be with the disciples to the close of the age.

Figure 7.10: The Great Commission

John 20:21-23	Luke 24:46-49	Matt. 28:18-20
Jesus said to them again, "Peace be with you. As the Father has sent me, even so send I you." And when he had said this he breathed on them, and said to them "Receive the Holy Spirit. If you forgive the sins of any, they are forgiven; if you retain the sins of any, they are retained."	[Jesus] said to them, "Thus it is written, that the Christ should suffer and on the third day rise from the dead, and that repentance and forgiveness of sins should be preached in his name to all nations, beginning from Jerusalem. You are witnesses of these things. And behold, I send the promise of my Father upon you; but stay in the city, until you are clothed with power from on high"	And Jesus came and said to them, "All authority in heaven and on earth has been given to me. Go therefore and make disciples of all nations, baptizing them in the name of the Father and of the Son and of the Holy Spirit, teaching them to observe all that I have commanded you; and lo, I am with you always, to the close of the age."

Note that among the three gospels, John renders the least formal of the commissions. The disciples do not go from Jerusalem, nor do they go to all nations; they are simply sent. Nor is there a formal message they are to take with them. In Luke, the formal message appears, along with a more structured commission to go from Jerusalem to all nations. Matthew adds the advanced liturgical formula *baptizing them in the name of the Father and of the Son and of the Holy Spirit.* This language is institutionalized; this phrase appears nowhere else in the gospels, and it is a significant sign that Matthew reflects a later tradition.

The Beatitudes

Another comparative study which indicates that Matthew is more advanced as compared to Luke is the texts commonly known as the Beatitudes. The Beatitudes do not exist as a distinct literary unit in John or Mark. However, there are passages in both of these gospels which are similar in tone and content to teachings in the Beatitudes, and may constitute earlier forms of the traditions:

> Truly, truly, I say to you, you will weep and lament, but the world will rejoice; you will be sorrowful, but your sorrow will turn to joy. (John 16:20)
>> *Blessed are you that weep now, for you shall laugh. (Luke 6:21b)*

> Whoever drinks of the water that I shall give him will never thirst. (John 4:14)
>> *Blessed are those who hunger and thirst for righteousness, for they shall be satisfied. (Matt 5:6)*

> For within, out of the heart of man, come evil thoughts . . . and they defile a man. (Mark 7:20-23)

>> *Blessed are the pure in heart, for they shall see God. (Matt. 5:8)*

> Whenever you stand praying, forgive, if you have anything against any one; so that your Father also who is in heaven may forgive you your trespasses. (Mark 11:25)

>> *Blessed are the peacemakers, for they shall be called sons of God. (Matt. 5:9)*

Figure 7.11: The Beatitudes

Luke 6:20b-23	Matt. 5:3-12
Blessed are you poor, for yours is the kingdom of God.	Blessed are the poor in spirit, for theirs is the kingdom of God Blessed are those who mourn, for they shall be comforted. Blessed are the meek, for they shall inherit the earth.
Blessed are you that hunger now,	Blessed are those who hunger and thirst for righteousness,
for you shall be satisfied. Blessed are you that weep now, for you shall laugh.	for they shall be satisfied.
	Blessed are the merciful, for they shall obtain mercy. Blessed are the pure in heart, for they shall see God. Blessed are the peacemakers, for they shall be called sons of God. Blessed are those who are persecuted for righteousness' sake, for theirs is the kingdom of heaven.
Blessed are you when men hate you, and when they exclude you and revile you, and cast out your name as evil, on	Blessed are you when men revile you and persecute you and utter all kinds of evil against you falsely on
account of the Son of man! Rejoice in that day, and leap for joy, for behold, your reward is great in heaven; for so their fathers did to the prophets.	my account. Rejoice and be glad, for your reward is great in heaven, for so men persecuted the prophets who were before you.

The Beatitudes from Luke and Matthew are shown in Figure 7.11. Note that Matthew's text is more extensive, for it includes several sayings which do not appear at all in Luke. In addition, of those sayings which are similar, it often appears as though Matthew has offered an enhanced or refined version of Luke.

In summary, the theory that there is an ascending refinement of ideological thought in the John-Mark-Luke-Matthew sequence is supported by comparative studies of common traditions. The Lord's Prayer, the Great Commission, and the Beatitudes all take their most advanced form in the Gospel of Matthew. Therefore, the apparent evolution of these texts echoes the statistical patterns noted earlier, confirming that they are not random or coincidental.

Matthew: Cleaning Up the Loose Ends

We have already seen ample evidence to conclude that Matthew is the most advanced of the four gospels. However, there is another fascinating aspect of the Gospel of Matthew which lends further support to this theory. Among the earlier gospels there are a number of stories which are disharmonious or confusing; they are the "loose ends" of the gospels. One of the most interesting characteristics of the Matthew is its propensity to tie up these loose ends. It resolves tensions which were left standing between the earlier gospels, and it provides new solutions to puzzling questions. Much of this appears to have been motivated by ongoing criticism or confusion stemming from the accounts in John, Mark, and/or Luke. One remarkable example of this begins with a puzzling statement in John:

> 25 Truly, truly, I say to you, the hour is coming, and now is, when the dead will hear the voice of the Son of God, and those who hear will live. 26 For as the Father has life in himself, so he has granted the Son also to have life in himself, 27 and has given him authority to execute judgment, because he is the Son of man. 28 Do not marvel at this; for the hour is coming when all who are in the tombs will hear his voice 29 and come forth, those who have done good, to the resurrection of life, and those who have done evil, to the resurrection of judgment. (John 5:25-29)

Within the context of John, this saying indicates that those who are in the tombs will be raised with Jesus at the time of his own resurrection. This is to happen in an hour which is coming *and now is*. Yet there is no fulfillment of this prophecy in John. With this as background, the astounding line in Matthew's death scene makes more sense:

> 50 And Jesus cried again with a loud voice and yielded up his spirit. 51 And behold, the curtain of the temple was torn in two, from top to bottom; and the earth shook, and the rocks were split; 52 the tombs also were opened, and many bodies of the saints who had fallen asleep were raised, 53 and coming out of the tombs after his resurrection they went into the holy city and appeared to many. 54 When the centurion and those who were with him, keeping watch over Jesus, saw the earthquake and what took place, they were filled with awe, and said, "Truly, this was the Son of God." (Matt. 27:50-54)

The resurrection of the saints in Matthew constitutes the most spectacular miracle of the NT, yet it is told in one sentence and passed over as if it were not a significant event. It has no counterpart anywhere else in the NT, and is foreshadowed only in the text of John. Further, its appearance here is unusual in that its summary treatment adds nothing to the meaning of the narrative.

Note that if verses 52-53 were deleted entirely the remaining text would be coherent and the story would not be missed. In fact the underlined text is unique to Matthew, whereas the remaining text in this quotation has direct counterparts in Mark 15:38-39. In these verses Mark records the tearing of the temple curtain and the exclamation of the centurion. However, there is no mention in Mark of an earthquake, the opening of the tombs, or the raising of the saints. Therefore, Matthew's text appears to be an embellishment of Mark's original text. At face value it accomplishes only one thing--it shows a fulfillment of the prediction in the Gospel of John.

There is a fundamental implication here. It is that the author of Matthew, in writing the last and greatest of the four gospels, had as one of his objectives the reconciliation of earlier traditions. Clearly, his advocacy of Peter, and his primary reliance on Mark as a key source, point to the political and ideological ascendancy of the Petrine sect by the end of the first century. However, for the author of Matthew, each of the three earlier gospels had value. A blending and reconciling of the earlier traditions appears to have been one of his essential goals.

The Problem of Jesus' Baptism

Another example of Matthew's tendency to reconcile loose ends is found in the account of Jesus' baptism by John the Baptist. Recall that the Fourth Gospel does not say Jesus was actually baptized by John:

> The next day he saw Jesus coming toward him, and said, "Behold, the Lamb of God, who takes away the sin of the world! This is he of whom I said, 'After me comes a man who ranks before me, for he was before me.' I myself did not know him; but for this I came baptizing with water, that he might be revealed to Israel." And John bore witness, "I saw the Spirit descend as a dove from heaven, and it remained on him." (John 1:29-32)

For the author of John, Jesus was an eternal being who was with God at the creation of the world. John the Baptist was calling people to repent of their sins, and he offered a baptism of repentance for the forgiveness of sins. Thus within Johannine theology it would be inappropriate to show Jesus, a sinless divine being, submitting himself to such a baptism.

For the author of Mark, on the other hand, there is no such difficulty. However we might interpret Mark's vision of Jesus' divine nature, Mark clearly understands him to have been fully human as well. For Mark the baptism represented no theological difficulty:

> In those days Jesus came from Nazareth of Galilee and was baptized by John in the Jordan. And when he came up out of the water, immediately he saw the heavens opened and the Spirit descending upon him like a dove. (Mark 1:9-10)

Therefore, Matthew inherited two opposing traditions from John and Mark. How might they be harmonized? He could not ignore the tradition that Jesus was baptized by John, but neither could he show this baptism without an attempt to answer the theological problem of a sinless man submitting to a baptism for the remission of sins. Here is Matthew's solution:

> Then Jesus came from Galilee to the Jordan to John to be baptized by him. John would have prevented him, saying, "I need to be baptized by you, and do you come to me?" But Jesus answered him, "Let it be so for now; for thus it is fitting for us to fulfill all righteousness." Then he consented. And when Jesus was baptized, he went up immediately from the water, and behold, the heavens were opened and he saw the Spirit of God descending like a dove." (Matt. 3:13-16)

Here Matthew adds a brief conversation which acknowledges that the baptism is unnecessary, but it is to be done for a greater symbolic purpose. Thus Matthew retains the essence of Mark's version of the story--that Jesus was actually baptized by John--but he does so with an interpretation that embraces the Johannine tradition.

The Problem of the Nearby Tomb

Another loose end in the movement's tradition is the problem of how Joseph and Nicodemus could have buried Jesus apparently on the spur of the moment in someone else's family tomb. Here is the report in the Gospel of John:

> [Joseph and Nicodemus] took the body of Jesus, and bound it in linen cloths and spices as is the burial custom of the Jews. Now in the place where he was crucified there was a garden, and in the garden a new tomb where no one had ever been laid. So because of the Day of Preparation, as the tomb was close at hand, they laid Jesus there." (John 19:40-42)

The phrase *where no one had ever been laid* identifies the tomb as a family tomb which had not yet been used. A large tomb made to accommodate numerous interments was a costly investment that someone had already made in anticipation of using it as a resting place for his own family members. Such tombs were not uncommon around Jerusalem in the first century. The problem here is that it would have been inappropriate to bury the body in a tomb such as this simply out of convenience. Yet Mark and Luke also report the use of this nearby tomb without further comment (Mark 15:46; Luke 23:53). However, Matthew adds a new element to the story to resolve the confusion:

> And Joseph took the body, and wrapped it in a clean linen shroud, and laid it <u>in his own new tomb, which he had hewn in the rock</u>; and he rolled a great stone to the door and departed. (Matt 27:59-60)

By introducing the detail that this tomb actually belonged to Joseph, the problem is neatly eliminated. This is a vital bit of information which would most likely have appeared in the other gospels if it had been in circulation earlier in the century. The fact that Matthew is the only gospel to include it is a sign that the question had been raised, and an attempt was made to reconcile the difficulty.

The Problem of Betrayal by an Apostle

Another fascinating problem in the gospel traditions centers on the figure of Judas Iscariot, the apostle who betrayed Jesus. The problem is this: How could an apostle who was chosen by Jesus and who traveled with Jesus during his entire ministry, be so unimpressed with him as to betray him?

The Gospel of John simply says Satan entered into him (John 13:27). Mark states that Judas decided to betray Jesus and was to be paid for it (Mark 14:10-11). Luke combines these two elements, saying that Satan entered into Judas *and* he arranged to betray Jesus for money (Luke 22:3-5). After the betrayal, Judas is seen no more in these three gospels. How is it that one of Jesus' closest associates, one who actually traveled with the Son of God and witnessed his teachings and his miracles, would have decided to betray him? Matthew adds a remarkable story to help resolve the problem:

> When Judas, his betrayer, saw that [Jesus] was condemned, he repented and brought back the thirty pieces of silver to the chief priests and the elders, saying, "I have sinned in betraying innocent blood." They said, "What is that to us? See to it yourself." And throwing down the pieces of silver in the temple, he departed; and he went out and hanged himself. (Matt. 27:3-5)

By including the story of the repentant Judas, Matthew casts an entirely new light on the issue. According to Matthew, Judas did not anticipate that Jesus would be condemned to death -- it was all a tragic mistake which overwhelmed Judas with such grief that he committed suicide. By showing that Judas did not anticipate or intend to cause the condemnation of Jesus, the author diminishes the heinous nature of the betrayal. Further, the repentant Judas who commits suicide after realizing what he has done presents much less of a doctrinal liability. The betrayal is transformed from a wanton and willful act of a renegade apostle into the sad miscalculation of a confused apostle.

The Problem of the Stolen Body Theory

A final example of Matthew's attempt to tie up loose ends is found in the passages which answer the criticism that the resurrection event was a hoax perpetrated by the disciples. John, Mark, and Luke say that Jesus' body was laid in the tomb and a rock rolled in front of the door to close it. On the morning of the third day, Mary Magdalene and other women go to the tomb only to find the rock rolled back and the body of Jesus gone. No one witnessed the actual resurrection--that is Jesus' body coming back to life--nor do they witness the opening of the tomb, or Jesus emerging from the tomb. Jesus is already gone by the time they arrive at the open tomb.

It is clear from Matthew's text that a common accusation was that the disciples had come at night, stolen the body, and fabricated the resurrection story. In response, Matthew introduces this encounter which occurs on the day after Jesus was crucified:

> Next day, that is, after the day of Preparation, the chief priests and the Pharisees gathered before Pilate and said, "Sir, we remember how that impostor said, while he was still alive, 'After three days I will rise again.' Therefore order the sepulchre to be made secure until the third day, lest his disciples go and steal him away, and tell the people, 'He has risen from the dead,' and the last fraud will be worse than the first." Pilate said to them, 'You have a guard of soldiers; go, make it as secure as you can." So they went and made the sepulchre secure by sealing the stone and setting a guard. (Matt. 27:62-66)

Here the author acknowledges the stolen body theory, and adds the detail of the sealed and guarded tomb to combat it. However, having introduced this story, the author created another problem. For now there is no way to follow the accounts of the other three gospels on the morning of the third day. Since the stone has been sealed, a supernatural force is now required to break it. Since the guards are watching, they must see the tomb actually opened:

> Now after the Sabbath, toward the dawn of the first day of the week, Mary Magdalene and the other Mary went to see the sepulchre. And behold, there was a great earthquake; for an angel of the Lord

descended from heaven and came and rolled back the stone, and sat upon it. His appearance was like lightening, and his raiment white as snow. And for fear of him the guards trembled and became like dead men. But the angel said to the women, "Do not be afraid; for I know that you seek Jesus who was crucified. He is not here; for he has risen, as he said. Come, see the place where he lay." (Matt. 28:1-6)

Note that even though the women and the guards watch as the stone is rolled back, Jesus does not emerge from the tomb. He is already gone before the tomb is opened, just as he is gone before the women arrive at the tomb in the other gospels. The fact that Jesus does not come out of the tomb is a telling omission. Matthew appears interested in altering the tradition just enough to defeat the accusation that the body was stolen, while at the same time retaining the essence of the earlier gospel accounts which say that Jesus was gone by the time the women arrived.

As a final note, this story in Matthew created yet another inconsistency which needed resolution. The guards, who have witnessed the angelic appearance and the unsealing of the tomb, are not part of the earlier gospel tradition. If they were there, why do they not appear as witnesses in John, Mark, and Luke? The author of Matthew goes to significant length to explain this problem away as well:

> . . . some of the guard went into the city and told the chief priests all that had taken place. And when they had assembled with the elders and taken counsel, they gave a sum of money to the soldiers and said, "Tell people, 'His disciples came by night and stole him away while we were asleep.' And if this comes to the governor's ears, we will satisfy him and keep you out of trouble." So they took the money and did as they were directed; and this story has been spread among the Jews to this day. (Matt. 28:11-15)

Here Matthew tells us that the guards do not act as witnesses to the resurrection because they were paid for their silence. Since none of this text pertaining to the sealed tomb and the guards exists in John, Mark, or Luke, it is further evidence that Matthew was the last of the four, and represents a tradition which was altered to meet the evangelical needs of the movement.

Summary

At this point we have seen an array of patterns in the gospels. The Gospel of John has been shown to be an anti-Petrine gospel which was later appended by a pro-Petrine editor. This appendix, John 21, was then demonstrated to contain an ideal literary and political conclusion to the Gospel of Mark. We found that once the Johannine features of John 21:1-19 are deleted, and the remaining text restored to Mark 16:8, the two gospels stand in ideological opposition to one another. The antithetical nature of Mark's text in relation to John suggested that Mark was composed after John for the purpose of correcting John.

The shift in perspective from John to Mark raised the question whether the shift was part of a larger trend of evolving perspective which might be detected in Matthew and Luke as well. In this chapter, we have seen that in the John-Mark-Luke-Matthew sequence there is a statistical progression of thought in the categories of supernatural events, eschatological issues, and moral vision. The distribution of these elements among the four gospels is not random. Therefore, we must either dismiss the statistical patterns as oddly coincidental, or seek an underlying formative influence which could account for them.

The most apparent formative influence on the data is time. The patterns suggest an evolution of thought in the Jesus movement during the first century. Supernatural mythologies such as the virginal conception and the resurrection of the saints did not exist in the primitive movement. They began to circulate only later in the first century. As the movement grew, and persecutions became more violent and deliberate, the notion of a violent day of judgment became more prominent in its preaching. Finally, the tradition of Jesus as a teacher of morality and wisdom evolved over the same time period.

The Problem of the Sayings Gospel "Q"

That a broader scope of moral vision should evolve in the Christian tradition as the Jesus movement grew from a small Jewish messiah cult to a religious movement with a more worldly expression is not unusual. It is consistent with the proposition that Luke and

254

Matthew were the later gospels, and John and Mark the more primitive. However, this observation has significant implications for the interpretation of the Q material.

Recall that one of the key assumptions made by the Jesus Seminar scholars is that the sayings common to Luke and Matthew which constitute the "double tradition," are derived from a primitive lost document--a "Sayings Gospel" which is thought to be a window into pre-Christian traditions of Jesus. Much historical Jesus research today is founded largely upon the notion that this double tradition material is the earliest and most historically authentic record of the teachings of Jesus.

Yet the evidence here would suggest just the opposite. The statistical patterns of development imply that the sayings common only to Luke and Matthew are later traditions developed by the movement. Thus there is reason to suspect that the double tradition material which scholars think came from Q is not primitive after all. It may bear little relation to the historical Jesus. Ironically, those sayings which the Jesus Seminar has red-lettered as originating with Jesus are for the most part taken from the Q material. Yet according to the present theory they are among the least likely candidates as authentic sayings of Jesus.

This is a contradiction of significant magnitude. It implies that modern historical Jesus research, which is influenced by the presumed priority and authenticity of Q, may be misguided. It suggests there could be an error in contemporary interpretations of the Q material. Indeed, it raises an alarming issue: Did the Q Gospel ever really exist?

❖   *8*   ❖

_____

The Lost Gospel

No study of the quest for the historical Jesus would be complete without an analysis of the most influential contemporary theory which bears on the subject--the alleged discovery of the lost gospel "Q." Arland Jacobson, in the introduction to his recent book *The First Gospel, An Introduction to Q*, writes:

> The earliest gospel about Jesus did not survive intact. Both Matthew and Luke undertook, independently, to improve upon this gospel by attaching chunks of it to a narrative framework. What we are left with, therefore, are fragments of a document scattered throughout Matthew and Luke. This gospel, a collection of sayings, did not survive independently so it has no name, only the non-descript designation "Q," abbreviated from the German Quelle, or "source."[1]

As noted in Chapter One, the Jesus Seminar identifies the Q theory as one of its operating presuppositions. The introduction to *The Five Gospels* states:

> The general acceptance of the Q hypothesis by scholars [has become] another of the pillars of scholarly wisdom. It plays a significant role in assessing the development of the Jesus tradition in its earliest stages.[2]

Though the Q theory is widespread, scholars vary on how they interpret Q as it relates to historical Jesus research. Burton Mack has produced several alarming speculations about the nature of Q and the

_____

[1] Jacobson, Ibid., p. 1
[2] Jesus Seminar, Ibid., p. 13

community in which it allegedly circulated. In his recent book *The Lost Gospel: The Book of Q and Christian Origins,* Mack writes:

> Q challenges the New Testament account of Christian origins by offering another, more plausible account of the first forty years. The Jesus movement [as revealed by Q] is a more believable group of people than the disciples and first Christians who are depicted in the narrative gospels. Q provides a documentation for the Jesus movement that the narrative gospels cannot provide for the congregational fiction they project. This is serious business, because the gospel story is the cornerstone of the Christian's mythic world.[3]

Mack's interpretations are not widely shared by scholars, even those who otherwise accept the Q hypothesis in some form. A more cautious appraisal of Q and its relevance to historical Jesus research is represented in John Meier's work *A Marginal Jew: Rethinking the Historical Jesus:*

> My previous work in redaction criticism of Matthew has convinced me that the two-source hypothesis [the "Q theory"], while not without its problems, is the most viable theory. It is also the one most used by the international community of scholars; hence it will be the hypothesis employed here. The important upshot of this position is that Mark and Q provide two different sources for comparison and verification.[4]

One cannot understate the influence of the Q theory on the contemporary quest for the historical Jesus. Though some scholars embrace the theory tentatively as Meier does, while others such as Mack are more aggressive, the basic fact is clear: the alleged existence of Q exerts a tremendous influence on modern scholars as they go about reconstructing the historical Jesus and the origins of Christianity.

This is not to suggest that scholars uniformly accept the Q theory. Over the last thirty years a significant minority of scholars has marshaled arguments against its viability. One leading critic, William Farmer, notes in his book *The Synoptic Problem*:

[3] Mack, Ibid., p. 238
[4] Meier, John P., *A Marginal Jew: Rethinking the Historical Jesus,* Doubleday, 1991, p. 44

> To those investigators who have preceded me in publishing views calling into question . . . the existence of "Q," I gladly acknowledge my profound indebtedness. Their companionship has been treasured during my own prolonged intellectual pilgrimage which has been marked first by a questioning of the existence of "Q," and later by a questioning of the priority of Mark to Matthew, and finally by a questioning of the priority of Mark to Luke as well. [5]

Farmer has promoted the view that Mark was the last of the three synoptic gospels, and that it represents a condensation of Luke and Matthew, both of which the author of Mark used as sources. He believes Matthew was the first, and Luke the second of the three, and that Luke's direct use of Matthew accounts for the double tradition material. Hence, for Farmer, this obviates the need to assume anything like Q every existed.

Unfortunately, scholars like Farmer who have argued against the existence of Q, have often done so within the context of a separate proposal that Matthew-Luke-Mark is the true chronological sequence of the synoptics. For reasons cited in the previous chapter, as well as a host of other reasons outside the scope of this book, this proposed sequence is very difficult to defend, and the large majority of scholars dismiss it. The result is that the cogent arguments which Farmer makes against the existence of Q tend to be lost in the confusion caused by his untenable position on sequence.

However, though the existence of Q and Farmer's proposed gospel sequence are related in Farmer's solution, they are in fact independent problems which need not be related to one another. This chapter will demonstrate that a substantial argument against the existence of Q can be sustained while affirming the academic community's widely accepted belief in the priority of Mark among the synoptics. The statistical patterns in the gospels suggest that the double tradition, or "Q material,"[6] could represent later tradition since it

---

[5] Farmer, Ibid., p. vii

[6] Since this study rejects the notion that Q existed as a single source document, the term "Q material" will be used in reference to the collection of traditions which are alleged to have come from this hypothetical source. In this book, the phrases "Q material" and "double tradition" are synonymous, as they both refer to the sayings common to Luke and Matthew, without presuming a single source behind them.

appears only in the later gospels. This warrants a look at the assumptions underlying the Q theory, or "Two-Document hypothesis."[7]

The Independence of Luke and Matthew

There is a key assumption on which the Two-Document hypothesis depends. It is that the authors of Luke and Matthew could not have been aware of each other's work. For if Matthew used Luke, or Luke used Matthew, the double tradition is explained by direct copying from one to the other, and the need to assume they used a common source document evaporates. Therefore, the validity of the Q theory is wholly dependent upon a reasonable demonstration that Luke and Matthew were written independently.

Oddly enough, this issue is not often discussed in contemporary Q literature. A few scholars have written entire studies on Q and the community which allegedly produced it without mentioning this vital assumption, much less defend it. Yet if it cannot be demonstrated beyond reasonable doubt that the later of Matthew or Luke did not know the earlier, one may easily conclude that the double tradition exists because one author copied from the other; in this case the hypothetical document Q may never have existed.

There are two separate questions to be addressed here. First, is it possible to demonstrate that the author of Luke could not have used Matthew? Second, can the reverse be shown that the author of Matthew could not have known Luke? Since we cannot establish with certainty the dates Matthew and Luke were composed, some may argue we cannot make assumptions about which was the later of the two. However, the previous chapter established that Matthew appears to be later than Luke. If this sequence is correct, then any direct dependence would derive from Matthew's use of Luke.

---

[7] The Two-Document Hypothesis is the formal name for the theory which states that Matthew and Luke each used Mark and Q as their two primary sources when they compiled their gospels. In some literature it is referred to as the Two-Source Hypothesis. In this chapter it will be referred to also as the "Q theory," in light of the fact that the notable component of the theory is that Q was a single source document from which the double tradition was taken.

It will be stipulated here that, apart from the statistical patterns developed in the previous chapter, there is good evidence that the author of Luke could not have known Matthew. In comparing the common traditions between them it is apparent that Luke has frequently rendered the more primitive version. Recall that our comparison of the texts of The Lord's Prayer showed that Luke appears to have the less developed version. It is difficult to imagine why the author of Luke would have rendered The Lord's Prayer in a more remedial fashion if he had been aware of Matthew's text. A similar observation can be made regarding the Beatitudes, and indeed most of the sayings Luke and Matthew have in common. So based strictly upon the superior refinement of the Matthean texts, it is not difficult to sustain an argument that the author of Luke could not have been aware of the Gospel of Matthew.

However, this argument does not work in reverse. It is entirely possible that the author of Matthew was fully aware of the Gospel of Luke, and that he edited and improved the traditions in Luke, thus creating what appear to be more refined and developed versions of the text. This would be compatible with the patterns identified in the previous chapter.

This chapter will argue that the author of Matthew must in fact have used Luke as a source, and because of this there is no reason to characterize the Q material, i.e., the double tradition in Matthew and Luke, as a lost gospel. Rather the double tradition is most easily explained by assuming Luke created his gospel by collecting an assortment of traditions and adding them to the narrative framework of Mark. Then Matthew used both Mark and Luke as sources for his own gospel. Some of the material which Luke had collected and added to Mark was duplicated by Matthew--this explains the double tradition. Furthermore, if this is the explanation for the double tradition, it will be shown that there is no reason to assume the Q material is primitive. All we may assume is the Q material had been developed by the time Luke was written, or by the early 80s.

As an aside, this theory is not new. In fact it was first proposed by the German scholar Christian Gottlob Wilke in 1838. Wilke is most remembered as the one who first put forth a compelling argument for the priority of Mark among the three synoptic gospels. For this his work is acclaimed. However, the balance of his theory, now obscured in the confusion over Q, was that Luke was the second of the synoptics, and that Matthew wrote last, combining the two earlier works. The theory was also promoted by several other 19th century scholars, including Bruno Bauer (1842) and Gustav Volkmar (1882).[8]

Defense of the Alleged Independence of Matthew and Luke

Why do scholars believe the author of Matthew could not have been aware of Luke? There are four arguments typically offered to support this assumption. However, upon close examination they do not hold up. Each will be taken in turn.

1. *Matthew and Luke contain different infancy narratives and genealogies.* Matthew and Luke each have stories about the birth of Jesus which include a family genealogy, the virginal conception by Mary, and the birth in Bethlehem. However, the two gospels present conflicting stories which cannot be reconciled. It is often presumed that if one author knew the other, he would not have intentionally introduced conflicting legends into the gospel records.

For example, consider the difference in the genealogies. Matthew states there were exactly 28 generations from David to Jesus-- fourteen from David to the deportation, and fourteen from the deportation to Jesus. However, Luke names 43 generations between David and Jesus. That there are an additional 15 generations in Luke's list creates an incompatibility. Further, according to the OT, David had two sons--Nathan and Solomon. Matthew says Jesus was descended from Solomon, and Luke reports descent from Nathan. At the opposite end of the genealogies, Matthew and Luke even disagree on the name of Jesus' grandfather; Matthew says it was Jacob, and Luke identifies him as Heli.

---

[8] For a comprehensive review of historical Jesus research in the 19th century, see Albert Schweitzer, *The Quest of the Historical Jesus*, first German edition, 1906; first English translation, 1910.

Regarding the birth narratives, Matthew reports Joseph and Mary were living in Bethlehem at the time Jesus is born, and the birth takes place in their own home. They subsequently flee Bethlehem in fear of a threat from Herod to kill all the infants in town in order to eliminate this future King of the Jews. They remain in exile for some time in Egypt before returning to Palestine, where they ultimately settle in Nazareth of Galilee.

In Luke, Joseph and Mary are already living in Nazareth at the time she conceives. A census of the population is ordered by Caesar Augustus which required that everyone register in the home town of their ancestors. This forces Joseph and the pregnant Mary to travel to Bethlehem, where Jesus is born and placed in a manger (feeding trough) because there was no room at the inn.

May we reasonably assume that if the authors were aware of each other's narratives, they would not have introduced such conflicts? The answer is *no*. First, we know from the letter of 1 Timothy that the creation of myths and genealogies was a subject of dispute in the early church; the author of this letter counsels to avoid these disagreements:

> As I urged you when I was going to Macedonia, remain at Ephesus that you may charge certain persons not to teach any different doctrine, nor to occupy themselves with myths and endless genealogies which promote speculations rather than the divine training that is in faith; whereas the aim of our charge is love that issues from a pure heart and a good conscience and sincere faith. Certain persons by swerving from these have wandered away into vain discussion, desiring to be teachers of the law, without understanding either what they are saying or the things about which they make assertions. (1 Tim 1:3-7)

It is obvious from Matthew and Luke that at least two genealogies and two different infancy stories were in circulation during the second half of the first century. The note in 1 Timothy[9] implies there may have been more than these two. There is no reason not to suspect

---

[9] The letters to Timothy and Titus are not generally accepted as authentic letters of Paul. They are later works, written sometime between 70 CE and 100 CE, by an author who appropriated Paul's name pseudonymously.

that the communities of Matthew and Luke may each have adopted their preferred traditions which appear in their respective gospels.

The question is whether we may assume Matthew would have used Luke's genealogy and infancy narrative if he had been aware of it. There are at least four possible reasons why he would have ignored Luke's tradition, opting for the one which he used instead.

First, Matthew may have recognized that Luke's infancy narrative contains several historical difficulties. For example, Luke 1:5 sets the time of the births of John the Baptist and Jesus "in the days of Herod, king of Judea." Then in Luke 2:1-2, we find that Joseph and Mary travel to Bethlehem in response to an enrollment when Quirinius was governor of Syria. However, Herod died in 4 BCE, and Quirinius did not become governor of Syria until 6 CE, ten years later. The references, therefore, create historical confusion.

Further, Luke's account contains other implausible references as well. Herod was not only "king of Judea" (Luke 1:5), but king of all Jewish Palestine. There is no historical record of Caesar Augustus ever issuing a decree for a world enrollment (Luke 2:1). If he had, such an enrollment would not have affected the citizenry under the sovereign rule of King Herod, but only those under Roman rule; thus residents of Galilee would not have been subject to such an enrollment. Even if there had been an enrollment, it would have been for tax purposes, and thus would have mandated enrollment in the current place of residence; enrollment in the town of one's ancestors would have served no useful government purpose.[10]

Therefore, if the author of Matthew was at all conscientious about recording authoritative traditions, he may reasonably have determined that Luke's account contained so many historical errors that it needed to be replaced by one which did not. Whether Matthew's account has any historical credence is beside the point; at least it sets the infancy events clearly within the reign of Herod, and is internally consistent in its historical representations. Therefore, the author may well have regarded it as a superior and more authentic tradition.

---

[10] For a more detailed examination of the historical problems in Luke's infancy narrative, see Robin Lane Fox, *The Unauthorized Version*, pp. 27-37.

A second possible reason why Matthew may have passed over Luke's account is that the infancy stories and genealogies are designed to support the theological concerns of the writers. Luke's gospel has little interest in rooting the Jesus movement within the prophetic traditions of Judaism; for Luke, Jesus has come as the savior of the world, and there is to be little distinction between Jew and gentile. The New Israel shall consist of all believing Jews and gentiles alike. So Luke has little concern for relating the gospel story to its Jewish origins by identifying specific events as fulfillments of prophetic expectation. Note that the genealogy in Luke spans all the generations of humankind, from Jesus back to the first man Adam, thus establishing Jesus as the Son of Man for all generations of humankind.

Matthew on the other hand is concerned with establishing that the Jesus movement emerged from the Jewish heritage, and that it is a fulfillment of Jewish expectations. Sprinkled throughout Matthew are references to specific fulfillments of OT prophecy.[11] The Matthean genealogy highlights the fact that Jesus is descended from Abraham and David. Furthermore, it is segmented into three distinct and even sections; Abraham to David (fourteen generations); David to the deportation (fourteen generations); and the deportation to the Christ (fourteen generations). Notice that the lists do in fact name fourteen generations from Abraham to David, and fourteen more to the deportation. However, there are only thirteen names after the deportation to Jesus--Jesus born of Mary is the thirteenth generation, and *the Christ* is the fourteenth.

This discrepancy is intentional on the author's part. First century readers would have been acutely aware of it since the author draws such deliberate attention to the three sequences of fourteen. The genealogy indicates that there have been three eras of Jewish history, and that the coming of the Christ heralds the fourth and final era, and by implication the fulfillment of the destiny of Judaism. The genealogy, then, is an effective preface for the thrust of Matthew's gospel--Christianity is a fulfillment of Jewish heritage:

---

[11] Matt. 1:22-23; 2:5-6; 2:17-18; 2:23; 3:3;4:14-16; 8:17;11:10; 12:17-21;13:14-15;13:35; 15:7-9;21:4-5

> Think not that I have come to abolish the law and the prophets; I have come not to abolish them but to fulfill them. For truly, I say to you, till heaven and earth pass away, not an iota, not a dot, will pass from the law until all is accomplished. (Matt. 5:17-18)

Note that Matthew's infancy narrative is constructed specifically to bring the story of Moses, the lawgiver, to mind. Just as the infant Moses was hidden to save him from Pharaoh's murder of the Hebrew male children (Ex 1:22-2:10), so Jesus is hidden to avoid King Herod's slaughter of all male children (Matt 2:16-17). Just as Moses led the Hebrews out of Egypt and into the promised land, so Jesus comes out of Egypt to save his people (Matt 2:14-15). Thus the Matthean narratives integrate the story of Jesus intimately with the tradition of Moses.

In short, the genealogies and infancy narratives of Luke and Matthew are intended to establish and support distinctive and unique themes which are carried through each of the gospels respectively. Luke's account would not have supported the theological objectives of Matthew's gospel nearly as well as those which appear in Matthew.

A third possibility for Matthew's passing over Luke's account is (as we will discover later in this chapter), that one of Matthew's literary objectives seems to have been to record the earliest version of a tradition when he had two to choose from. Hence, he may have chosen to use the one he did because he perceived it to be earlier and, therefore, more authoritative than the Lukan version.

Finally, Matthew appears to have had a high regard for the Gospel of Mark, following it much more closely than did Luke. Thus, the author of Matthew appears to have had a close affinity with the community which produced Mark. If this community had embraced one genealogy and infancy narrative, while Luke's community accepted another, Matthew may have chosen to stay with the tradition he was more closely allied with.

Therefore, it is possible that Matthew was fully aware of Luke's genealogy and infancy narratives, yet elected not to use them for any of the reasons above, or perhaps for other reasons of which we are not aware. Thus, we cannot infer from the fact that Matthew did not reproduce Luke's genealogy or infancy narratives, that he must not have been aware of them.

2. *Matthew and Luke contain different resurrection narratives.* Matthew and Luke each follow the Gospel of Mark (Matthew closely; Luke quite loosely) up to the point where the text is truncated at 16:8. From this point forward they give markedly different reports of the resurrection appearances of Jesus. It is often assumed that if Matthew had been aware of Luke, such a divergence would not have been as pronounced as it is.

Yet this does not follow either. Mark establishes a significant theme that Jesus will first appear to his disciples in Galilee; it is forecasted twice (Mark 14:28; 16:7). Matthew duplicates this Markan tradition, and also twice records the prediction (Matt. 26:32; 28:7). If Matthew is to show these predictions fulfilled, he must show a resurrection appearance in Galilee, which of course he does (28:16-20).

On the other hand, Luke omits the Markan prediction of the resurrection appearance in Galilee. Since he does not record this prophecy, Luke does not follow this tradition in his resurrection account. Instead, Luke shows an appearance to two unnamed disciples on the road to Emmaus, and subsequent appearances within the environs of Jerusalem. Thus Luke's account is in direct conflict with the Markan predictions.

Matthew elected to follow Mark closely through the entire passion and resurrection sequence up to Mark 16:8. This decision would have precluded the use of Luke's resurrection narrative since it conflicts with Mark's predictions. Since Mark was an earlier gospel than Luke, and since it appears to have reflected Petrine ideology with which Matthew was in sympathy, it is consistent that Matthew would defer to Mark as the earlier and more authoritative source. From this we cannot infer that Matthew was not aware of Luke.

3. *Matthew sometimes records more primitive versions of sayings than their counterparts in Luke.* Every once in a while, when comparing the texts of Matthew and Luke, it is apparent that Matthew has the older or more original version of a particular saying. Some infer from this that Matthew could not have been using Luke as a source. Helmut Koester makes this argument:

The numerous verbal agreements of these parallel [double tradition] passages cannot be explained as dependence of either Matthew upon Luke or dependence of Luke upon Matthew because, in numerous instances, Luke's version is evidently the more original one. But there are also passages in which Matthew rather than Luke has preserved words and phrases which cannot be explained as the product of Matthew's editorial work.[12]

It is the exception to find passages in Matthew's double tradition material which appear more primitive than their counterparts in Luke, but some instances of this do in fact occur. Most notable are Matthew's duplication of structured sayings which are known as Semitic parallelisms. These are poetic sayings which retain their poetic form in Matthew, but which have been broken and paraphrased by Luke. Two examples of this are found in figures 8.1 and 8.2.

Figure 8.1: The House Built Upon the Rock

Luke 6:47-49	Matt. 7:24-27
47 Every one who comes to me and hears my words and does them, I will show you what he is like; he is like a man building a house, who dug deep, and laid the foundation upon the rock; and when a flood arose, the stream broke against that house, and could not shake it, because it had been well built.	**24 "Everyone then who hears these words of mine and does them will be like a wise man who built his house upon the rock;**
	25 and the rain fell, and the floods came, and the winds blew and beat upon that house, but it did not fall, because it had been founded on the rock.
But he who hears and does not do them is like a man who built a house on the ground without a foundation; against which the stream broke, and immediately it fell, and the ruin of that house was great.	**26 And everyone who hears these words of mine and does not do them will be like a foolish man who built his house upon the sand;**
	27 and the rain fell, and the floods came, and the winds blew and beat against that house, and it fell, and great was the fall of it.

---

[12] Koester, Ibid., p. 131

Figure 8.2: Treasures in Heaven

Luke 12:33-34	Matt. 6:19-21
Sell your possessions and give alms; provide yourselves with purses that do not grow old, with a treasure in the heavens that does not fail, where no thief approaches and no moth destroys.	**Do not lay up for yourselves treasures on earth,** *Where moth and rust consume and where thieves break in and steal,* **But lay up for yourselves treasure in heaven,** *Where neither moth nor rust consumes and where thieves do not break in and steal.*
For where your treasure is, there will your heart be also.	For where your treasure is, there will your heart be also.

In both of these examples the poetic structure of the original parallelism is recorded in Matthew. The Matthean texts are highlighted in alternating bold and italic type to emphasize the latent structure which is not evident when read directly from most modern translations of the Bible. Parallelisms such as this are thought to have developed in the early Semitic origin of the Jesus movement for the accurate oral transmission of certain teachings. So Matthew's versions, since they retain the parallel structure, appear to be closer to the original oral units. Conversely, Luke has rendered them in prose which appears to have been derived from the originals.

May we infer that since Matthew contains the original form of these sayings that he must not have been aware of Luke's paraphrased versions? Once again the logic does not follow. For if Matthew was intent upon documenting the earliest and most authentic traditions, it is not surprising that he would record the earlier oral units rather than Luke's loose rendition of them. We only need to assume that, in these cases, Matthew was aware of both Luke's paraphrasing as well as the earlier formal parallelisms, and that he opted to record the more authentic forms of the sayings.

In general, it is widely acknowledged that Luke contains the more primitive versions of sayings in the double tradition, with only occasional exceptions. This has led Q theorists to suggest that Matthew may even have used a later edition of Q than that used by Luke:

> Luke preserves the original wording of sayings more faithfully than Matthew, although even Luke occasionally edited his Q materials and Matthew cannot be ruled out as the document in which the original wording of its source is still extant.[13]

> Q probably underwent one additional redaction [editorial revision] before it was used by Matthew . . .[14]

So the comparison between Matthew and Luke indicates that Luke records, in most cases, the earlier form of the double tradition sayings. On occasion there are sayings which "cannot be ruled out" as more original in Matthew. Certainly the parallelisms would fall into this category. The remaining few are uncertain and do nothing more than raise the question of which may have been an earlier version.

However, if we assume that Matthew's objective was to record the earliest and most authentic tradition that he was aware of, such a policy would allow for an occasional appearance of earlier versions than those found in Luke. On the other hand, for all of Luke's non-Markan material which did not have a significant pre-history, Luke's wording would have appeared to Matthew to be the earliest. Hence, in these cases he would have copied or edited Luke's wording directly.

In short, the fact that Matthew occasionally renders a saying more primitive than its counterpart in Luke does not indicate that Matthew was not aware of Luke. Indeed, the grand pattern identified by the Q theorists that Luke generally contains the earlier traditions is entirely compatible with what we would expect if Luke were indeed the earlier document, and Matthew had used Luke as a source.

4. *Matthew and Luke contain no major agreements against Mark.* Another argument which has been advanced to support the idea that Matthew could not have known Luke is that there are no major textual agreements between Matthew and Luke against Mark. If

---

[13] Koester, Ibid., p. 134
[14] Koester, Ibid., p. 134

Matthew had used both Mark and Luke as sources, he would have often seen two different versions of the same story--one in Mark, and the other in Luke. Yet in these cases, Matthew always reproduces Mark's version rather than Luke's. Would we not expect Matthew on occasion to have opted for Luke's wording rather than Mark's had he been aware of it?

There is no reason to believe that he would have. If the author of Matthew perceived Mark to have been an earlier gospel, and one which reflected the pro-Petrine tradition of which he was a part, it would make sense that he would routinely defer to Markan authority. Under this scenario, we would expect to find few if any major agreements between Matthew and Luke against Mark. So the fact that there are none is no indication that Matthew was not aware of Luke; it simply indicates once again that Matthew may have seen Mark as the more authoritative of the two sources.

The Minor Agreements

While there are no major textual agreements between Matthew and Luke against Mark, there are a host of minor agreements. These appear to be circumstances where the author of Matthew decided that the editorial changes made by Luke to the Markan original were appropriate; therefore Matthew follows Luke on these occasions. Figures 8.3 through 8.9 illustrate the phenomenon of the minor agreements.

Figure 8.3: The Cleansing of the Leper

Mark 1:40-41	Luke 5:12-13	Matthew 8:2-3
" If you will, you can make me clean." Moved with pity, he stretched out his hand and touched him, and said to him, "I will, be clean"	"Lord, if you will, you can make me clean." -------------------- And he stretched out his hand and touched him, saying, ----------------- "I will, be clean."	"Lord, if you will, you can make me clean." -------------------- And he stretched out his hand and touched him, saying, ----------------- "I will, be clean."

Figure 8.4: The Choosing of the Twelve

Mark 3:16-18	Luke 6:14	Matthew 10:2-3
Simon, whom he surnamed Peter;	Simon, whom he named Peter, <u>and Andrew, his brother,</u> and James and John, ---------------- ------------------------ ------------------------ ------------ and Philip and Bartholomew	Simon, who is called Peter, <u>and Andrew, his brother,</u> and James the son of Zebedee, and John, his brother; ---------------- ------------------------ ------------------------ ------------------ Philip and Bartholomew
James the son of Zebedee and John the brother of James, whom he surnamed Boanerges that is, sons of thunder; Andrew, and Philip, and Bartholomew		

Figure 8.5: Plucking Grain on the Sabbath

Mark 2:25	Luke 6:3	Matthew 12:3
he said to them, "Have you never read what David did when he was in need and was hungry, he and those who were with him; how he entered the house of God, when Abiathar was high priest, and ate the bread of the Presence . . .	Jesus answered, "Have you <u>not</u> read what David did when he was ----------------- hungry, he and those who were with him; how he entered the house of God, ---------- ------------------------ ------ and took and ate the bread of the Presence . . .	He said to them, "Have you <u>not</u> read what David did when he was ----------------- hungry, he and those who were with him; how he entered the house of God, --------- ------------------------ ------ and ate the bread of the Presence . . .

Figure 8.6: New Wine in Old Wineskins

Mark 2:22	Luke 5:37-38	Matthew 9:17
And no one puts new wine into old wine-skins; if he does, the wine will burst the skins, and the wine is lost, and so are the skins; but new wine is for fresh skins.	And no one puts new wine into old wine-skins; if he does the new wine will burst the skins and it will be <u>spilled, and the skins</u> will be <u>destroyed.</u> But new wine must be <u>put into fresh wineskins.</u>	Neither is new wine put into old wine-skins; if it is the skins burst and the wine is <u>spilled, and the skins</u> are <u>destroyed;</u> but new wine is <u>put into fresh wineskins.</u>

Figure 8.7: The Healing of the Paralytic

Mark 2:9	Luke 5:23	Matthew 9:5
Which is easier, to say to the paralytic, "Your sins are forgiven," or to say, "Rise, take up your pallet and walk?"	Which is easier, to say ------------------ "Your sins are forgiven," or to say, "Rise, ------------- -------- and walk?"	which is easier, to say ------------------ "Your sins are forgiven," or to say, "Rise, ------------- --------- and walk?"

Figure 8.8: Salt of the Earth

Mark 9:50	Luke 14:34-35	Matthew 5:13
Salt is good; but if the salt has lost its saltness, how will you season it?	Salt is good; but if the salt has lost its <u>taste, how shall its saltness be restored?</u> It is fit neither for the land nor for the dunghill; men throw it away.	You are the salt of the earth; but if the salt has lost its <u>taste, how shall its saltness be restored?</u> It is no longer good for anything except to be thrown out and trodden under foot by men.

Figure 8.9: Stilling the Storm

Mark 4:38	Luke 8:24	Matthew 8:25
and they woke him and said to him, "Teacher, do you not care if we perish?"	And they <u>went and</u> woke him, <u>saying,</u> "Master, Master, <u>we are perishing!</u>"	And they <u>went and</u> woke him, <u>saying,</u> "Save, Lord, <u>we are perishing!</u>"

From these examples it is clear that some of the minor agreements are the result of common deletions by Matthew and Luke from Mark's text; others occur when Matthew and Luke make the same additions or changes. This represents a problem for the Q theorists--if Luke and Matthew were not aware of each other's work, how is it that they so frequently make identical small changes to Mark's text? Farmer highlights this problem in his argument against the existence of Q. He maintains that the only satisfactory explanation for the minor agreements is to assume that the later of Matthew or Luke used the earlier.[15]

Though the minor agreements constitute evidence of direct dependence between Matthew and Luke, Q theorists argue that the evidence is not conclusive. They are well aware of the minor agreements and have developed ideas about how they could have occurred without Luke and Matthew being aware of each other's work. Helmut Koester helps identify the possibilities. First, he suggests that Matthew and Luke may have used a different edition of Mark than the one we have in the NT:

> I shall argue . . . that many of the minor agreements between Matthew and Luke result from the fact that both Matthew and Luke used a text of Mark that was different from the text which is preserved in the manuscript tradition of the canonical Gospel of Mark.[16]

However, he concedes that this is not in itself a comprehensive solution:

> It is hardly possible to argue that all these minor agreements can be explained by the assumption that Matthew and Luke used a Markan text that differed from the one preserved in the canonical manuscript tradition. A large number of the minor agreements are due to common stylistic or grammatical corrections of the sometimes awkward Markan text or are caused by accidental common omissions. There is also the possibility that later scribes altered the text of Luke under the influence of the better-known text of Matthew, thus creating secondary agreements of Matthew and Luke against Mark.[17]

Koester argues that many but not all of the minor agreements may be explained by assuming Matthew and Luke used a different version of the Gospel of Mark than the one we find in the NT, which is lost to us today. Other agreements may be explained by obvious grammatical corrections that both authors could have been expected to make independently. Still others were the result of accidental common

---

[15] See William Farmer, *The Synoptic Problem: A Critical Analysis*, Mercer University Press, 1976, for a full review of his alternative solution to the synoptic problem.

[16] Koester, Ibid., p. 129

[17] Koester, Ibid., p. 275

omissions. Finally, perhaps later copy editors changed some of Luke's text to read in accordance with the better known text of Matthew.

All of these suggestions are conceivable. In essence they are dismissed as an odd array of coincidences and/or the result of the use of a hypothetical source. The simpler solution is that Matthew had the gospels of Mark and Luke sitting in front of him, and from time to time he judged Luke's editing to be worthwhile, and used it himself.

Koester's proposal that the minor agreements are partly explained by two editions of Mark is speculative and unable to be demonstrated one way or the other. It is interesting to note however that Koester proposes that Matthew and Luke each independently used yet another hypothetical document (a lost edition of Mark) in addition to using the hypothetical Q. This is quite a bit of speculative theory, and it begins to grow rather cumbersome in light of the fact that there is a much simpler alternative.[18]

Summary

The validity of the Q theory depends upon an adequate demonstration that the authors of Matthew and Luke could not have been aware of one another's work. While a demonstration that Luke was not dependent upon Matthew is rather straightforward due to the array of comparatively remedial Lukan sayings in the double tradition, there is no direct evidence to show that Matthew was not aware of Luke.

Matthew's unawareness of Luke is often inferred from the fact that (a) Matthew does not follow Luke's genealogy, infancy narrative, and resurrection narrative, (b) Matthew occasionally contains a more primitive version of a saying that does Luke, and (c) Matthew never reproduces Luke's paraphrasing of Mark's gospel. Yet all of these can be explained by supposing Matthew's objective was to document the earliest and most authoritative traditions of which he was aware. All

---

[18] This is not to dismiss the idea that more than one edition of each gospel existed; most likely they did. In fact, if anything is probable, it is that Matthew and Luke used *different* editions of Mark, rather than the same lost edition, a point which Koester makes as well (Ibid., pp. 284-5)

we need to assume is that Matthew saw Luke's gospel as relatively late and, therefore, less authoritative than his other sources.

Since the double tradition may therefore be explained simply by Matthew's direct use of Luke, it is not necessary to characterize the double tradition material as deriving from an earlier common source. Instead, it is possible that the author of Luke assembled an assortment of oral and written traditions which had accumulated with time. Using the Gospel of Mark as a literary framework, he added the various new traditions which he had collected, and ended up with a much larger gospel which we know today as Luke.

This solution makes sense when we consider the diversity of the non-Markan material in Luke. The author combined a host of unrelated new traditions with Mark's basic narrative. They include stories about the virginal conception, the birth in Bethlehem, Satan's temptations of Jesus, additional sayings of John the Baptist, a collection of moral teachings, many new parables and miracles, and a more urgent vision of the end of the world. There is no reason to suspect these miscellaneous traditions had any common origin, or that they reflect the thought of a single community of Jesus' followers. Rather they may be unrelated legends which evolved in various communities over time, just as they appear to be at face value.

Now the fact that one cannot demonstrate the independence of Matthew and Luke is only the first step in the puzzle. For it only establishes a viable alternative to the Two-Document hypothesis without providing any evidence that it may be the preferred solution. The minor agreements constitute favorable evidence, but Q theorists have attempted to explain them away as largely coincidental. A more substantive argument is needed to bring the hypothetical Q theory into further doubt. So the next step will be to show that the Two-Document hypothesis itself manifests internal inconsistencies which, apart from all the evidence seen thus far, make it highly questionable.

Textual Analysis of the Synoptic Problem[19]

In order to illustrate the inconsistencies of the Two-Document hypothesis, it is necessary to review a series of texts side by side. Each set of texts will illustrate a relationship between the gospels that must ultimately be explained. After looking at each set of texts, we will consider how they affect the validity of the Two-Document hypothesis on the one hand, and the idea that Matthew used both Mark and Luke on the other.

1. Some passages which appear only in Matthew and Luke are identical to one another. Figures 8.10, 8.11, and 8.12 illustrate the phenomenon of textual duplication between Matthew and Luke.

Figure 8.10: Jesus' Lament over Jerusalem

Luke 13:34	Matt. 23:37
34 "O Jerusalem, Jerusalem, killing the prophets and stoning those who are sent to you! How often would I have gathered your children together as a hen gathers her brood under her wings, and you would not!	37 "O Jerusalem, Jerusalem, killing the prophets and stoning those who are sent to you! How often would I have gathered your children together as a hen gathers her brood under her wings, and you would not!

Figure 8.11: On Serving Two Masters

Luke 16:13	Matt. 6:24
13 "No servant can serve two masters; for either he will hate the one and love the other, or he will be devoted to the one and despise the other. You cannot serve God and mammon."*	13 "No servant can serve two masters; for either he will hate the one and love the other, or he will be devoted to the one and despise the other. You cannot serve God and mammon."*

* *Mammon* is a Semitic word for wealth.

---

[19] The Synoptic Problem is the formal term for the study which analyzes the literary interrelationships of the synoptics gospels. The Two-Document hypothesis is one proposed solution to the Synoptic Problem; the idea that Matthew used both Mark and Luke is another.

Figure 8.12: Jesus' Prayer

Luke 10:21b	Matt. 11:25-26
21b "I thank thee, Father, Lord of heaven and earth, that thou hast hidden these things from the wise and understanding and revealed them to babes; yea, Father, for such was thy gracious will."	25 "I thank thee, Father, Lord of heaven and earth, that thou hast hidden these things from the wise and understanding and revealed them to babes; 26 yea, Father, for such was thy gracious will."

Here are three examples of word-for-word textual duplication between Matthew and Luke, an occurrence which is fairly common in the double tradition. Both theories under consideration easily explain duplicate texts. If Matthew copied from Luke, or if they both independently copied from the same source Q, the result would be as we see in the examples above. Of course from the identical texts alone there is no way to tell which of these is correct. For the moment, it is only important to note that textual duplication is rather common between Matthew and Luke.

2. It is most often apparent that between Matthew and Luke when there is a textual variation, it is Matthew that has the later or more refined version.

Figure 8.13: John the Baptist's Preaching of Repentance

Luke 3: 7-8	Matt 3:7-9
7 He said therefore to the multitudes that came out to be baptized by him, "You brood of vipers! Who warned you to flee from the wrath to come? 8 Bear fruits that befit repentance, and do not **begin** to say to yourselves, 'We have Abraham as our father'; for I tell you, God is able from these stones to raise up children to Abraham.	**7 But when he saw many of the Pharisees and Sadducees coming for baptism, he said to them,** "You brood of vipers! Who warned you to flee from the wrath to come? 8 Bear fruits that befit repentance, 9 and do not **presume** to say to yourselves, 'We have Abraham as our father'; for I tell you, God is able from these stones to raise up children to Abraham.

In Figure 8.13 we again find quite a bit of identical language, but it is apparent that some of the text has been changed by one of the authors. In Luke's version, the Baptist gives a tongue-lashing to the faithful multitudes who came out to be baptized. In Matthew the focus of the Baptist's attack is limited to the religious leaders, the "Pharisees and Sadducees." Also we see the word *begin* in Luke's version appears as *presume* in Matthew.

Which of these is the original version? It seems that Matthew could have been uncomfortable with the suggestion that the Baptist's sharp tongue was directed at the faithful who had come for baptism. Hence, he alters the story to show the Baptist's wrath focused on the religious leaders. Further, the difference in the words *begin* and *presume* indicates someone's careful attention to editing. Most would infer that *presume* is the stronger and more appropriate word in this context.

Note that Matthew routinely eliminates or alters the use of the word *begin* when he feels it has been improperly used in Mark. The following examples illustrate:

And they <u>began</u> to beg Jesus to depart from their neighborhood
(Mark 5:17)
when they saw him, they begged him to leave their neighborhood
(Matt. 8:34)

Peter <u>began</u> to say to him   (Mark 10:28)

Peter said in reply   (Matt. 19:27).

when the ten heard it, they <u>began</u> to be indignant at James and John
(Mark 10:41)
when the ten heard it, they were indignant at the two brothers.
(Matt. 20:24)

They <u>began</u> to be sorrowful, and to say to him one after another
(Mark 14:19)
And they were very sorrowful, and <u>began</u> to say to him one after another
(Matt. 26:22)

So from a study of Matthew's use of Mark, it is evident that Matthew was sensitive to the proper use of *begin*. Thus when we consider the difference in wording of *began* vs. *presume* in Figure 8.13, it is reasonable to conclude that Matthew has edited the text in Luke, and that Luke's is therefore the earlier version.

With respect to our two solutions, the simplest interpretation is that Matthew used Luke as a source and modified the text directly as we see it. However, Q theorist argue that in this case Luke copied the original text verbatim as it appeared in Q. Matthew, also using Q, performed the editing from the Q text to generate his version. So even though it *looks* like Matthew edited Luke directly, the phenomenon occurred as a result of both authors' use of Q. From this data alone there is no way to tell which of these solutions is correct.

Figure 8.13 is not a unique example of Matthew's apparent tendency to edit Luke, or Luke's version of Q. Rather, it is a common phenomenon in the double tradition texts; Figure 8.14 is another example.

Figure 8.14: John the Baptist's Question

Luke 7:18-23	Matt 11:2-6
18 The disciples of John told him of all these things. 19 And John, calling to him two of his disciples, sent them to the Lord, saying, "Are you he who is to come, or shall we look for another?" 20 And when the men had come to him, they said, "John the Baptist has sent us to you, saying, 'Are you he who is to come, or shall we look for another?'" 21 In that hour he cured many of diseases and plagues and evil spirits, and on many that were blind he bestowed sight. 22 And **he** answered them, "Go and tell John what you **have seen and heard:** the blind receive their sight, the lame walk, lepers are cleansed, and the deaf hear, the dead are raised up, the poor have good news preached to them. 23 And blessed is he who takes no offense at me."	2 Now when John heard in prison about the deeds of the Christ, he sent word by his disciples 3 and said to him, "Are you he who is to come, or shall we look for another?" 4 And **Jesus** answered them, "Go and tell John what you **hear and see:** 5 the blind receive their sight, and the lame walk, lepers are cleansed, and the deaf hear, and the dead are raised up, and the poor have good news preached to them. 6 And blessed is he who takes no offense at me."

280

In Figure 8.14 it seems Matthew has introduced prudent editorial changes to Luke. Luke's version contains redundant and irrelevant language; it also has an inappropriate change of verbal tense at v. 22. Matthew eliminates the redundant and irrelevant information and changes the verbs to uniformly present tense.

Once again the simplest explanation for these two texts is that Matthew edited Luke directly. The complex answer is posed by the Two-Document hypothesis, which says there was a common edition of Q which Luke copied verbatim and Matthew edited. Once again, this produces the coincidence that Matthew looks as though he edited Luke.

A substantial portion of the double tradition displays exactly this phenomenon.[20] In each case, Matthew appears to be a precision editor and a greater master of language and communication. Luke is often a verbose storyteller whose text is in need of editing. In each instance, Matthew looks as though he has edited, refined, and improved Luke directly. However, Q theorists argue that Luke copied his version of Q accurately, while Matthew independently edited from the same Q document. This coincidentally created the appearance that Matthew edited Luke directly.

Therefore, it is important to note that a critical assumption has materialized which the Q theory is founded upon:

> *Luke must have copied his Q source verbatim in most instances, and stayed very close to the original text in the rest; for this is the only way to explain the continuing coincidence that Matthew appears to have copied or edited Luke directly.*

This is a vital link in the argument, and one which we will return to after looking at several other implications which arise from comparing the double tradition material.

---

[20] Further examples include Luke 6:20-23 = Matt. 5:3-12; Luke 11:1-14 = Matt. 6:9-13; Luke 12:2-9 = Matt. 10:26-33; Luke 12:22-32 = Matt. 6:25-34; Luke 12:51-53 = Matt. 10:34-36; Luke 14:26-27 = Matt. 10:37-38; Luke 15:3-7 = Matt. 18:10-14.

3. *Luke very rarely copies Mark verbatim. Rather, he most frequently paraphrases Mark, following it closely, but rendering it in his own words.* Figures 8.15, 8.16, and 8.17 illustrate Luke's typical use of Mark.

Figure 8.15: Jesus Departs from Capernaum

Mark 1:35-38	Luke 4:42-43
35 And in the morning, a great while before day, he rose and went out to a lonely place, and there he prayed. 36 And Simon and those who were with him pursued him, 37 and they found him and said to him, "Everyone is searching for you." 38 And he said to them, "Let us go on to the next towns, that I may preach there also; for that is why I came out."	42 And when it was day, he departed and went into a lonely place. And the people sought him and came to him, and would have kept him from leaving them; 43 but he said to them, "I must preach the good news of the kingdom of God to the other cities also; for I was sent for this purpose."

Figure 8.16: The Healing of the Demoniac in the Synagogue

Mark 1:23-28	Luke 4:33-37
23 And immediately there was in their synagogue a man with an unclean spirit; 24 and he cried out, "What have you to do with us, Jesus of Nazareth? Have you come to destroy us? I know who you are, the Holy One of God." But Jesus rebuked him saying, "Be silent and come out of him!" 26 And the unclean spirit, convulsing him and crying with a loud voice came out of him. 27 And they were all amazed, so that they questioned among themselves, saying, "What is this? A new teaching! With authority he commands even the unclean spirits, and they obey him." 28 And at once his fame spread everywhere throughout all the surrounding region of Galilee.	33 And in the synagogue there was a man who had the spirit of an unclean demon; and he cried out with a loud voice, 34 "Ah! What have you to do with us, Jesus of Nazareth? Have you come to destroy us? I know who you are, the Holy One of God." 35 But Jesus rebuked him saying, "Be silent and come out of him!" And when the demon had thrown him down in the midst, he came out of him, having done him no harm. 36 And they were all amazed, and said to one another, "What is this word? For with authority and power he commands the unclean spirits, and they come out." 37 And reports of him went out into every place in the surrounding region.

282

Figure 8.17: Stilling the Storm

Mark 4: 35-41	Luke 8:22-25
35 On that day, when evening had come, he said to them, "Let us go across to the other side." 36 And leaving the crowd, they took him with them in the boat, just as he was. And other boats were with him. 37 And a great storm of wind arose, and the waves beat into the boat, so that the boat was already filling. 38 but he was in the stern, asleep on the cushion; and they woke him and said to him, "Teacher, do you not care if we perish?" 39 And he awoke and rebuked the wind, and said to the sea, "Peace! Be still!" And the wind ceased, and there was a great calm. 40 He said to them, "Why are you afraid? Have you no faith?" 41 And they were filled with awe, and said to one another, "Who then is this, that even wind and sea obey him?"	22 One day he got into a boat with his disciples, and he said to them, "Let us go across to the other side of the lake." So they set out, 23 and as they sailed he fell asleep. And a storm of wind came down on the lake, and they were filling with water, and were in danger. 24 And they went and woke him, saying, Master, Master, we are perishing!" And he awoke and rebuked the wind and the raging waves; and they ceased, and there was a calm. 25 He said to them, "Where is your faith?" And they were afraid, and they marveled, saying to one another, "Who then is this, that he commands even the wind and water, and they obey him?"

The three illustrations above show that Luke's style is usually to rewrite Mark in his own words. While there are occasional verbatim reproductions, they are unusual. Note the underlined text in Figure 8.16 (Luke 4:34-35a). This is the longest continuous duplication of Markan text found in the Gospel of Luke. There are no other duplications which match the length of this passage, and there are only a few which exceed half its length. Hence, it stands out as a remarkable exception when Luke and Mark are compared. In contrast there are numerous instances of exact, or very close to exact, reproductions in Luke and Matthew's double tradition.

In studying the texts in Figures 8.15, 8.16, and 8.17, there is no discernible motive on Luke's part to change the meaning of the stories for any reason. For example, in 8.16, Mark's *unclean spirit* becomes *the spirit of an unclean demon* in Luke. In Mark, the man *cries out*; in Luke, the man *cries out with a loud voice*. Again in Mark, Jesus commands *with authority;* in Luke he commands *with authority and power.* These additions to the text have no purpose other than to add color and drama to the story without changing its essential meaning.

Luke's propensity to rewrite Mark is not surprising; rather, it is the norm. That an author would rewrite his sources was an accepted and well-established practice in the Hellenistic world of the first century. Thus Luke's paraphrasing of Mark would not have raised any concern among his readers. However, it raises a huge question for us today. For the Q theory depends upon the assumption that Luke copied large portions of his Q source essentially verbatim. If he did not, the exact or nearly exact duplications in the double tradition would not exist. Nor would we be able to detect the precise editing which seems apparent in Matthew against Luke's texts.

Therefore, the Q theory is based upon a suspicious assumption. It assumes that Luke copied Q essentially verbatim, yet the only direct evidence we have (Luke's use of Mark) indicates that Luke followed the common practice of paraphrasing his sources. This apparent stylistic inconsistency on Luke's part is vital to the issue at hand. For if Luke did not copy large portions of Q verbatim, the Q theory cannot account for the exact duplications of text in the double tradition.

The Semitic Parallelisms

Some will wonder whether it is possible that Luke treated his sources differently. For instance, we might speculate he had a higher regard for the integrity and authority of Q than he did for Mark, and so felt obligated to reproduce Q more exactly than he did Mark. Fortunately the Semitic parallelisms we considered previously are part of the double tradition. They provide a vital key to understanding how Luke may have treated this hypothetical source.

Recall that Matthew retains the parallel structure of the original oral units while Luke paraphrases them. It is widely assumed that since Matthew's version is closer to the original oral tradition, it is older, and hence the version more likely to have appeared in Q. Luke, in using Q, is assumed to have rendered the parallelisms in his own words.   Therefore, Luke's paraphrasing of the parallelisms indicates that he rewrote his Q source in the same manner that he did Mark.

While it is not surprising that Luke would have paraphrased all of his sources, this observation constitutes a grave, and perhaps fatal, inconsistency in the assumptions underlying the Two-Document hypothesis.   For the theory maintains that Luke rendered large portions of his Q source verbatim, even though all direct evidence indicates that this practice was contrary to Luke's style.   This inherent contradiction is the Achilles' heel of the Two-Document hypothesis. When this contradiction is brought to light, it becomes clear that the Q theory fails as a solution to the Synoptic Problem.

4. *Matthew does not rewrite or paraphrase Mark for the purpose of saying the same thing in different words.   He either copies Mark verbatim, or edits Mark.   Either way the result in Matthew bears the stamp of the Markan original.*   In the triple tradition, Matthew most frequently preserves Mark's text either verbatim, or edits from Mark's text.   Luke's rendering is normally the odd one of the three.

In Figure 8.18, Matthew has virtually duplicated Mark with the exception of several minor changes to improve the clarity of the text. On the other hand, Luke's method of putting the story in his own words is evident; only one sentence (v. 33) is duplicated from Mark without change.

Figure 8.19 illustrates Luke's tendency to embellish the story by adding dramatic elements.   Luke changes the word *alarmed* in Mark to *terrified*; in Luke *earthquakes* become *great earthquakes*; he renders the single word *famines* to *famines and pestilences,* and to ensure his readers get the point, he adds *and there will be terrors and great signs from heaven.*   On the other hand, Matthew simply refines Mark's text without altering its dramatic intensity.   When Mark writes, *And Jesus began to say to them*, Matthew changes it to *And Jesus answered them.* Mark's phrase *there will be earthquakes in various places; there will be famines,* is edited by Matthew to read more concisely: *there will be famines and earthquakes in various places.*

Figure 8.18: The Parable of the Fig Tree

Mark 13:28-32	Luke 21:29-33	Matthew 24:32-36
28 From the fig tree learn its lesson: as soon as its branch becomes tender and puts forth its leaves, you know that summer is near. 29 So also, when you see all these things taking place, you know that he is near, at the very gates. 30 Truly, I say to you, this generation will not pass away before all these things take place. 31 Heaven and earth will pass away, but my words will not pass away. 36 But of that day or that hour no one knows, not even the angels in heaven, nor the Son, but only the Father.	29 And he told them a parable: "Look at the fig tree, and all the trees; 30 as soon as they come out in leaf, you see for yourselves and know that the summer is already near. 31 So also, when you see these things taking place, you know that the kingdom of God is near. 32 Truly, I say to you, this generation will not pass away till all has taken place. 33 Heaven and earth will pass away, but my words will not pass away.	32 From the fig tree learn its lesson: as soon as its branch becomes tender and puts forth its leaves, you know that summer is near. 33 So also, when you see all these things, you know that he is near, at the very gates. 34 Truly, I say to you, this generation will not pass away till all these things take place. 35 Heaven and earth will pass away, but my words will not pass away. 36 But of that day and hour no one knows, not even the angels of heaven, nor the Son, but the Father only.

In general, Matthew reproduces Mark's text more faithfully than Luke, often copying large sections of text verbatim. For the most part, when he makes changes they are intended to clarify or streamline a passage without altering its meaning. On the infrequent occasions when Matthew does alter Mark's meaning (as in the reference to the mother of the sons of Zebedee in Fig. 8.20), the changes appear to be motivated by the theological or political needs of the church, rather than by the author's intent to rewrite the text.

In the opening lines of Figure 8.20, Mark states that the two sons of Zebedee approached Jesus directly to ask for preferential treatment in the new kingdom. Recall that Mark was an early gospel which cast these two disciples in a negative light in political response to the Johannine treatment of Peter as a negative character. It would not be surprising to find that as the movement matured it would have reconciled these earlier conflicts in its traditions. We have already seen editing in John and Mark which accomplished precisely this objective.

Figure 8.19: Signs Before the End

Mark 13:3-8	Luke 21:7-11	Matthew 24:3-8
3 As he sat on the Mount of Olives opposite the temple, Peter and James and John and Andrew asked him privately, saying, 4 "Tell us, when will this be, and what will be the sign when these things are all to be accomplished?" 5 And Jesus began to say to them, "Take heed that no one leads you astray. 6 Many will come in my name, saying, 'I am he,' and they will lead many astray. 7 And when you hear of wars and rumors of wars, do not be alarmed; this must take place, but the end is not yet. 8 For nation will rise against nation, and kingdom against kingdom; there will be earthquakes in various places, there will be famines; this is but the beginning of the birth-pangs.	7 And they asked him, "Teacher, when will this be, and what will be the sign when this is about to take place?" 8 And he said, "Take heed that you are not led astray' for many will come in my name, saying, 'I am he!' and 'The time is at hand!' Do not go after them. 9 And when you hear of wars and tumults, do not be terrified; for this must first take place, but the end will not be at once." 10 Then he said to them, 'Nation will rise against nation, and kingdom against kingdom; 11 there will be great earthquakes, and in various places famines and pestilences; and there will be terrors and great signs from heaven.	3 As he sat on the Mount of Olives the disciples came to him privately, saying, "Tell us, when will this be, and what will be the sign of your coming and of the close of the age?" 4 And Jesus answered them, "Take heed that no one leads you astray. 5 For many will come in my name, saying, 'I am the Christ,' and they will lead many astray. And you will hear of wars and rumors of wars; see that you are not alarmed for this must take place, but the end is not yet. 7 For nation will rise against nation, and kingdom against kingdom, and there will be famines and earthquakes in various places; all this is but the beginning of the birth-pangs.

Figure 8.20: The Request of the Sons of Zebedee

Mark 10:35-45	Matt. 20:20-28
35 **And James and John, the sons of Zebedee,** came forward to him, and said to him, "Teacher, we want you to do for us whatever we ask of you." 36 And he said to them, "What do you want me to do for you?" 37 And they said to him, "Grant us to sit, one at your right hand and one at your left, in your glory." 38 But Jesus said to them, "You do not know what you are asking. Are you able to drink the cup that I drink, or to be baptized with the baptism with which I am baptized?" 39 And they said, "We are able." And Jesus said to them, "The cup that I drink you will drink; and with the baptism with which I am baptized, you will be baptized; 40 but to sit at my right hand or my left is not mine to grant, but it is for those for whom it has been prepared." 41 And when the ten heard it they began to be indignant at James and John. 42 And Jesus called them to him, and said to them, "You know that those who are supposed to rule over the Gentiles lord it over them, and their great men exercise authority over them. 43 But it shall not be so among you; but whoever would be great among you must be your servant, 44 and whoever would be first among you must be slave of all. 45 For the Son of man also came not to be served but to serve, and to give his life as a ransom for many."	20 **Then the mother of the sons of Zebedee** came up to him, with her sons, and kneeling before him she asked him for something. 21 And he said to her, "What do you want?" She said to him, "Command that these two sons of mine may sit, one at your right hand and one at your left, in your kingdom." 22 But Jesus answered, "You do not know what you are asking. Are you able to drink the cup that I am to drink?" They said to him, "We are able." 23 He said to them, "You will drink my cup, but to sit at my right hand and at my left is not mine to grant, but it is for those for whom it has been prepared by my Father." 24 And when the ten heard it, they were indignant at the two brothers. 25 But Jesus called them to him and said, "You know that the rulers of the Gentiles lord it over them, and their great men exercise authority over them. 26 It shall not be so among you; but whoever would be great among you must be your servant, 27 and whoever would be first among you must be your slave; 28 even as the Son of man came not to be served but to serve, and to give his life as a ransom for many."

Figure 8.20, then, appears to be another example of Matthew reconciling earlier hostile traditions which originated in factional conflict. Note that Matthew says it was the two disciples' *mother* who had asked Jesus for special treatment of her sons. This would have

been a forgivable thing for any mother to ask. Thus the Markan story which intended to make the sons of Zebedee appear self-serving is altered by Matthew to mitigate the harsh implication.

In Figure 8.20 there are several instances where Matthew has removed redundant phrases, or changed words for the purpose of improving clarity. However, in its totality, the story remains largely Mark's; Matthew has simply improved the language.

By examining Matthew's use of Mark, we find that he tended to duplicate Mark's text whenever it did not require editing for clarity or for deliberate alteration to meet ecclesiastical objectives. Further, it is apparent that he attempted to render the parallelisms in their original form as well. Thus it is consistent with the author's demonstrated use of his sources to propose that the verbatim duplications in the double tradition are the result of Matthew's copying from Luke.

Additional Evidence that Matthew used Mark and Luke

Before we close this inquiry into the Synoptic Problem, there are two further observations which support the present theory. First, if it is true that Matthew used Luke as a source, then the material which is common between them would have been defined by Matthew's editorial decisions--Matthew would have selected which of Luke's stories and sayings he would include in his own gospel, and which he would leave out. Modern scholars, by defining Q as the material which is unique to Luke and Matthew, have in so doing limited their definition of Q to just those traditions which Matthew saw fit to reproduce from Luke. In essence, Matthew would have "composed" Q.

If this is were the case, the Q material should not be thematically divergent from the Gospel of Matthew at large, but rather should show a noticeable affinity with Matthean thought. Has such a phenomenon been detected? Burton Mack provides an answer:

> If one were to ask which of the narrative gospels most nearly represents an ethos toward which the community of Q may have tended, it would be the Gospel of Matthew."[21]

---

[21] Mack, Ibid., p. 173

There is no reason a pre-Christian "community of Q" should have had a particular ethos toward any of the four Christian gospels. Yet this finding is no coincidence: the Q material as a distinct set of traditions has a theological and philosophical affinity with Matthew because Matthew selected them from Luke's gospel and copied them into his own. Therefore, Matthew's editorial decisions effectively composed the material scholars have alleged came from Q.

The second observation relates to the nature of the double tradition material itself. If Q was not a lost gospel, then what is the source of this material? The statistical patterns in the gospels suggest that most of the Q material, and in fact most of all the non-Markan tradition which appears in Luke, is a miscellaneous collection of traditions which developed later in the first century. The author of Luke collected these emerging traditions, added them to Mark, and created a revised and enhanced gospel story.

If it is correct that the non-Markan traditions in Luke derive from oral and recently written sources, we might imagine they would bear signs of oral origin. This would be the case for the Q material; it would also be the case for the material that is unique to Luke among the four gospels, which is referred to as Luke's "special" material. Does Luke show evidence of having made direct use of oral traditions? Helmut Koester comments on Luke's Q material:

> The sequence in which certain groups of sayings occur in the Gospel of Luke *often reveals an association and composition of sayings that is more directly related to the process of the collection of oral materials,* while Matthew interrupts or disturbs such sequences whenever his motivations as an author of literature are evident."[22]

So it is evident to researchers that the Q material in Luke has a closer association with oral tradition than does the same material in Matthew. Can the same be detected in Luke's special material? Koester has found that it can:

---

[22] Koester, Ibid., p. 131, emphasis added

The diversity of the special materials included in Luke's Gospel warn against the assumption of just one major special source for Luke. It is more likely that an educated and widely traveled author like Luke had access to a variety of written as well as orally circulating materials. Luke wrote at a comparatively late date, several decades after Matthew, that is, after the turn of the 1st century, when more of the gospel materials had been collected in written form . . . *On the other hand, Luke's church does not seem to have lost the connection to the continuing and still developing free (oral) tradition of sayings of Jesus and stories about him. Luke is therefore a remarkable witness for the continuing free circulation of oral and written collections of sayings of Jesus and of narratives about him as late as three generations after his death.*[23]

Luke is a remarkable witness indeed. Most of the material in Luke which is not derived from Mark bears a close affinity with the process of orally developing legends. This is precisely what one would anticipate if Luke had combined Mark with a collection of newly developed legends and sayings attributed to Jesus.

The Improbability of the Q Gospel

The idea that two independent writers each selected the same source materials and produced separate gospels that were virtually identical in literary scope has always been one of the puzzles of Q. How did the later writer manage to assemble all the same sources without being aware of the earlier gospel itself? The scenario seems unlikely, but since it is conceivable, the problem is most often written off as coincidental. Similarly, the array of minor agreements between Luke and Matthew against Mark point toward a direct dependence of one writer upon the other. Yet these are also in one way or another explained away as coincidental. Although these are two of the common arguments against the Q theory, they are not the most compelling ones.

---

[23] Koester, Ibid., p. 337, emphasis added. Note Koester's belief that Luke wrote several decades after Matthew is not generally accepted by most scholars. The evidence presented in this book shows that Koester's sequencing of Luke and Matthew is in error. The purpose of this quotation is to illustrate the recognition of Luke's materials as being derived from oral traditions.

The idea that there was a common Q Gospel used by Matthew and Luke fails on two counts. First, scholars cannot advance a strong argument that Matthew could not have been aware of Luke. Once this possibility is admitted, the notion that Q must have been a single document with its own literary integrity is undermined. Second, it requires that Luke copied large portions of Q verbatim in spite of the fact that all evidence indicates this was not Luke's style. That the theory can stand in the light of this inconsistency is remarkable.

The evidence further shows that the literary style of Matthew allowed for frequent verbatim duplication of his Markan source, though at the same time he felt free to edit for clarity, efficiency of language, and occasionally for doctrinal reasons. When Matthew and Luke are compared, the same style is evident. There are frequent duplications of text, and when text is not duplicated it most often looks as though it has been edited in the same manner that the Markan texts were edited. So the credibility of the Two-Document hypothesis also suffers from the fact that the data are easily explained by Matthew's use of Luke as a source.

The Alleged Literary Unity of Q

Scholars on the leading edge of Q research have identified what they believe to be a literary unity within the Q material. Such a finding would lend credence to the proposal that the Q material was derived from a single document which had been composed with some unity of ideological purpose and literary style. Assertions that Q does indeed display such a unity are often made by Q theorists interested in advancing the idea that Q can be reasonably understood as a lost gospel.

At face value, however, the Q material looks like a miscellaneous collection of traditions which seem rather detached from one another once they are removed from their contexts in Luke and Matthew. Had there been an obvious unity to the material, it would have been detected some time ago. The fact that scholars can detect a subtle unity once they look for it is not surprising. It is likely that the thematic unity some believe exists in the Q material derives from the fact that it is the discrete subset of non-Markan traditions in Luke which Matthew decided to reproduce in his gospel. Editing activity on the part of two successive authors would have been adequate to impart an inconspicuous literary unity to the Q texts.

Q scholars have also tried to isolate distinctive literary features which would support the notion of Q as a single document which was distinct in tradition from Mark. Arland Jacobson highlights what he believes to be a "small but very striking example" of different language usage between Q and Mark:

> In Q, the quotation formula, "I say to you" never occurs with the word "truly" . . . . In fact, the word "truly" does not occur anywhere in Q . . . . But Mark has fourteen instances of the "I say to you" formula, and in all but two, he has "truly." . . . The consistency of Markan usage is as dramatic as the fact that "truly" is never found in Q, even though it occurs often in Matthew and six times in Luke. Not only does this illustrate the difference in usage between Mark and Q, but it is also a potent argument for the Two-Document hypothesis.[24]

What Jacobson has pointed to is a unique phrase "Truly, I say to you," which is a Markan idiom. He implies that its absence from the Q material is evidence of the literary unity of Q. However, this cannot be sustained. There is no reason to think that an assortment of legends which evolved in the decades after Mark would reproduce a distinct Markan formula such as this. So the fact that it is absent from the Q material is no particular surprise. Jacobson's observation only demonstrates the literary integrity of Mark, which of course is not the point at issue. His conclusion that the lack of the Markan formula in Q is a potent argument for the Q theory does not follow.

In general, much of the work being done to demonstrate the uniqueness and unity of Q begins with the assumption that Q was a single literary source. Hence, many of the observations which are no more than compatible with the theory are advanced as firm evidence in its favor. It is often overlooked that the same observations can as easily be explained by assuming Q to have been a miscellaneous assortment of oral and written traditions which took on distinct

---

[24] Jacobson, Ibid., p. 62, 63

literary similarities when they were first collected and arranged by Luke, and subsequently edited by Matthew.

Q and the Quest for the Historical Jesus

The Jesus Seminar identifies the Two-Document hypothesis as one of its pillars of scholarly wisdom. It is upon this pillar that a great deal of historical Jesus research depends. Many of the sayings of Jesus identified by the Jesus Seminar as having the highest historical authenticity come from the Q material. However, the evidence shows that there is a different way to interpret the texts which leads to an opposite conclusion. For if the Q theory does not hold, and the Q material is found to be a collection of legends and attributions which evolved during the second half of the first century, then many of the sayings judged by the Jesus Seminar to be the most authentic may in fact be the least.

The statistical patterns in the previous chapter indicate that an evolution of mythology and moral vision is apparent in the John-Mark-Luke-Matthew sequence. The data harmonize with the findings in this chapter that the most comprehensive solution to the synoptic problem is that the author of Matthew compiled his gospel using Mark and Luke as sources.

In short, the notion that Q is a "discovered lost gospel" has led us up a long blind alley in the quest for the historical Jesus. For it is not a lost gospel at all; rather, it is a collection of legends and attributions which the Jesus movement assimilated as it grew from its roots as a struggling Jewish Messiah cult into a movement with an expanded world vision. Efforts to recover Q and the community that allegedly produced it have been motivated by the best of intentions, and by the universal desire to discover who Jesus really was. However, in the end, the notion that the historical Jesus can be glimpsed through the window of Q is in error. The lost gospel Q never existed.

❖ 9 ❖

The Historical Jesus

At first it may appear that the quest for the historical Jesus has been set back to square one. For two key assumptions which undergird much contemporary thought on Jesus have been shown herein to be untrustworthy. The first is that the Gospel of John is historically irrelevant to the quest. The second is that Q provides reliable and unique insights into the primitive Jesus movement. Since neither of these assumptions is well founded, reconstructions of the historical Jesus which are based upon them are likely to be inaccurate.

Does this mean that the quest is hopeless? Fortunately, it does not. For though these common notions about the gospels are not viable, the results of this study suggest a new method for recovering historical elements of the life of Jesus. Based on the priority of John, and the demonstration that the Q material is a legendary overlay, a new and more fruitful quest may reasonably begin with the Gospels of John and Mark.

John and Mark are the earliest surviving records of the historical Jesus. John appears to have been composed by one very close to eyewitness sources, if indeed, he was not an eyewitness himself. Mark is the earliest record of the teachings of Peter. Since John and Mark are in ideological opposition to one another, a good starting point will be to isolate the common elements on which these two gospels are in agreement. Independent attestation from two opposing sects of the primitive Jesus movement increases the probability that an event or saying has historical foundation. The common elements found in John and Mark, when drawn together as a subset of gospel traditions, may constitute a more probable core of historical fact from which a credible portrait of Jesus may be derived.[1]

Before pursuing this more closely, we must recognize that there are indeed limits to what may be recovered with certainty. There are few sayings of Jesus which appear in both John and Mark. This means that there are very few data with which to reconstruct the content of his preaching. Yet the absence of a clearly defined historical message is, in itself, an important clue. Scholars have long recognized that the words of Jesus as recorded by John are often motivated by the desire of the author to present Jesus in a certain theological light. However, the same is true of Mark, and no less so than John.

Since there is little agreement between John and Mark on the sayings of Jesus, and since their attributions are often influenced by a theological agenda, it appears that John and Mark (unlike Luke and Matthew) did not perceive Jesus as one who had taught a distinct collection of authoritative teachings as an objective of his ministry. For John and Mark, the dominant issue is the resurrection. They record teachings of Jesus which bear primarily upon the interpretation of this event.

In John, Jesus says, "I am the resurrection and the life; he who believes in me, though he die, yet shall he live" (John 11:25). In Mark, Jesus says, "If any man would come after me, let him deny himself and take up his cross and follow me" (Mark 8:34). Sayings such as these would have been meaningless to Jesus' historical audience. If we were to delete all sayings from John and Mark which make sense only in the light of resurrection theology, there would be few teachings left which would have been comprehensible to Jesus' historical audience. Though Mark contains more sayings which could survive such an edit, both gospels would be drastically altered.

---

[1] Technically, critical historical method requires that two sources be entirely independent of one another before double attestation is recognized. However, since all four gospel traditions are based upon one another, there is no demonstrable independent double attestation of any Jesus tradition. Thus the closest we can come to double attested traditions are the elements common to John and Mark. Even though Mark was produced using John as a reference, the fact that the two gospels are products of sects which are in conflict on so many fundamental issues, we have reason to believe they have evolved from two different eyewitness traditions. Hence the points upon which they agree have greater potential to have been derived from historical events.

Furthermore, as independent evidence, the apostle Paul does not seem to be aware of a substantive message derived from Jesus' teaching either. For Paul, the entire message is Jesus as the resurrected Lord. Paul remembers little, if any, substance in the teachings of Jesus. "We preach Christ crucified . . ." proclaims Paul (1 Cor. 1:23). Whatever Jesus' teachings might have been, they were of little relevance to the central Pauline message of resurrection and redemption.

Thus, we have three early and somewhat independent witnesses which do not seem concerned to document a concrete message of Jesus, or at least one which would have been understood by his historical audience. Therefore, we must allow the possibility that, contrary to popular notions about him, Jesus did not have an extensive repertoire of teachings which his earliest disciples recognized as an authoritative message of their Lord. His historical ministry did not consist of moral revelations, or memorable wisdom teachings which gave his followers personal strength.

As we proceed through this chapter, we will find that the absence of such traditions from John, Paul, and to a lesser degree Mark, most likely derive from the fact that they were, in fact, absent from the message of the historical Jesus. The explosion of faith and confidence manifested by the primitive Jesus movement was not based upon a substantive message of Jesus, but on his perceived resurrection.

Finding the Historical Jesus in John and Mark

Since John and Mark are the earliest gospels, the most rational way to proceed will be to isolate elements common to both which may help us to sketch his ministry. The elements of mutual agreement between John and Mark are these:

1. Jesus came from Nazareth of Galilee.

2. His ministry began within the context of the ministry of John the Baptist.

3. He gathered a band of followers about him, and moved about the regions of Judea and Galilee during the course of his ministry.

4. He designated a group of twelve followers as special disciples; Peter was a prominent disciple.

5. He taught in the synagogue at Capernaum.

6. According to the Pharisees, he broke the Sabbath law.

7. He proclaimed himself to be the "Messiah" or "Christ."

8. He performed several miraculous healings:
   a. restored the sight of a blind man
   b. healed a paralyzed man
   c. raised a person from death

9. He performed non-healing miracles:
   a. fed 5,000 persons with five loaves of bread and two fish
   b. walked on the sea

10. His activities threatened the Jewish authorities in Jerusalem.

11. He had recurring disputes with the Pharisees over interpretations of the law.

12. He created a violent disturbance in the temple.

13. He staged a public entry into Jerusalem the week before Passover and the Feast of Unleavened Bread.

14. The people who witnessed this public entry anticipated the arrival of a new "kingdom" being ushered in by Jesus.

15. He was anointed with expensive oil at Bethany.

16. He had a Last Supper with his disciples.

17. He was betrayed by Judas Iscariot, who disclosed where he was to authorities.

18. He was troubled by his impending arrest.

19. He was arrested at night in an unknown location outside Jerusalem by armed representatives of the Jewish authorities.

20. Upon his arrest, his disciples fled.

21. He was interrogated first by Jewish authorities, then by the Roman governor Pontius Pilate.

22. During his interrogation, the issue at hand was whether he had proclaimed himself to be King of the Jews.

23. Pilate was initially noncommittal in his condemnation of Jesus; he finally condemned Jesus at the urging of the Jewish authorities.

24. He was mocked as a would-be king by being dressed in a purple robe and a crown of thorns.

25. He was executed by crucifixion on the day of Preparation.

26. The inscription on the cross read, "King of the Jews."

27. He was buried by Joseph of Arimathea in a nearby tomb.

28. On the morning of the first day of the week, the tomb was found vacant by Mary Magdalene.

29. Jesus appeared to his disciples after his crucifixion.[2]

Analyzing the Common Elements

We have seen that a wide assortment of mythological and legendary material was added to the story of Jesus during the course of the first century. Due to the mythical quality of some of the stories in the above list, the miracle stories in particular, we may assume the myth-making process had begun prior to the compilation of John. Hence, though a particular story may appear in both John and Mark, we cannot automatically presume it is historical.

The opposite is also true. There are a host of traditions which appear in either John or Mark, but not both. The fact that they are not recorded in both does not automatically disqualify them from consideration. We have already seen that a number of stories in John have greater historical plausibility than do their synoptic counterparts. Thus it may also be that a variety of traditions in John which have no synoptic parallel, may be historically valid anyway. However, the first step is to see whether a coherent general outline of the life of Jesus may be gleaned from the traditions attested by both John and Mark, which will be referred to as the *core* material. To such an outline, further traditions might be added from John, or indeed any source, if they are found to be in harmony with the core material.

---

[2] Common element based on restoring the traditions in John 21 to the end of Mark.

Jesus as Religious Insurgent

The most fundamental element of the picture which emerges from the core traditions is that of Jesus as a religious insurgent who challenged the authority of established Jewish leadership in Jerusalem. The observation is based upon two key traditions. First, Jesus had launched his activities within the context of John the Baptist's movement. Recall that John the Baptist was also arrested and executed as one who threatened the authorities with the potential for leading an uprising. That Jesus' ministry emerged out of the religious unrest which had found its voice in the Baptist's movement would indicate that Jesus was capitalizing upon the same restless mood of the people.

Second, the fact that Jesus was himself arrested and executed is evidence that he was perceived as a threat to the ruling authorities. Even the Romans, as brutal as they often were, were not in the habit of crucifying gentle teachers of morality and wisdom for no apparent reason. The execution of Jesus indicates that his activities were a visible threat to Jewish leaders and/or the Roman administration. He was crucified as an enemy of the state. The most obvious inference is that Jesus had demonstrated himself capable of leading an uprising in defiance of established authority, and that he was executed before he could do so.

Jesus as Moral Visionary

It would be inappropriate to characterize Jesus as a gentle moral sage who went about preaching admonitions to turn the other cheek, love one's enemies, and let the children come to him. These sayings do not appear in the core tradition, and they are incompatible with the portrait of Jesus as a revolutionary activist. Of all attempts to portray the historical Jesus, this is probably furthest from the truth. However, the core tradition shows that Jesus was motivated in part by a righteous indignation against religious hypocrisy. The moral authority behind his revolutionary spirit stemmed from an indignation toward institutionalized religion which was being used to control and suppress its adherents.

A key element in the core material is that Jesus regularly violated the Sabbath:

> If on the Sabbath a man receives circumcision, so that the law of Moses may not be broken, are you angry with me because on the Sabbath I made a man's whole body well? Do not judge by appearances, but judge with right judgment. (John 7:23-24)

> And he said to the man who had the withered hand, "Come here." And he said to them, "Is it lawful on the Sabbath to do good or to do harm, to save life or to kill?" But they were silent. And he looked around at them with anger, grieved at their hardness of heart, and said to the man, "Stretch out your hand." He stretched it out, and his hand was restored. (Mark 3:3-5)

> And he said to them, "The Sabbath was made for man, not man for the Sabbath." (Mark 2:27)

In John and Mark, the institutionalized regulations regarding observation of the Sabbath epitomize the manner in which religion had become distorted. In the core tradition, Jesus speaks out with indignation against the Pharisees who have produced a stifling legalism that exists not to serve the people but to control them. It is apparent that the revolt Jesus intended to instigate had gained a great deal of its moral vitality and authority from conflicts with the Pharisees over a freer interpretation of the law.

John and Mark also agree that Jesus created a violent disturbance in the temple. The temple, as the physical and symbolic center of Judaism, had for many years been under the administration of Jewish authorities who were politically allied with the Romans. The temple actually served Roman interests as a place where sacrifices to the emperor were performed, although Jews were not required to make such sacrifices. Nevertheless the temple was not functioning as the sacred house of God that it was envisioned to be in Jewish tradition. The core material indicates that Jesus reacted against the profaning of the temple. Though his confrontation was with money-changers who facilitated the purchase of sacrificial animals and the payment of the temple tax, we may assume the issue was more fundamental. Jesus objected to the use of the temple for institutional purposes which were incompatible with its function as the house of God.

Thus the earliest traditions show how Jesus held the high moral ground in his conflict with authorities. It is not surprising that as the first century progressed, the moral teachings attributed to him grew in number and scope as his legend evolved.

Jesus as Messiah

The core material indicates that Jesus represented himself as the anticipated Messiah. As noted previously, both Jesus and John the Baptist were identified by their followers as messianic figures.

Though the earliest traditions agree that Jesus appropriated the title *Messiah*, it is difficult to say exactly what he and his followers may have understood the role of Messiah to represent.[3] There is no prophecy in the OT that the Messiah would be executed or resurrected. Neither is there any expectation that the Messiah would perform miracles as a sign of his identity. Indeed, the very anticipation of the Messiah is almost non-existent as an OT theme.[4] So we cannot define the first century usage of the term *Messiah* by reference to OT tradition. For the most part we must infer the meaning of the term from its contextual usage in the gospels, and in John and Mark in particular, since we may suspect its definition within Christian expression would have changed by the time Luke and Matthew were composed.

John and Mark are in unison on the fact that a common perception of the day was that a Christ (Messiah) was in fact anticipated, and

---

[3] It is important to recognize that the definition of "Messiah" as it was used in the time of Jesus was nothing like its definition in Christian theology today. As Christianity evolved, its proclamation of Jesus as Messiah became loosely synonymous with other Christian titles such as the Son of God, and the Savior of the world. Sometimes the messianic role of Jesus is equated with his substitutionary death and resurrection. However, Christianity did not exist during the time of Jesus, and Christian interpretations of the nature and role of the Messiah would not have been in the consciousness of the people Jesus encountered. Therefore, the question is what Jesus intended to communicate to his historical audience by proclaiming himself as the Messiah.

[4] Out of seventeen books of prophecy in the OT, the anticipated coming of an "anointed one" (the literal meaning of the term *Messiah*), only occurs once (Daniel 9:25,26). There are several references to an anticipated future Davidic king, but in these instances the phrase "anointed one" is not used to describe this figure.

that he would be a descendent of David (Mark 12:35-37; John 7:40-43). However, in these passages both John and Mark agree that Jesus claimed messianic status without the credentials of descent from David. The descent from David and the birth in Bethlehem are later myths which appear in Luke and Matthew. They were apparently developed by the movement to make the tradition of Jesus conform to the popular understanding of the Messiah as a "son of David."

Descent from David implies a political role for the Messiah. Historically, David was Israel's greatest king. It was David who had first captured Jerusalem and established it as the capital of the nation of Israel ten centuries prior to Jesus. Thus if the Messiah was to be a Son of David, the most apparent expectation would have been that he would fulfill the role of a king in the manner of David.

In Jesus' day, Judea[5] was occupied by the Romans. The Jewish authorities had aligned themselves politically with the Roman administration. Caiaphas, the high priest, had been in office for many years, and was to serve a total tenure of eighteen years, according to Josephus. He was clearly in favorable standing with the Romans. In Christian tradition, this alliance of the Jewish authorities with the Romans is often characterized as the result of self-serving opportunism on the part of the Jews. However, it is likely that this "alliance" had originally stemmed from a prudent deference to Roman occupation in the face of Roman military superiority. Regardless of the root cause of the alliance, it appears to have created enough political animosity among Jews who did not receive any benefit from Roman occupation that an uprising was perceived as a real threat.

Hence messianic expectation would have carried a political connotation, albeit one which is difficult to define. We may infer from the core material in John and Mark that the uprising contemplated by Jesus would have been directed against the Jewish authorities who controlled the temple activities. One of his objectives would have been to restore the religious integrity of the temple. Perhaps there were other roles the Messiah may have been expected to fulfill, but it is difficult to imagine that a Messiah was expected who would not

---

5 Judea was the province in which the city of Jerusalem was located.

address the political issue of the Jewish establishment's association with the Roman administration, and the consequent secularization of the temple.

Therefore, the proclamation of Messiahship by Jesus is consistent with the indications that he was capable of, and intent upon, leading a popular uprising which threatened the stability of the Jewish establishment. When Jesus announced himself as the Messiah, he was proclaiming himself to be one who would literally lead a revolt to install a new Jewish leadership and (consequently) bring about a new relationship with the Romans. He was the one who would be the new King of Israel.

Jesus as King of the Jews

Messiahship and kingship were closely related terms in first century Palestine; both were political in nature. John and Mark agree that Jesus proclaimed himself to be King of the Jews. Both gospels report that he staged a dramatic entry into Jerusalem riding upon a young ass. Both gospels also report that this event was pre-planned. Jesus did it for the purpose of illustrating the fulfillment of an OT prophecy that the new king would arrive riding upon a young ass:

> Rejoice greatly, O daughter of Zion!
> Shout aloud, O daughter of Jerusalem!
> Lo, your king comes to you; triumphant and victorious is he,
> humble and riding on an ass, on a colt the foal of an ass.
> (Zechariah 9:9)

During the "triumphal entry" the people who assembled for the event (no doubt Jesus' own followers), proclaimed Jesus to be the new King of Israel (according to John 12:13), and the one who was to usher in the coming kingdom of David (according to Mark 11:10). So both gospels identify Jesus' entry into Jerusalem as a triumphant arrival of a king. Both indicate that it was a premeditated and carefully staged event to achieve dramatic visual effect.

According to John, Jesus conducted his triumphal entry five days before Passover and the concurrent commencement of the seven day Feast of Unleavened Bread. In other words, Jesus did this at a time when tens of thousands of pilgrims were arriving in Jerusalem to celebrate the holy days. The Fourth Gospel implies that Jesus' prior activities had already created an expectation among many that he would be a significant presence at this festival, and that his anticipated activities would be related to the temple:

> Now the Passover of the Jews was at hand, and many went up from the country to Jerusalem before the Passover to purify themselves. They were looking for Jesus and saying to one another as they stood in the temple, "What do you think, that he will not come to the feast?" (John 11:55-56)

Thus Jesus appears to have conducted the triumphal entry in preparation for his move at precisely the time that the riotous consequence of a popular uprising would have been at its maximum. At face value, Jesus' announcement that he had arrived as the new king implies that he expected to force a political confrontation with Jewish authorities. If it is historical, the triumphal entry would appear not only to have been a signal of his intent, but an attempt to rally support for his impending confrontation. The Christian notion that he was marching on Jerusalem to proclaim the new spiritual kingdom of God would have made no sense to anyone at the time. Hence a political interpretation of Jesus' action is the most plausible solution.

John and Mark are in unison on the fact that the accusation against Jesus was that he had announced himself to be the King of the Jews. They agree that upon his condemnation, Jesus was dressed in a purple robe and crowned with a crown of thorns in order to mock his alleged kingship. They agree that the inscription on the cross read, "King of the Jews."

Within Christian tradition, it is common to interpret that his accusers all sadly misunderstood the true spiritual kingship of Jesus, and that his condemnation was an ignorant mistake based on a mis-comprehension of Jesus' true purpose. However, these interpretations were developed later to accommodate the vision of Jesus as the Son of God who had come on a universal mission to save the world. A literal reading of the core tradition does not support such interpretations. Jesus had a political objective, and he evoked a political response.

The evidence indicates that Jesus had intended to lead a popular uprising which would install him as the new King of Israel. Such a role would enable him to assume influence over, or control of, the temple's use. He would restore it to sacred use, and eliminate practices which he perceived to be in the service of the establishment rather than true religion. His self-proclamation as Messiah and anticipated king were to this end. His move on Jerusalem was timed to capitalize upon the fact that thousands of visitors were arriving from all over Palestine, many of whom he may have believed were in support of his objectives. As there is strength in numbers, Jesus must have understood that his best odds for success lay with an uprising during the high holy days when the crowds were present.

Meanwhile, it is also clear from the core tradition that the Jewish authorities anticipated such an uprising. The Fourth Gospel is specific on the point that they feared Jesus would lead a revolt which would result in a bloody suppression by the Romans:

> So the chief priests and Pharisees gathered the council, and said, "What are we to do? For this man has performed many signs. If we let him go on thus, every one will believe in him, and the Romans will come and destroy both our holy place and our nation." (John 11:47-48)

The gospel traditions are unanimous in their reports that it was the Jewish authorities who arrested and condemned Jesus. Through the centuries this has been the source of a bizarre anti-Semitism in Christianity, one which professes hatred of Jews while remaining comfortably oblivious to the fact that Jews founded Christianity.

In order to mitigate the unfortunate effects of the tradition that the Jewish authorities arrested and condemned Jesus, an effort has been made periodically to emphasize the Romans as the true villains. After all, the Roman governor held the final say in condemning and crucifying Jesus. How can the Jewish leaders be blamed when they did not have the power to condemn anyone under Roman law?

While it is easy to agree with the motive for such a reinterpretation, the fact remains that the gospels place the blame squarely upon the Jewish authorities. However, we must bear in mind once again that the gospels were written by dedicated followers of Jesus with an evangelical objective. Thus they had a significant bias. The gospels are story-telling documents in which the conflict is simplified; Jesus was the hero and the Jewish authorities the villains. Real historical conflicts, of course, are rarely this simple. Further, it is clear from numerous incidental references in John that it was not this simple.

From the Gospel of John, we know that the Jewish leaders were confronted with the potential for a revolt led by Jesus. Since it was to take place during the festival when the city streets would be jammed, we may presume the Roman legion would have been on alert and ready to suppress any civil unrest. The Jewish leaders' fear that an uprising would result in a violent suppression by Roman troops may have been well-founded. If they perceived that Jesus had threatened to instigate a riotous calamity, fueled by a messianic fever to occupy and seize control of the temple, they may legitimately have believed that he needed to be stopped in order to avoid a bloody conflict with the Romans. That they actually perceived him as a threat to their own political stability is remote. However, given the violent consequences of a riot, it would have been their duty as a governing body to ensure that peace was maintained during the holy days.

Given the political dilemma they faced, their action against Jesus becomes more understandable. From their perspective, to eliminate a religious and political insurgent in order to maintain the peace would have been entirely justifiable. For them, the arrest of Jesus would reduce the threat of a violent disturbance, and thereby save hundreds, or perhaps thousands, of lives. Remarkably, the Gospel of John says the high priest Ca'iaphas used this very logic in his address to the assembled council:

> But one of them, Ca'aiphas, who was high priest that year, said to them, "You know nothing at all; you do not understand that it is expedient for you that one man should die for the people, and that the whole nation should not perish." (John 11:49-50)

This statement by Ca'aiphas is an excellent example of the author's use of irony as a literary device. Of course, the statement has double meaning as a reference to the Christian belief that Jesus died in order to secure the salvation of the world. Thus in this statement, the author portrays Ca'aiphas as saying something of much greater significance than he is aware. However, perhaps the greatest irony is that the ironic interpretation itself serves to obscure the fact that the statement literally depicts the political trade-off the authorities were faced with. Should they allow Jesus to proceed and risk an uncontrolled violent confrontation with the Romans, or should they arrest Jesus and maintain social stability? Clearly they acted to preserve the peace. The arrest warrant was issued.

Jesus as Fugitive

John and Mark agree that Jesus and his disciples operated in a clandestine manner, especially during the last week of his life. This is indicated by the tradition of the betrayal by Judas Iscariot. The implications of this well-known story are not often considered: What exactly did the betrayal consist of, and why was it necessary? We need look no further than the Gospel of John. For this gospel is explicit that Jesus was in hiding, and that the authorities were actively seeking those who would report his whereabouts:

> Jesus therefore no longer went about openly among the Jews, but went from there to the country near the wilderness, to a town called E'phraim; and there he stayed with his disciples (John 11:54)

> Now the chief priests and the Pharisees had given orders that if any one knew where he was, he should let them know, so that they might arrest him. (John 11:57)

Clearly, the betrayal by Judas consisted of his revealing to authorities where Jesus was hiding the night of his arrest:

> When Jesus had spoken these words, he went forth with his disciples across the Kidron Valley, where there was a garden, which he and his disciples entered. Now Judas, who betrayed him, also knew the place; for Jesus often met there with his disciples. So Judas, procuring a band of soldiers and some officers from the chief priests and the Pharisees, went there with lanterns and torches and weapons. (John 18:1-3)

While the synoptic gospels retain the story of the betrayal, they omit the information that Jesus went into hiding to avoid arrest. Mark places an entirely different interpretation on it by saying that Jesus and his disciples went to Gethsemene to pray and to come to terms with his impending death (Mark 14:32-42). In addition, Mark adds another element into the arrest scene which is intended specifically to reverse the Johannine claim that Jesus was acting as a fugitive:

> And Jesus said to them, "Have you come out as against a robber, with swords and clubs to capture me? Day after day I was with you in the temple teaching, and you did not seize me. But let the scriptures be fulfilled." (Mark 14:48-49)

Both John and Mark indicate that a large armed band was needed to capture Jesus. They both say that one of Jesus' disciples pulled a sword of his own during this confrontation. Finally, they say that Jesus' disciples scattered and fled during the arrest scene. From the fact that Jesus was in hiding we may deduce that he was well aware that his activities made him subject to arrest. From the fact that the disciples fled, we may infer that they could have been arrested as well.

The cumulative evidence suggests that Jesus and his disciples were planning to stage a dramatic public event which was intended to ignite a revolt during the festival. Jesus and his band were in hiding. He had already telegraphed his intentions with the triumphal entry. The authorities were highly motivated to arrest him before the festival began. Due to a tip from one of his own followers, they were able to locate and arrest Jesus just twenty-four hours prior to the Passover. As the soldiers arrived, his disciples fled; Jesus was apprehended. He was quickly condemned and crucified as a warning to all that those who would conspire to revolt would not be tolerated.

Since Jesus' plans were cut short, we will never know with certainty what he had intended to do. However, the Gospel of John remembers people in the temple awaiting his appearance during the last week of his life (John 11:55-56). It also recalls a disturbance in the temple early in Jesus' ministry which was prompted by his indignation at the profaning of the temple with inappropriate business practices

(John 2:13-17). Furthermore, the Gospel of Mark places the disturbance in the temple on the day after the triumphal entry. Mark identifies this as the act which mobilized Jesus' opposition (Mark 11:15-19), and led directly to his arrest. Thus Mark associates the end of Jesus' career with the action at the temple. Collectively, these elements of the tradition are compatible with the theory that Jesus was planning to seize the temple during the festival, and by popular acclaim of the assembled crowds, to assume a role as their new king.

The Political Dilemma

Ever since their fateful confrontation with Jesus, the Jewish authorities who acted to arrest and condemn Jesus have been maligned in Christian tradition. Since the story is told by those who had great sympathy for Jesus, the tradition vilifies the Jews without any reflection upon the magnitude of the dilemma Jesus posed for them. Though many of them enjoyed benefits deriving from their political association with the Romans, some of them may have been in sympathy with restoring the temple to a more sacred use.

However, when the situation was weighed with a sober mind, it was apparent to the Jewish council that an uprising posed grave risks to life and to the security of Jerusalem. They knew the mood of the people. They also knew the attitude and resolve of the Roman governor. They knew that he would not hesitate to suppress an uprising with brutal force. Whatever they may have felt personally about the Roman occupation, or the institutionalized use of the temple, this festival was not the time to allow anyone to incite a riot. The loss of life could be great, and the risk to the temple unacceptable.

Christian tradition has reduced the Jewish council's decision to arrest Jesus from a complex political, religious, and social dilemma to a spiteful and mean-spirited act on the part of a few self-serving Jews. However, from the evidence embedded within the Gospels of John and Mark, it is clear that the decision was not that simplistic.

The Message of Jesus

With this as background, the fact that the earliest traditions do not record a substantial collection of sayings of Jesus makes more sense. If Jesus' historical role was to restore the temple and to establish himself as a new king, the content of his teachings would have been oriented toward that objective. John and Mark clearly recall an ideological conflict between Jesus and the Pharisees regarding which included disputes about purification, the observance of the Sabbath, and other issues related to the Judaic law. John and Mark both recall the conflict surrounding the temple and the fact that it had been profaned. These recollections are consistent with his apparent historical mission.

Hence, from these elements we may envision the essential message of the historical Jesus as one which was related to the furtherance of his revolutionary objectives. However, once Jesus died, the political context of his movement ended. Much of his rhetoric which served the political agenda would have found little use in a spiritual movement with radically redefined objectives. Thus it is not surprising that John and Paul, as the earliest of the traditions, do not recall an array of teachings on morality and wisdom which were, in and of themselves, an important part of Jesus' message. The absence of a developed teaching content in John and Paul, and the relatively limited content in Mark, is evidence that the substance of Jesus' historical message was not relevant to the subsequent portrait of Jesus as the eternal resurrected Savior of the world.

Neither it is a surprise that John characterizes the ministry of Jesus as one of hostile conflict with the Jewish establishment. Much of the caustic rhetoric of the Johannine Jesus is consistent with his historical role as that of a religious insurgent whose objective was to challenge established authority. Thus the recollections in John which portray Jesus as aggressively confrontational are likely derived from historical roots.

Within the context of his anti-establishment movement, Jesus cultivated among his followers a sense of moral indignation against the Jewish authorities. No doubt this served to strengthen their resolve and commitment to support Jesus in his objectives. However, after Jesus' death it also provided grounds for the remembrance of Jesus as a moral luminary. This in turn fostered the growth of his legend in this regard. As the first century progressed, an array of teachings of a moral or philosophical nature were attributed to him which were not at all related to his historical activities. They served to enhance his legend as a moral sage, and added a much needed universal vision and substance to the portrait of Jesus as resurrected Lord.

From Revolutionary Leader to Resurrected Lord

John and Mark agree on one other critically important item: On the morning of the first day of the week his tomb was found empty, and he subsequently appeared to his disciples. John tells us this explicitly; Mark predicts it, and from this study it is apparent that the missing ending of Mark was explicit about it as well. Further, the letters of Paul, which are thought by most to be the earliest documents in the NT, are resoundingly clear on this key issue. Jesus was resurrected from death and appeared to his disciples afterward.

How are we to comprehend the transformation of a religious insurgent with political objectives into a resurrected Lord and God? Some say it is pure mythology and has no foundation in historical reality. Others say it may stem from psychological hysteria associated with the shock and grief of Jesus' tragic end. For it is not unusual to mythologize heroes, especially those who have been violently cut down in the prime of life.

These may be plausible explanations for a modern society which easily dismisses ancient myths. Yet there is something oddly tangible, even earthy, about the story of the resurrection. It is not a typical myth, at least not in the Gospel of John. The angels appear at the tomb, but they do nothing and say little. Jesus does not emerge from the tomb wrapped in burial shrouds as Lazarus did when Jesus raised him from the dead. No one sees the body of Jesus come back to life as they do the body of Jairus' daughter in Mark. If these miraculous representations of resurrection are already present in the movement's consciousness, why do they not appear in the story of Jesus' own resurrection?

The Gospel of John says that Jesus was a man from heaven. Yet this gospel's resurrected Jesus is not a spiritual being manifesting himself in ghostly form. He is not a heavenly being on his way back home. He appears in flesh and bones. His wounds are not healed--he asks Thomas to place his finger in them to verify his physical presence. To dismiss the resurrection as pure myth is the simple solution, for resurrection is one of the great mythical themes of human civilization. However, to be confronted with a Jesus who has *not* been mythically transformed by his resurrection--that is another problem entirely.

The Resurrection

What historical events could account for the origin of the resurrection story? During the time of Jesus, there was no historical or religious precedent for the resurrection of a single person within the context of Jewish tradition. Nor was there a prophecy that the Messiah would rise from the dead. Therefore, the resurrection story is inconsistent with the religious milieu from which it evolved. Christian theological interpretations, which later identified the event as a substitutionary and sacrificial death on behalf of all believers, did not exist at the time. The disciples in the weeks and months following the crucifixion could not be expected to have understood or proclaimed such a grand theological agenda.

Persons today who seek a rational faith are often reluctant to believe that the resurrection of Jesus was a supernatural act intended by God to inspire the faith of humankind. They are further reluctant to accept some of the Christian theological reasoning which associates belief in this miraculous event with an exclusive salvation. Why would a God of infinite love and forgiveness--a God who commanded that we forgive each other our trespasses--consign millions of human beings to eternal damnation for the forgivable failure to believe in the resurrection? How is it that a person's reluctance to attribute a non-rational act to God is to be judged by God as an unforgivable sin? This is part of the non-rational essence of Christianity. Problems such as these have caused Christianity to lose its force in contemporary culture.

However, the typical rationalist interpretations of the resurrection are not compelling either. The common allegation that the resurrection is pure myth does not adequately explain how such an odd myth could have developed out of its historical milieu. That simple belief in such a strange event would magically link all believers to eternal life is an idea so foreign to the politically oriented message of the historical Jesus that its incongruity cannot be ignored. How did a movement with a goal to establish Jesus as King of the Jews, suddenly transform itself into a spiritual movement preaching eternal life and promoting a resurrected Jewish Messiah to the gentiles? Though the story does indeed have significant mythical elements, the notion that it is pure myth begs the fundamental issue that the story bears no relation to its historical roots. For those who accompanied Jesus in his historical mission are those who are attributed with having created the myth. How were they able to visualize such unrelated agendas? The connections here are as tenuous as the Christian claim that God simply performed a miracle.

Did Jesus Survive the Crucifixion?

One possibility that is often proposed is that Jesus may have survived the crucifixion. The appearances to his disciples were indeed actual appearances. Unfortunately, this solution is often accompanied by groundless speculations about Jesus having married, had children, moved to India, and so forth. So the extra baggage with which the theory is typically burdened tends to make it sound rather ludicrous.

However, from a purely rational perspective, the possibility that Jesus survived the crucifixion could account for the traditions of his being seen in physical form, wounds and all, after the crucifixion. Thus it is worthy of closer examination. However, pure speculation on such a solution is not worth much. The question is whether we might find any tangible evidence in the gospels themselves that Jesus may have survived the crucifixion.

The Gospel of John

This book has argued that the Gospel of John is the earliest gospel. With surprising frequency its textual details seem credible. It contains many key references which have been omitted from the synoptics. So if there is evidence to be found that Jesus may have survived the crucifixion it will most likely be found in John. Remarkably, such clues do indeed exist, and they are unique to John.

The first clue is based on the assumption that if Jesus survived the crucifixion, he would not have traveled great distances immediately following such a traumatic physical ordeal. Therefore, reports that his resurrection appearances occurred near the site of the crucifixion are more compatible with this historical scenario than are reports that he appeared in Galilee or other relatively dispersed locations.

John 20 reports three resurrection appearances. The first is in the garden near the tomb. The second and third are in Jerusalem. Conversely, Mark, though its ending is missing, predicts the first appearance would be in Galilee. Luke depicts a first appearance on the road to Emmaus, some seven miles from Jerusalem, although a subsequent appearance occurs in Jerusalem. Matthew says the first appearance was to Mary and another woman as they ran from the tomb, but the first appearance to the disciples was in Galilee. So of the four different scenarios, John's is most compatible with the theory that Jesus may have survived the crucifixion, since it alone reports all appearances to have been in the immediate vicinity of the crucifixion.

The second clue is based upon the further assumption that Jesus would have remained in hiding after the crucifixion. Public appearances would have put him at great risk for another arrest and crucifixion. John states that the first appearance was to Mary near the tomb at dawn. Remarkably, the second is at a secret meeting of the disciples in a closed room:

> On the evening of that day, the first day of the week, the doors being shut where the disciples were, for fear of the Jews, Jesus came and stood among them . . . (John 20:19)

Here Jesus' first appearance to the disciples is at a secret meeting behind closed doors. The disciples are still fugitives as they fear arrest by the authorities; Jesus is himself intent upon remaining hidden. Thus he meets his disciples at night in a private meeting. John is the only gospel of the four which indicates this meeting took place secretly and at night "for fear of the Jews." Eight days later, another meeting is held, again in the same room with the doors shut (John 20:26). These are the only appearances of Jesus to his disciples in the Fourth Gospel. It is clear in John that Jesus did not appear in public.

Since a resurrection story which does not depict a public appearance of Jesus is contrary to what we might expect from a mythologized representation of the event, the account in John is notable in this detail. A mythologized resurrection story might be expected to have proclaimed a visible and victorious resurrection, thematically consistent perhaps with the triumphal entry or the dramatic resurrection of Lazarus. Thus the account in John is remarkable in its avoidance of such a glorified vision. Jesus appears only twice to his disciples, and only at night in secret meetings. John's story is noteworthy precisely because if Jesus had indeed survived the crucifixion, this is exactly what he would have been expected to do. Hence, John's account contains the remembrance of a plausible historical event rather than a fabrication for the purpose of theological proclamation.

These two observations, that Jesus appeared only in the vicinity of the crucifixion, and only in private to his disciples, are strong enough to justify examination of the Johannine crucifixion and resurrection accounts for further evidence that Jesus did indeed survive the crucifixion. For there is now reason to suspect that these accounts may be connected closely to eyewitness testimony. Indeed, as we will soon see, these are only the first of many details in the Fourth Gospel which lend credence to the theory that Jesus survived the crucifixion.

Now it is certain that John was written by someone who was convinced Jesus died on the cross and that he was raised from the dead; the story at face value tells us exactly this. However, though the author is writing from a perspective of belief, the apparent eyewitness integrity of John's texts may allow us to find clues as to how the entire sequence of events of the crucifixion and resurrection may have honestly been perceived by witnesses as miraculous, while at the same time enabling us to interpret them in the light of reason.

We will assume for the purpose of this inquiry that the author of John was either an eyewitness to the events, or that he relied upon eyewitnesses as sources. We will assume that he reported events as he saw them or heard about them from contemporaries. Clearly what he experienced made him believe that Jesus was raised from the dead. What was it that really happened?[6]

The Crucifixion

Every once in a while we encounter stories which force us to confront the dark side of humanity, and the unspeakable depravity to which we as humans are capable of descending. The use of crucifixion as a method of execution is just such a story. Though it is difficult to think about it is unfortunately necessary to understand a few aspects of crucifixion in order for the story in John to become coherent.

Crucifixion was a sadistic method of execution which was intended to inflicted agony over a long period of time prior to death. It was also intended to degrade and humiliate the victim to the greatest extent possible. Gerald O'Collins explains the process:

> Under the Roman Empire, crucifixion normally included a flogging beforehand. At times, the cross was only one vertical stake. Frequently, however, there was a crosspiece attached either at the top to give the shape of a "T" (*crux commissa*) or just below the top, as in the form most familiar in Christian symbolism (*crux immissa*). The victims carried the cross or at least a transverse beam (*patibulum*) to the place of execution, where they were stripped and bound or nailed to the beam, raised up, and seated on a *sedile* or small wooden peg in the upright beam. Ropes bound the shoulders or torso to the cross. The feet or heels of the victim were bound or nailed to the upright stake. As crucifixion damaged no vital organs, death could come slowly, sometimes after several days of atrocious pain.[7]

---

[6] Before moving through this meditation on the Gospel of John, the reader may want to be familiar with John's entire account of the crucifixion (John 19) and the resurrection (John 20). Key verses from these two chapters will be cited here along with comment.

[7] O'Collins' excerpt from *Anchor Bible Dictionary*, Doubleday, 1992, Vol. 1, p. 1209

The Gospel of John's report that Jesus was forced to carry his own cross, and that the soldiers took his clothes, are consistent with what is known of the typical procedure in Roman crucifixion:

> So they took Jesus, and he went out, bearing his own cross, to the place called the place of the skull, which is called in Hebrew Golgotha. There they crucified him, and with him two others, one on either side, and Jesus between them (19:17-18)

> When the soldiers had crucified Jesus they took his garments and made four parts, one for each soldier; also his tunic. (19:23)

A notable element in John's account is Jesus' apparent rapid death. The gospel says he was condemned at the sixth hour (19:14), which would have been 12 noon. Allowing an hour to make preparations and have Jesus and the other prisoners carry their crosses out to the execution site, we might suppose he was crucified around 1 PM. The passage depicting Jesus' death is rather brief:

> But standing by the cross of Jesus were his mother, and his mother's sister, Mary, the wife of Clopas, and Mary Magdalene. When Jesus saw his mother, and the disciple whom he loved standing near, he said to his mother, "Woman, behold your son!" Then he said to the disciple, "Behold your mother!" And from that hour the disciple took her to his own home. After this Jesus, knowing that all was now finished, said (to fulfill the scripture), "I thirst." A bowl full of vinegar stood there; so they put a sponge full of the vinegar on hyssop and held it to his mouth. When Jesus had received the vinegar, he said, "It is finished"; and he bowed his head and gave up his spirit. (19:25-30)

With these brief sayings, Jesus is seen to expire. The story concludes with his body being taken down off the cross, prepared for burial, and transported to the tomb before sundown. So in this account he could have been on the cross no more than three to four hours. Crucifixion was not designed to cause its victims to succumb so quickly. It is conceivable but unlikely that he would have died in so short a time.

Another important detail in John's account is the breaking of the legs of the two who were crucified with Jesus:

Since it was the day of Preparation, in order to prevent the bodies from remaining on the cross on the Sabbath (for that Sabbath was a high day), the Jews ask Pilate that their legs might be broken, and that they might be taken away. So the soldiers came and broke the legs of the first, and of the other who had been crucified with him; but when they came to Jesus and saw that he was already dead, they did not break his legs. But one of the soldiers pierced his side with a spear, and at once there came out blood and water. He who saw it has borne witness -- his testimony is true, and he knows that he tells the truth -- that you also may believe. For these things took place that the scripture might be fulfilled, "Not a bone of him shall be broken." And again another scripture says, "They shall look on him whom they have pierced." (19:31-37)

Since the crucifixions did not take place until early afternoon, the authorities did not *expect* the crucifixions to be fatal to the victims before sundown. Yet to have the bodies of the condemned on the crosses after sundown would have defiled the Passover. Hence, they requested that the legs of the victims be broken. This was a conventional method for hastening death by crucifixion, for it induced shock and caused the victim's body weight to be supported fully by the arms; this soon created intense pressure on the chest cavity, and the victim would die by suffocation.

As expected, the other two victims had not died and the procedure of breaking their legs was necessary. However, it was *unexpected* to find Jesus already dead. The soldier no doubt intended to thrust a spear into his heart to ensure he was dead, but his aim was off and the spear struck his side, inflicting another nonlethal wound.

As a side note, the breaking of the victims' legs provides another clue which turns out to be a key link in the inquiry. For Jesus' ability to walk after the crucifixion is requisite to a natural interpretation of the resurrection appearances. If his legs had been broken, of course he would not have been able to walk. Furthermore, nail wounds to his feet would have seriously impaired his ability to walk also.

It is typically assumed that Jesus' feet had been nailed to the cross. We assume this from images of the crucifixion provided by centuries of Christian art and symbolism, which depict both the hands and the feet of Jesus nailed to the cross. However, there is no reason to presume these artistic renderings are historically precise, for this was not the typical or preferred method of crucifixion. Sometimes the hands, or the feet, or both were bound rather than nailed to the cross. Further, the gospels contain no description of the specific procedure used in Jesus' crucifixion. The Gospel of John says several times that the wounds inflicted upon Jesus during the crucifixion were to his *hands and side only*; there is never any mention of wounds to his feet:

> Jesus came and stood among them and said to them, "Peace be with you." When he said this he showed them his hands and his side. Then the disciples were glad when they saw the Lord. (John 20:19b-20; see also 19:34; 20:25; 20:27).

The synoptic gospels do not record the details regarding the breaking of the legs of the other two victims, nor of the spear wound to Jesus' side. Matthew and Mark are silent on the issue except to say that Jesus was crucified. There is one statement in Luke which is often interpreted as a reference to Jesus' wounds, but the reference is not clear. The scene is Jesus' first resurrection appearance to the disciples in Jerusalem:

> . . . Jesus himself stood among them. But they were startled and frightened, and supposed that they saw a spirit. And he said to them, "Why are you troubled, and why do questionings rise in your hearts? See my hands and my feet, that it is I myself; handle me, and see; for a spirit has not flesh and bones as you see that I have." (Luke 24:36b-40).

Given the long-standing assumption that Jesus' hands and feet were pierced with nails, the phrase *"see my hands and feet"* is assumed to imply that Jesus is displaying his wounds. However, within the context of the passage, it is not his wounds which are the issue, but rather whether he is a physical presence or a ghostly one. The hands and feet are the parts of the body which are exposed when a person is dressed in a tunic as Jesus would have been. His intent here is to prove he is in the midst of them in bodily form--that indeed he has flesh and bones. His wounds are not mentioned; one might even suspect the author of Luke envisioned that the resurrected body of Jesus was healed and showed no marks of the crucifixion.

Thus the only NT references to actual wounds from the crucifixion are found in John, and this gospel says several times that Jesus had nail wounds in his hands, and a spear wound in his side. However, there is another intriguing reference in the work known as the Gospel of Peter. This gospel is not known in its entirety, for it is not a NT gospel, and only a fragmentary manuscript has been recovered. However, the portion of text recovered contains an account of the crucifixion:

> And the Lord called out and cried, "My power, O power, thou hast forsaken me!" And having said this he was taken up. And at the same hour the veil of the temple in Jerusalem was rent in two. *And then the Jews drew the nails from the hands of the Lord and laid him on the earth.* (Gos. Pet. 5:19-6:21a)

Here we have what appears to be an independent tradition which could not have been drawn from the Gospel of John. The cry that Jesus has been forsaken is foreign to John, as is the indication that the veil of the temple was rent in two. However, it agrees with John in the critical detail that Jesus suffered nail wounds only to his hands. Therefore, the explicit textual evidence available to us is clear that Jesus sustained nail wounds to his hands, and is silent regarding any wounds to his feet.

Actually, the breaking of the legs may add further support to this observation. For the legs of the victims were broken in order to prevent them from maintaining body weight on the feet, thereby alleviating pressure on the chest cavity. Yet this would have been exceedingly difficult if the feet had been nailed to the cross. The need to break the legs of the victims in this case may have derived from the fact that the feet had been bound rather than nailed.

There are numerous clues, then, which tacitly support the theory that Jesus may not have actually died on the day of his crucifixion. None of the wounds reported in the text were lethal. He had not been on the cross long enough for the authorities to expect that he would have died. Finally, John's resurrection appearances describe a scenario which is consistent with what we would anticipate if Jesus had survived. Thus we may suspect that Jesus had lost consciousness from the grueling ordeal, and that as his body hung by the arms, he had stopped breathing just prior to being examined by the soldiers. There is no doubt, however, that the author (or his sources), as well as the soldiers, thought he was dead.

> After this, Joseph of Arimathea, who was a disciple of Jesus, but secretly, for fear of the Jews, asked Pilate that he might take away the body of Jesus, and Pilate gave him leave. So he came and took away his body. Nicodemus also, who had at first come to him by night, came bringing a mixture of myrrh and aloes, about a hundred pounds' weight. They took the body of Jesus, and bound it in linen cloths with the spices, as is the burial custom of the Jews (19:38-39).

At this point in the account there is another intriguing anomaly. It would have been typical for the soldiers to remove the victims' bodies from the crosses and arrange for a shallow burial, or to leave the bodies exposed to be consumed by scavenging animals. But in this case two friends gain permission to handle the body of Jesus directly. Though victims of crucifixion were not typically granted an honorable burial, on the eve of holy days such as Passover it was not unusual for the Romans to make exceptions to this rule.[8]

Once Jesus' body was removed from the cross, Joseph of Arimathea took it, and he and Nicodemus began the process of preparing it for burial. There is no clue in the Fourth Gospel as to who Joseph of Arimathea was, other than that he was an undeclared disciple of Jesus. The author implies that Joseph was able to attend to Jesus' burial because he was not known as a disciple. The known disciples were keeping themselves concealed, for to have been involved with Jesus' burial directly may have placed them at risk of arrest.

There is another interesting side note to this story which was pointed out by Rudolf Bultmann. This was the day of Preparation; the Passover meal was to be taken this evening after sundown. The handling of a corpse would have been an unclean act for a Jew, and

---

[8] It is not likely that the Roman governor would have been involved in the details of the disposition of Jesus' body. It is possible that permission was granted by the soldier in command of the crucifixion detail, and that as he had acted as Pilate's agent, the author recorded Pilate's permission.

such acts were to be avoided on the day of Preparation. Joseph's and Nicodemus' handling of Jesus' body would have rendered them unclean, which would have prevented them from participating in the Passover meal. So there is no compelling reason why they would have needed to be home before sundown.[9]

The story so far has established several important facts: Jesus was only on the cross several hours; he did not sustain any certain mortal wounds; and he was not expected to die in this length of time. Though Jesus was unconscious and not breathing, he may not have been clinically dead at the time the soldiers delivered his body to Joseph and Nicodemus.

A Speculation on the Resurrection

The following discussion is a speculation about events which could have led to the resurrection story. Though it is based upon clues in the text, the final interpretation must be left to the reader, and must remain, as always, within the domain of faith and intuition. There is not enough historical evidence to prove what actually happened to Jesus and the disciples. This is all to the good, for the true power of the gospel story consists in its ability to make us wonder and reflect.

Without imagining anything too unusual, an intriguing scenario fits the evidence of the text. Once Joseph and Nicodemus take possession of Jesus' body from the soldiers, they busy themselves about the preparation of his body for burial. They wash it, and begin to prepare the body with the spices they had brought with them. Suddenly, they detect a heartbeat or a fitful breath. They recognize he is still alive. Stunned by this turn of events, they whisper between themselves and quickly agree to keep working so as not to arouse suspicion. They do not want anyone to know for fear he will be killed by the soldiers, so they work secretly and quickly to bandage his wounds. At this point they want to move him to a secure location, hidden from view, so that they may give him the medical attention he needs without causing alarm. Since he is on the verge of death, they do not want to move him far.

---

[9] Bultmann, Ibid., p. 679

Joseph and Nicodemus do not know which if any of the disciples can be trusted at this point. They know the disciples abandoned Jesus upon his arrest, and they know at least one had betrayed him. However, they have no way to know how widespread the disaffection was among his followers. So they agree between themselves to tell no one.

> Now in the place where he was crucified there was a garden and in the garden a new tomb where no one had ever been laid. So because of the Jewish day of Preparation, as the tomb was close at hand, they laid Jesus there. (19:41-42)

Clearly, this tomb had not been prepared for Jesus ahead of time, since he had been executed in such short order. Further, the phrase *where no one had ever been laid* indicates this was a large family tomb intended to accommodate multiple burials. The comment implies that someone had prepared this tomb as a family resting place, and that no family member had yet died. A family tomb would have been an ideal place to hide Jesus, since it would have been large enough to accommodate those who would be attending to him in the hours and days to come. The author's comment that the tomb was selected because it was "close at hand" implies that Joseph and Nicodemus decided to use it on the spur of the moment.

Since they were using someone else's family tomb without any apparent notice to the owner, we may assume they expected this to be a *temporary* use of the tomb. A traditional explanation for this has been that they were running out of time and planned to give his body a more proper burial after the Passover. However, Rudolf Bultmann's observation is key here. Joseph and Nicodemus cannot celebrate the Passover due to their handling of Jesus' body.

Thus there is an incongruity in the literal reading of the text. On the one hand, they do not want Jesus' body to be handled with dishonor by the Roman soldiers, as would normally have been the case. They want to ensure that his body is treated with respect. In attending to his burial, Joseph and Nicodemus disqualify themselves from celebrating the Passover. So they have already made a personal commitment to see that Jesus' body is treated with dignity. They have brought spices with which to give him a burial with honor. Then suddenly they decide to deposit his body in a temporary tomb and hurry off to a Passover meal for which they are not qualified to participate. This final action does not follow from the premise of the story.

It is just as likely that the sudden use of the large, nearby tomb derived from the fact that Jesus was alive; Joseph and Nicodemus found this unused tomb to be a safe and secure place to conceal Jesus temporarily. Though the author assumes their haste to bury him is due to the Passover, what he recorded as their haste in burying him was in fact an effort to move him quickly in order to administer prompt medical attention.

Joseph and Nicodemus attend to Jesus as best they can without being discovered. He would need to be nursed round the clock, as they would not have wanted to leave him alone in the tomb. They enlist the help of family members, trusted friends, or household servants. They work in shifts, making sure that someone is always with Jesus.

By Sunday morning, Jesus has recovered enough to be able to stand up and walk; two unidentified persons are with him. They help him out of the tomb, and stand by as he walks in the garden to get some fresh air. Suddenly, Mary arrives and finds the tomb empty and no one there; she does not look around in the garden but immediately runs away in alarm:

> Now on the first day of the week Mary Magdalene came to the tomb early, while it was still dark, and saw that the stone had been taken away from the tomb. So she ran, and went to Simon Peter and the other disciple, the one whom Jesus loved, and said to them, "They have taken the Lord out of the tomb, and we do not know where they have laid him." (20:1-2)

Jesus and the two attendants are still in the garden and away from the tomb. They hear the commotion of two men running toward the tomb, and not knowing who they are, they remain hidden in the garden. Jesus has been unwrapped from his burial linens, but they have been using them as bedding, and they still remain where Jesus was laying. The napkin which was used to treat his head wounds has been set aside:

Peter then came out with the other disciple, and they went toward the tomb. They both ran, but the other disciple outran Peter and reached the tomb first; and stooping to look in, he saw the linen clothes lying there, but he did not go in. Then Simon Peter came, following him, and went into the tomb; he saw the linen clothes lying, and the napkin which had been on his head, not lying with the linen clothes but rolled up in a place by itself. Then the other disciple, who reached the tomb first, also went in, and he saw and believed; for as yet they did not know the scripture, that he must rise from the dead. Then the disciples went back to their homes. (20:3-10)

Those assisting Jesus watch as the two disciples examine the empty tomb and leave. They decide it is no longer safe to keep him hidden in the tomb; Jesus stays in the garden while the attendants return to the tomb to retrieve the linens which have been used for his bed. Peter and the Beloved Disciple, in running to the tomb, had left Mary behind. However, Mary has now returned and is distraught. Suddenly she hears something in the tomb. She looks in and sees two persons dressed in white, one at the head and one at the foot of the bed. They see her and do not associate her with Jesus; the sight of a woman crying as she wanders in the garden alone at dawn is puzzling to them. They ask why she is crying:

> But Mary stood weeping outside the tomb, and as she wept she stooped to look into the tomb; and she saw two angels in white, sitting where the body of Jesus had lain, one at the head and one at the feet. They said to her, "Woman, why are you weeping?" She said to them, "Because they have taken away my Lord, and I do not know where they have laid him." (20:11-13)

Mary displays none of the fright or alarm that normally accompanies the appearance of an angel or supernatural being -- she recognizes these two as human. She simply responds to their question. The author will assume later, when Mary reports that she saw two figures in the tomb, that these two unrecognized beings must have been angels attending Jesus' resurrection.

Note the "angels" do not say, "He is not here, he is risen!" as they do in the other three gospels. Here they say nothing; they do not know what to say, as they have been instructed to keep the fact that

Jesus is alive a secret. It is remarkable that the author did not add angelic or supernatural embellishments to this angelic appearance or to their dialogue, even though the story seems to demand it. If the author was inventing this story for dramatic purposes, the angels would have been sketched with a more deliberate angelic presence. So the understatement of the appearance is an intriguing clue that the author tried to report the facts as he heard them. Mary reported seeing two beings in the tomb, and the author assumed they were angels.

Mary hears someone else approach and turns. She has been crying, and her eyes are full of tears. It is dawn and the light is dim. In her grief she avoids looking directly at him. She had seen Jesus die on the cross, so the idea that this could be Jesus does not occur to her. She thinks it must be the gardener:

> Saying this, she turned around and saw Jesus standing, but she did not know that it was Jesus. Jesus said to her, "Woman, why are you weeping? Whom do you seek?" Supposing him to be the gardener, she said to him, "Sir if you have carried him away, tell me where you have laid him, and I will take him away." Jesus said to her, "Mary." She turned and said to him in Hebrew, "Rabboni!" (which means Teacher). (20:14-16)

Jesus does not know who this woman is at first. Her back is turned and her head is veiled. He wants to know who she is and why she is staring into the tomb. As she turns and answers, he recognizes her. Once she is called by name, she recognizes him also. Mary's immediate reaction is to approach Jesus and attempt to embrace him, but Jesus is stiff with pain from his ordeal and does not want to be touched:

> Jesus said to her, "Do not hold me, for I have not yet ascended to the Father; but go to my brethren and say to them, "I am ascending to my Father and your Father, to my God and your God." Mary Magdalene went and said to the disciples, "I have seen the Lord"; and she told them that he had said these things to her. (20:17-18)

Jesus' statement here is astounding and without precedent heretofore in the gospel. Jesus refers to the disciples as his *brethren*. This word in Greek, *adelphoi*, has only occurred four times thus far in the gospel, and in each instance it refers to Jesus' blood brothers (2:12; 7:3; 7:5; 7:10). Further, the saying that he is ascending to "my Father and your Father, to my God and your God," signals a radical change in Jesus' self-perception. No longer is he the anticipated Messiah, the King of the Jews. Jesus puts himself on equal footing with the disciples, calling them "brethren" for the first time. We will return to this remarkable change of tone later.

Since the two disciples had discovered the empty tomb and had undoubtedly gone to spread the word, it was determined the tomb was no longer a safe place to hide Jesus. Since he was now able to walk the attendants decide to take him into town, perhaps to the home of Joseph or Nicodemus. Meanwhile, the disciples have called a clandestine meeting after dark to discuss the mysterious disappearance of Jesus' body and Mary's claim that she had seen him alive. They are fearful and bewildered; they plan to meet secretly to avoid arrest.

Joseph and Nicodemus, since they buried Jesus, are told of the meeting and where it is to be held; they in turn tell Jesus. He is able to walk to the meeting as it is nearby. It is after dark, so he can proceed unseen to the meeting. He enters the room quietly to avoid a stir:

> On the evening of that day, the first day of the week, the doors being shut up where the disciples were, for fear of the Jews, Jesus came and stood among them and said to them, "Peace be with you." When he had said this, he showed them his hands and his side. Then the disciples were glad when they saw the Lord. Jesus said to them again, "Peace be with you. As the Father has sent me, even so send I you." And when he had said this, he breathed on them, and said to them, "Receive the Holy Spirit. If you forgive the sins of any, they are forgiven; if you retain the sins of any, they are retained." (20:19-23)

Once again the uniqueness of Jesus' speech is notable. This is the first and only time the word "forgive" *(aphiemi)* appears in the Gospel of John. The formulation "forgiveness of sins" is absent from Jesus' teaching until now. Further, the reference to "peace" has only been made twice before in the Gospel (14:27; 16:23), and the phrase "Peace be with you", which occurs three times in Chapter 20 (vv. 19, 21, 26), is unique to the resurrection appearances.

The remainder of the chapter tells of Thomas, who was not at the meeting, expressing his doubt it was actually Jesus who appeared. He would not believe unless he personally placed "his finger in the mark of the nails . . . and his hand in [Jesus'] side." (John 20:25). At another meeting of the disciples eight days later, again under cover of darkness, Jesus appears and confronts Thomas:

> Then [Jesus] said to Thomas, "Put your finger here, and see my hands; and put out your hand, and place it in my side; do not be faithless, but believing." Thomas answered him, "My Lord and my God." (John 20:27-28)

This is the third and last appearance of Jesus in the original Gospel of John. Jesus has not had to travel far to effect these appearances. After these he does not appear again, and the gospel is silent about what happened to him.

What actually happened to Jesus?

The foregoing scenario is speculative and based on limited textual evidence. Though this is so, the realm of speculation is also the realm of faith; it is where we may allow our reason to be informed by intuition. It is where things cannot be proven, only believed; and it is where the final answers to what happened to Jesus must be found. So having come this far, we may travel a bit farther down this road to see how we might fully explain the origin of the resurrection story.

We can start by summarizing what the Gospel of John tells us. First, Jesus has suffered severe wounds from the flogging, the crucifixion, and from the spear in his side. These would have produced ample opportunity for infection. One possibility, therefore, is that he eventually died from complications of his wounds. This would explain his disappearance after the eleventh day.

Second, there is an indication by his resurrection sayings that Jesus had a change in perspective after the death/resurrection experience. As noted above, his disciples are now "brethren." He does not say, "I am going to my Father" in an exclusive sense as we would expect from his prior proclamations in this gospel. Instead, he now represents the Fatherhood of God as applying to all the brethren. This is a notable change of tone given the thrust of the gospel to this point. Further, the appearance of the twice repeated phrase "Peace be with you" and the statement for the first time in the gospel that if the disciples forgive sins, they will be forgiven, also contribute to a picture of Jesus as somehow changed in his spiritual orientation.

A change in demeanor may be detected also by what is absent from the text. There is no bold proclamation of victory nor is there a hint of talk of his own glorification. Recall that the raising of Lazarus from the dead was announced by Jesus to be "for the glory of God, so that the Son of God may be glorified by means of it." (John 11:4) Later on Jesus prays, "Father, the hour has come; glorify thy Son that the Son may glorify thee." (John 17:1) So it would not have been surprising to find language in the resurrection appearances indicating the glorification of the Son is the result of this final and greatest sign. This language is highly conspicuous by its absence.

All of this is consistent with what we would expect the frame of mind of Jesus and the disciples to have been. Hopes for the revolution have been dashed; Jesus will not lead an overthrow of the establishment; he will not assume his role as triumphant King of the Jews. Jesus is alive but severely wounded, and he and his disciples are staying out of public view. Thus it makes sense that Jesus would not at this point be proclaiming victory as the one who was sent from God.

Therefore, the account in John has a unique air of historical plausibility. Many of the elements in the story are more probable as recollections of historical events rather than fabrications of myth.

Yet there is something else going on in John's resurrection account. Jesus is more humble, more compassionate, more forgiving, than he was shown to be during his ministry, at least as he is portrayed in John. He believes he is about to "ascend" to the Father, which appears to be a calm anticipation of his impending death. Though the movement has failed, there is no sense of anger, defeat, or frustration. Jesus is truly at peace with himself for the first time in the gospel.

What has happened here? All of these indications could be explained by one solution: it is possible that during the crucifixion Jesus may have had what has become known in the twentieth century as a "near-death-experience." This phenomenon is rather common, and occurs frequently enough that the reports of persons who have had such experiences are well documented. The near-death-experience (NDE) has been studied in thousands of persons who were close to death, or actually clinically dead, for a short period of time before being revived. The NDE is a powerful psychological and spiritual experience which has a transforming effect on the personality.

Melvin Morse at the University of Washington has done extensive research in near-death studies and written two books on the NDE. He writes:

> By examining thousands of near-death experiences, medical researchers have been able to identify the common stages or elements that define the NDE. There are basically nine traits that characterize this experience. . [10]

He summarizes the nine experiential traits as follows:

1. A Sense of Being Dead. NDE'ers often report while they were having the experience they felt an absolute separation from their own body and the physical world which was recognizable to them as a state of death.

2. Peace and Painlessness. Frequently reported is a sense of tranquillity and peace that was heretofore unknown in their earthly existence.

3. Out-of-Body Experience. Many describe a state of awareness of having left their bodies. Some who were being operated on reported they were able to look down upon the doctors from above as they worked to save them.

---

[10] Morse, Melvin, *Transformed by the Light*, Villard Books/Random House, 1992, p. ix

4. Tunnel Experience. A commonly reported phenomenon is a sense of traveling through a tunnel toward a brilliant light at the other end. It is a peaceful experience, and there is a positive expectancy of arriving into the light.

5. People of Light. Some report having seen loved ones, others say they saw persons unknown. Often these people are described as glowing with an internal radiance, as a lantern.

6. Being of Light. Another common element of the NDE is the sense of having seen or been in the presence of God or some other radiant being of light.

7. Life Review. Some have reported they saw a review of their life, including all its good and bad aspects. This experience is a positive one and does not have the sense of judgment.

8. Reluctance to Return. Many have reported that they wanted to continue the journey up the tunnel or into the light. The idea of returning to their body for further existence on earth is strongly unappealing and some fight the return to the body, even to the extent of being angry with doctors who saved them. Some say they were given a choice whether to return or not, and decided to return to finish some specific task or work.

9. Personality Transformation. NDE'ers have certain unique personality traits after their experience. The most common reactions are that they exhibit a calm and tranquil nature that may not have existed before, and they have little or no fear of death since they are convinced their first time experience of it was positive.

The near-death-experience has been identified in persons of all ages and beliefs. There is no correlation between religious faith and the NDE; many NDE'ers describe themselves as having been agnostic or atheistic prior to the experience.

This is not the place to examine the possible explanations for the phenomenon of the near-death-experience. Some suggest that it derives from natural neurological impulses of the traumatized brain which are not well understood. Others believe that human beings are essentially spiritual beings who move into a spiritual plane of existence upon death, and that the NDE occurs when a person hovers on the threshold of this non-physical reality. They interpret the NDE as tangible evidence of an afterlife. Virtually all of those persons who have had the experience understand it as clear evidence of an afterlife, and it is this recognition which causes their transformation in attitudes and beliefs subsequent to the experience.

The nature and causes of the NDE will be debated for years to come, and it is certainly beyond the scope of this book to suggest what causes it. The point here is limited to the observation that the NDE is a common and scientifically documented psycho-spiritual phenomenon which alters people's outlook and behavior after they have experienced it. Further, the circumstances surrounding the crucifixion of Jesus, and his reported demeanor in his risen state, match closely with the physical trauma and spiritual reaction we find in persons who have reported a near-death-experience.

Thus there is no reason Jesus could not have had just such an experience. He believed he had returned from the dead. He believed he had not yet ascended to the Father, but would be ascending soon. These things are consistent with the glimpse of eternity reported in the near-death-experience.

In his brief period of life after his crucifixion, he seems to have been changed by the experience. He speaks of peace in a new way; the disciples are now his brothers; the Father is Father of all of them; God is the God of all. In the same breath he speaks of receiving the Holy Spirit and encourages them to forgive the sins of others.

If Jesus did have a near death experience, he would not have believed that he had experienced a close brush with death; he would have believed that he had actually died, and returned from death. He would have believed that he had gained firm evidence of an afterlife in which there was peace, harmony, and no condemnation.

For Jesus, death would no longer have been anything to be feared, for life on this earth was just a prelude to eternal life. Most importantly, he would have tried to explain everything that he had just experienced to his disciples.

The disciples would have seen the spiritual calm and peace of the risen Jesus; they would have heard his encouragement; they would have sensed in him the transformation of his spirit. Their would-be King, in whom they had believed and hoped and trusted, now stood in their presence as one who had conquered death. They would have listened in wonder and awe as he described his experience of eternity. Within the limits of their understanding, and given everything they had seen and heard, the disciples would have believed they had witnessed the resurrection of the Lord.

❖   *Epilogue*   ❖

Perhaps the greatest sign of the historical integrity of John's Gospel is that it recalls two distinct portraits of Jesus. It shows us Jesus the religious insurgent, aggressively challenging and condemning the Jewish authorities for using their interpretations of Judaism toward institutional and political ends. Yet it also portrays the tranquil, spiritual Jesus who speaks of peace, forgiveness, and eternal life. The author remembers this transformation of Jesus' character and spirit to be associated with the crucifixion and resurrection.

These remembrances appear to be historical in origin. The fact that two distinct portraits exist in John is an indication that the myth-making process had not yet integrated them. Both of them must be taken seriously in our attempt to understand Jesus and the origin of Christianity.

If Jesus survived the crucifixion, then what may we say eventually happened to him? Certainly he would have died at some point. From the gospel traditions it appears that he died soon afterward. John's story implies that he was not seen again after the eleventh day. The Book of Acts says Jesus appeared to them over a forty day period (Acts 1:3). Matthew and Luke report only two appearances each. Thus the various traditions are unanimous in their indication that Jesus was not present with them long after his crucifixion. It is not unreasonable to suspect he succumbed to infections or other complications from the wounds sustained during his scourging and crucifixion. The subsequent death of Jesus is the final element necessary for a rational interpretation of Christian traditions. However, if Jesus had died, surely his death would have been remembered? Indeed, it was.

The Ascension as the Subsequent Death of Jesus

In the Gospel of John, the resurrected Jesus anticipates his imminent ascension to the Father (John 20:17). Matthew implies that Jesus departs from his disciples after the last scene in which Jesus gives the Great Commission (Matt. 28:16-20). Luke tells explicitly of a day when Jesus "parted from them and was carried up into heaven." (Luke 24:51). The story of the ascension is the disciples' spiritualized interpretation of the subsequent death of Jesus. He had told them that he had experienced the eternal, and that he was soon to ascend to the Father. He had revealed that this was not death, but rather the beginning of eternal life. Death was to be anticipated with joy and expectation rather than fear. Hence, they do not recall his subsequent death as a tragic event. Rather, after he "parted from them, and was carried up into heaven" Luke says "they returned to Jerusalem with great joy, and were continually in the temple blessing God" (Luke 24:51-52).

Some may wonder whether this suggestion of Jesus' subsequent death renews the need to assume a cover up or a deliberate misrepresentation of the facts? The answer is *no*. Joseph and Nicodemus concealed Jesus during his post-crucifixion days not to propagate a hoax or conspiracy, but simply to protect him. They knew if he was found alive, he would be killed. We may easily imagine Joseph and Nicodemus attended to him in his final days, and upon his death arranged for his burial as they had originally intended to do.

The charge that a hoax was then perpetrated by the disciples would be based on two indefensible assumptions. First, it assumes that a substantial resurrection theology would have developed within a matter of weeks after Jesus' crucifixion. Second, it assumes the disciples would have seen Jesus' subsequent physical death as negating that theology and hence requiring a cover up. There is no reason to believe either of these propositions.

Christianity did not exist in the weeks immediately following Jesus' crucifixion. There was no concept of his death and resurrection as the doctrinal cornerstone of a new religion. It would be years before they would develop the theological meaning of the cross. For the disciples, Jesus' resurrection had no meaning or purpose other than

336

what Jesus would have told them directly in the post-crucifixion appearances. If the theory of his near-death-experience is correct, Jesus would have told his disciples that he had died, that he had overcome death, and that there was an eternal spiritual afterlife in which there was no condemnation. Death was not to be feared.

At its core, this is precisely the message Christianity would be built upon. If this is what the disciples heard, the subsequent physical death of Jesus would not have created a theological conflict. Indeed, his subsequent death would have been perceived as an ascension to a spiritual reality which had been revealed to them by the Lord. Hence, no hoax or cover up would have been required.

The Jesus movement would eventually begin to think that his death and resurrection were instrumental in bringing eternal life within reach of the believers, for had he not died and been resurrected, there would have been no glimpse of eternity. They would begin to infer that only those who believed Jesus' message of an eternal afterlife would participate in it. They would eventually interpret his brutal death as a substitutionary payment for their own sins, for how else could there be no condemnation for one's sins? How else could the crucifixion of the one who had brought them eternal life be explained?

The idea that Jesus survived the crucifixion only to die a matter of weeks later is not part of Christian orthodoxy. Nor is the proposal that he had a near-death-experience which was the source of his vision of eternal life. Yet this scenario fits hand-in-hand with the textual details in the Gospel of John. It is fully adequate to explain the explosion of confident faith which emanated from the event of the crucifixion. As an historical scenario, it is a plausible and sufficient explanation for the event which gave birth to Christianity.

The Doctrine of the Holy Spirit

We cannot conclude an interpretation of the Gospel of John without considering its unique treatment of the Holy Spirit. The gospel's reflections on the Holy Spirit occur within the spiritualized interpretations of the events surrounding the crucifixion and resurrection. There is confusion in John regarding the essence of the

Holy Spirit, and whether it is the Holy Spirit or Jesus himself who will dwell in the believer. There is also confusion regarding whether the Holy Spirit is sent from the Father, or sent by Jesus. The functional role of the Holy Spirit as counselor or advocate is identified, but otherwise not developed theologically as it is in the letters of Paul.

The idea of a separate and distinct Holy Spirit is not present in the Old Testament. Since the discovery of the Dead Sea Scrolls, many now believe that Holy Spirit theology in Christianity was drawn from the Qumran community. While Qumran influence on the development of Holy Spirit teaching is likely, there is a further possibility which must be considered from the results of this study. One of the hallmarks of near-death-experience is a transformation of spirit. If Jesus had had such an experience, the disciples would have witnessed a distinctly new spiritual orientation in Jesus' own personality. The change might easily have been perceived as the indwelling of a new *holy spirit* which Jesus received as a result of his resurrection experience. Something must have accounted for such a change, and for the disciples to have associated it with the indwelling of a Holy Spirit from heaven would have been a natural interpretation. This would explain John's locating of the Holy Spirit teachings around the time of the resurrection (John 14-16; 20). It would also explain the specific association of the Holy Spirit with peace and the forgiveness of sins (John 20:21-23).

Ultimately, the deeply spiritualized portrait of Jesus, which is so well recognized as unique to John among the four gospels, may have been derived from the intensely spiritual revelations of Jesus during his post-crucifixion appearances. In the brief time between the resurrection and Jesus' final death, his encounters with the disciples would have had a profound spiritual impact upon them. It is perhaps not surprising that this experience would be reflected most prominently in the earliest gospel.

The Evolving Gospel

What we recognize today as the Christian "gospel" is a melting pot of ideas which evolved over many decades. It represents the thought of several generations of believers as they attempted to interpret the meaning of Jesus and his resurrection. He was interpreted as the one uniquely sent by God to reveal the things of heaven. He was seen as the Savior through whom humankind may gain eternal life. As time progressed, a host of mythical traditions appeared which were to tell of his miraculous powers, his magical birth, his descent from David, his temptations from Satan, and so forth. His moral and philosophical vision would grow in universal scope as his legend increased.

As the Jesus movement pressed its proclamation of exclusive revealed truth, it began to elicit hostile reactions from non-believers. The movement experienced several waves of violent persecutions. Out of these experiences, the movement developed the notion of an imminent end of the world which would be attended by a judgment of the ungodly. Though they faced hostility and rejection on earth, their faith would ultimately be vindicated on the day of judgment.

Thus the gospel tradition evolved over time as believers grappled with the meaning of Jesus within their own social and religious milieu. For the first believers, the gospel was not dogmatic truth authorized by a church. Rather, it was an ongoing inquiry--a living, changing meditation on the meaning of Jesus for their own lives. It consisted of dialogues and letters and gospels in which ideas were debated, refuted, and advanced. The New Testament documents are a remarkable historical record of the ongoing struggle to define who Jesus was, and what his resurrection meant for believers and the world.

Eventually, the Jesus movement began to assume formal organizational structures of its own. Consensus opinions were formed. The authorized canon of the New Testament was identified, and the documents of the first century dialogue were elevated to the status of sacred scripture. The evolving gospel was frozen as official doctrine.

By the fourth century, the leaders of the institutionalized church had formed their own political alliance with the Romans. The state participated in the construction of churches, and it actively enforced the doctrines of the Roman Catholic Church. In return, the church leadership supported state policy. Thus ironically, the Jesus movement, which had begun as an uprising against politicized and institutionalized religion, became an official state religion in the service of the Roman Empire.

Over the last two millennia, institutionalized Christianity has claimed to be the revealer of God's absolute truth on earth. The Roman Catholic Church developed the notion of papal primacy in the fourth century, and eventually would advance the doctrine of the infallibility of the Pope. Martin Luther's defiance of certain papal decrees in 1517 would mark the beginning of the Protestant Reformation, the hallmark of which was the rejection of the authority of the Pope. However, Protestantism itself quickly assumed its own institutional forms. In place of the infallibility of the Pope, it taught the inerrancy of scripture, effectively replacing one oracle of absolute truth with another. In Hans Kung's words, Protestantism made of the scriptures a "paper pope."

The history of Christianity has demonstrated how susceptible humankind is to institutionalizing its religious experience, and to defining in creeds and doctrines those things which must always remain within the domain of faith and mystery. For this very reason, religious doctrine is particularly easy for governing bodies to appropriate as a tool for motivating and controlling a population. That institutionalized forms of Judaism, Christianity, and other revealed religions, have historically been allied with political power is no accident. Religion too often serves the interests of state admirably. It is precisely this that Jesus of Nazareth warned against.

If Jesus were here today, he would be as sharply critical of modern institutionalized Christianity as he was of the regulated Judaism of his day. He would challenge Christianity's formulation of truth in creeds, sacraments, and dogmas. He would decry the depiction of God as one who would consign human souls to eternal torment for failing to accept arbitrary doctrines. He would tell us that man was not made for the gospel; rather the gospel was made for man.

In the earliest days of the primitive Jesus movement, the gospel was a living, changing entity. It produced a tremendous spiritual awakening as the first followers struggled to interpret the meaning of Jesus and his resurrection. There were no answers, and there was no established doctrine. This forced them to think, to meditate, and to wonder about this world and the next. Jesus had given them a brief vision of a new spiritual dimension which they had not previously known, and it was left to them to make the vision intelligible. In the process of seeking to understand, a new spirituality was born.

Ironically, the apostle Paul was right all along. The gospel of Jesus has power precisely because it is *not* comprehensible by the human mind. Jesus revealed truths which exceeded the limits of the disciples' understanding, and which exceed our understanding today. He inspired in the disciples a fervent desire for greater comprehension of the eternal, and of the nature of God. The gospel was a powerful influence in their lives *because* it was incomplete, and because it left them without a fully revealed truth. They had seen a glimpse of heaven, and they wanted to know more.

If Jesus were here today, he would tell us that the power of the gospel abides in its incompleteness. It is the partial revelation of truth which inspires us to seek further. It is the process of seeking, not the act of finding, which invigorates the soul. If the gospel is to remain a vital living force, and lead us toward a true spiritual awareness, it must never provide final answers. It must always leave us to wonder. If the gospel of Jesus is to endure, it must forever remain unfinished.

Author Index

Scripture Index

346